XBRL for Interactive Data

Roger Debreceny · Carsten Felden ·
Bartosz Ochocki · Maciej Piechocki ·
Michal Piechocki

XBRL for Interactive Data

Engineering the Information Value Chain

Springer

Prof. Dr. Roger Debreceny
School of Accountancy
Shidler College of Business
University of Hawai`i at Manoa
2404 Maile Way
Honolulu, HI 96822
USA
roger@debreceny.com

Prof. Dr. Carsten Felden
TU Bergakademie Freiberg
Wirtschaftswissenschaft
Lessingstraße 45
09599 Freiberg
Germany
carsten.felden@bwl.tu-freiberg.de

Bartosz Ochocki
Lermontowa 17
60-461 Poznan
Poland
bartosz.ochocki@br-ag.eu

Dr. Maciej Piechocki
Flat 27, Wheel House
1 Burrells Wharf Square
London E14 3TA
UK
mpiechocki@iasb.org.uk

Michal Piechocki
Sloneczna 9
62-064 Plewiska
Poland
michal.piechocki@br-ag.eu

ISBN 978-3-642-01436-9 e-ISBN 978-3-642-01437-6
DOI 10.1007/978-3-642-01437-6
Springer Dordrecht Heidelberg London New York

Library of Congress Control Number: 2009928425

Printed on acid-free paper

Springer is part of Springer Science+Business Media (www.springer.com)

Foreword

"The period of promoting XBRL for its potential is over.
Promises are being realized"

Olivier Servais, Director of XBRL Activities, International Accounting Standards Committee (IASC) Foundation

With the market turmoil of the early 2000's, perhaps we should look back through history and seek lessons from the past. In 1139, during the Catholic Church's second Council of Lateran, Pope Innocent II advised against the use of crossbows or *ballistas* – a type of medieval catapult – because their arrows and darts were launched so far ahead that the soldiers could not see the consequences of their actions. Investment bankers and others who took excessive risks would do well to remember this basic principle of caution. The good news is that today stakeholders are getting closer to the information they need.

XBRL, or "Interactive Data" plays an important role in this new era of transparency. The period when XBRL was perhaps excessively promoted for its potential benefits – remember the 'better, faster, cheaper' mantra? – is over. Promises are already being realized. I believe that most of the requisite conditions for the efficient implementation of XBRL are now in place: political decisions have been made, taxonomies are available and software solutions, including ERPs, are affordable.

The financial crisis of the early 2000's is playing an ambiguous role. Few people doubt XBRL's potential to improve information exchange and therefore assist in the restoration of market confidence by providing transparency. Yet at the same time few, if not forced, are willing to dedicate the time and money to implement it. This applies to all countries and regions as all are affected, though some have been quicker on the uptake than others. I was highly impressed that XBRL as a concept or idea in Japan is no longer discussed because it is already implemented. It is a similar situation in Belgium, where all non-listed and non-financial companies – approximately 280,000 of them – have been filing in XBRL for some time.

In this sense, XBRL is becoming a non-issue. Why? Commitment and endorsement from high level decision-makers, who want to see XBRL embraced in their markets. As well as Japan and Belgium, there are interesting examples of XBRL adoption in Australia, China, France, India, Italy, Poland, Spain and the US.

As the Director for XBRL Activities at the IASC Foundation – whose standard-setting body the International Accounting Standards Board (IASB), is responsible for developing International Financial Reporting Standards (IFRS) – I am closely involved in the development and implementation of XBRL for international financial reporting. The IASC Foundation is promoting XBRL because we believe in the benefits it offers all stakeholders and end-users such as investors and banks. Our commitment is to provide IFRS in XBRL – the IFRS taxonomy – to the highest quality and at the same time as the IFRS are released. At present, more than 100 countries worldwide are either allowing or mandating IFRS and very few are doing so without also considering XBRL. It is no coincidence that the main expected benefit of Belgium switching to XBRL was to ease the transition to IFRS. The world's financial markets are desperately seeking greater accuracy; in this respect, they have much in common with Pope Innocent II.

An important pre-requisite for success of standards such as XBRL is not only the taxonomies and software tools that I mentioned above, but also knowledge about the standard in the wider community. That is why this book is both timely and valuable. The authors traverse all the key technologies within the XBRL domain. They provide many practical examples that allow the reader to become thoroughly familiar with the design of taxonomies and the production of instance documents within a wide range of settings. So now is the perfect time for the international community to familiarise itself with XBRL and to reap the benefits from it. It is simply time to get to work with XBRL. I wish you a lot of success with this book.

The opinions expressed are those of the author and do not necessarily reflect the views of the IASB or the IASC Foundation.

About the Authors

Prof. Roger Debreceny – Professor, University of Hawai'i at Mānoa

Roger Debreceny is the Shidler College Distinguished Professor of Accounting in the Shidler College of Business at the University of Hawai'i at Mānoa. Dr. Debreceny teaches accounting, auditing and accounting information systems. His research interests are in IT governance; information systems auditing and assurance; XBRL; corporate reporting on the Internet and accounting information systems. He has published widely in professional and academic journals in accounting and information systems. Debreceny holds the degrees of Master of Commerce, Master of Public Policy and PhD and is a FCPA. He previously served on the International Steering Committee of XBRL International. Dr. Debreceny serves as President of the Strategic and Emerging Technologies section of the American Accounting Association.

Prof. Dr. rer. oec. Carsten Felden – Full Professor, University of Technology and Mining of Freiberg (Saxony, Germany)

Prof. Dr. Carsten Felden is a full professor for Management Information Systems in the faculty of business administration at the University of Technology and Mining of Freiberg. Prof. Dr. Felden teaches Information Systems with the focus on business intelligence, predictive analytics, and IT governance. This in respect to his main research topics which are predictive analytics, data warehousing, XBRL, business process intelligence, information systems within the European utility sector and maturity in IT governance. He has published in professional and academic journals and conferences in accounting and information systems. Felden is member of the XBRL Germany strategy advisory board and consults at the Business Intelligence Research Center and The Data Warehouse Institute (TDWI) Germany.

Bartosz Ochocki – CTO, Business Reporting – Advisory Group

Bartosz Ochocki is co-owner and Chief Technology Officer of Business Reporting - Advisory Group (BR-AG). The company's main activities are consulting services, conducting trainings and software development in the area of business reporting solutions utilizing XBRL. As the CTO of BR-AG, Bartosz advises public institutions, regulators, software vendors and reporting entities on implementation of XBRL.

Prior to his work for BR-AG, Bartosz was a member of the XBRL Team at the International Accounting Standards Committee (IASC) Foundation.

Bartosz graduated from the Poznan University of Economics (Management Department with majors in Capital Investments and Corporate Financial

Strategies) where he received Master's degree in economics and continues his education as a PhD candidate.

Dr. Maciej Piechocki – XBRL Project Manager, IASC Foundation

Maciej Piechocki is Project Manager for International Accounting Standards Committee Foundation (IASCF) where he is responsible for the IFRS and XBRL related projects. His main areas of activities include technological aspects of the IFRS Taxonomy development.

Maciej Piechocki holds a PhD in Economics (dr. rer. pol.) with major in Management Information Systems and his doctoral dissertation covered the area of "XBRL Financial Reporting Supply Chain Architecture". He was awarded the 2008 Outstanding Dissertation Award from the Strategic Emerging Technologies Section of the American Accounting Association. Maciej Piechocki holds an MSc in Management and Marketing from the University of Economics in Poznan, Poland where he majored in Investment and Corporate Financial Strategy. He also holds an MSc in Business Administration from the Freiberg University of Technology, Germany with majors in Information Technologies and Information Systems, Accounting and Corporate Governance.

Maciej is the author of the insolvency prediction model commonly used by auditors in Poland using the analysis of financial statements and financial ratios. Maciej is an initiator of Polish XBRL Jurisdiction and the founding member of the XBRL Poland Association.

Formerly, he was the Head of the Competence Centre Information Logistics at the Chair of Information Systems at the Freiberg University of Technology. In the industry related projects of the Competence Centre, he was responsible for topics such as data warehouses, business intelligence, ontologies and XBRL concerning the Information Logistics. Maciej was also an advisor to a number of XBRL projects including central and commercial banks, stock exchanges and IT companies.

The views expressed in this book are those of the author and not those of the IASC Foundation.

Michal Piechocki – CEO, Business Reporting – Advisory Group

Michal Piechocki is a Chief Executive of the Business Reporting – Advisory Group (BR-AG) - a leading advisory company helping institutions and companies implement business reporting solutions using XBRL. As a CEO Michal advises international governmental and supervisory institutions on adoption of XBRL. His expertise contributed to projects in Europe, Australia and North and South America. Michal serves also as an At-Large Representative at the XBRL International Steering Committee and a member of the XBRL Quality Review Team at the IASC Foundation. He is also a judge in several Polish and international IFRS and XBRL related competitions.

Prior to his leadership of BR-AG Michal worked as a member of the International Accounting Standards Committee (IASC) Foundation XBRL Team developing the International Financial Reporting Standards (IFRS) XBRL taxonomy and related projects.

Michal graduated from the Poznan University of Economics (Management Department with majors in Capital Investments and Corporate Financial Strategies) where he received Master's degree in economics and continues his education as a PhD Candidate at the Technische Universitat Freiberg, Germany. Michal is a speaker at various international IFRS and XBRL conferences.

The authors express our thanks to Stefan Krebs for his invaluable assistance with the production of the manuscript.

Contents

Figures

Tables

Code Examples

Abbreviations

AGA	Association of Government Accountants
AICPA	American Institute of Certified Public Accountants
ASB	Auditing Standards Board
ASCII	American Standard Code for Information Interchange
BIOML	BIOpolymer Markup Language
CAFR	Comprehensive Annual Financial Report
CDATA	Character Data
CDR	Centralized Data Repository
CEBS	Committee of European Banking Supervisors
CFA	Chartered Financial Analyst
COREP	COmmon REPorting
CPA	Certified Public Accountant
CRD	Capital Reporting Directive
CSS	Cascading Style Sheets
DTS	Discoverable Taxonomy Set
ebXML	Electronic Business eXtensible Markup Language
EDGAR	Electronic Data-Gathering, Analysis, and Retrieval
EDI	Electronic Data Interchange
ELR	Extended Link Role
ERP	Enterprise Resource Planning
FDIC	Federal Deposit Insurance Corporation
FFIEC	Federal Financial Institutions Examination Council
FINREP	FINancial REPorting
FpML	Financial Products Markup Language
FRIS	Financial Reporting Instance Standards
FRS	Federal Reserve System
FRSC	Financial Reporting Supply Chain
FRTA	Financial Reporting Taxonomy Architecture
FRVC	Financial Reporting Value Chain
FSA	Financial Services Authority
GAAP	Generally Accepted Accounting Principles
GLFTA	GL Taxonomy Framework Technical Architecture
GLIS	XBRL GL Instance Standards
HTML	Hypertext Markup Language
IAS	International Accounting Standards
IASB	International Accounting Standards Board
IASCF	International Accounting Standards Committee Foundation
IEEE	Institute of Electrical and Electronics Engineers
IFAC	International Federation of Accountants
IFRS	International Financial Reporting Standards
ISO	International Organization for Standardization

IT	Information Technology
ITMM	IFRS Taxonomy Modules Manager
iXBRL	Inline XBRL
LRR	Link Role Registry
MathML	Mathematical Markup Language
OASIS	Organization for the Advancement of Structured Information Standards
OCC	Office of the Comptroller of the Currency
OECD	Organisation for Economic Co-operation and Development
PDF	Portable Document Format
SQL	Structured Query Language
SRCD	Summary Reporting Contextual Data
SSADM	Structured Systems Analysis and Design Method
SSAE	Standards for Attestation Engagements
SWIFT	Society for Worldwide Interbank Financial Telecommunication
URI	Uniform Resource Identifier
URL	Uniform Resource Locator
US SEC	U.S. Securities and Exchange Commission
VFP	Voluntary Filing Program
W3C	World Wide Web Consortium
WWW	World Wide Web
XBRL	eXtensible Business Reporting Language
XBRL FR	XBRL for Financial Reporting
XBRL GL	XBRL Global Ledger
XBRL VR	XBRL Visual Reporting
XDT	XBRL Language Dimensional Taxonomies
XFRML	eXtensible Financial Reporting Markup Language
XII	XBRL International
XLink	XML Linking Language
XML	eXtensible Markup Language
XP	eXtreme Programming
XPointer	XML Pointer Language
XSD	XML Schema Description
XSL-FO	XSL Formatting Objects
XSLT	eXtensible Stylesheet Language Transformations
XVS	XBRL Versioning Specification

How it all began…

Letter from Charles Hoffman "The Father of XBRL"

More than ten years ago in April 1998 my personal journey toward what was to become XBRL began. To me it is pretty amazing where XBRL is today. I think that everyone should be quite proud of what our little group has been able to achieve in this time. I think XBRL is a wonderful gift to the world. It has taken a lot of people with a lot of different skills in a lot of different areas to pull what we have together. Thank you to each and every one involved in this initiative for your efforts in turning our little dream into a reality.

For me, it was a Wednesday when I took the first step in this journey. Why I remember that it was a Wednesday, I really don't know. But it was on a Wednesday that during a lunch break during a class I was taking I went to the University of Washington Bookstore in Bellevue, Washington in search of a book on XML. I had heard of XML, but I really did not understand what it was. At that time I was worked with the public accounting firm of Knight, Vale and Gregory (now RSM McGladery).

The book was published by the W3C and explained what XML was by providing a collection of articles on how people were making use of XML. I remember one example that described how the chemicals industry had written an XML language and the book described how that all worked, explained the benefits, etc. I noticed there was nothing in the book about the accounting profession or financial reporting.

I knew immediately that XML was "the last piece of the puzzle". Over the prior 15 years, I had spent much of my time integrating one system that had some data/information to another system which needed that data/information. As a CPA, usually as a controller for smaller companies, I had learned about stuff like relational databases, fixed field formats, comma separated values. I had gotten quite good at using Microsoft Access as the intermediary application, pulling information from one place, testing it to be sure everything was OK, and then pumping that data somewhere else. The reason I used Access was that it supported so many different data formats.

After reading the book I called my friend and colleague Wayne Harding. I got to know Wayne because I read a letter to the editor he had written about something and out of the blue I called him to chat about it. As it turned out, several years later I did a lot of work with Great Plains Software (now Microsoft Business Systems), the company for which Wayne worked.

I was excited and tried to explain to Wayne that there was this new thing XML that was going to revolutionize the world and we needed to use XML for financial reporting. Wayne told me to slow down, and that we were both going to be in Chicago in about a month so why don't we talk about it then. I knew Wayne had a lot of connections at the AICPA.

So we met in Chicago. I handed Wayne a stack of documents an inch thick, which I had photocopied and highlighted for him. Wayne looked through the documents and said that it just so happened that he was the chair of the AICPA High Tech Task Force and that they were having a meeting in Sedona, Arizona sometime in September; why don't I come down and explain what XML was?

Before that September meeting I was doing some experimenting with XML. I built some samples for audit schedules, financial statements, and other things to just dink around and learn how to work with XML. I even built a little prototype that pulled inventory data (for a candy company, a client of KVG) out of a Great Plains Dynamics SQL based accounting system and rendered live inventory information on the Internet. As it turns out, what we learned at Knight, Vale and Gregory about this prototype has dramatically influenced the business of another friend and colleague who took this information, learned more about XML, and uses that base in his business today.

In September, I took my prototypes and a PowerPoint and went to Sedona, Arizona to present my idea to the AICPA High Tech Task Force that was chaired by my friend Wayne Harding. Also members of the task force were Karen Waller (with the AICPA, who many of you from the early days of XBRL know), John Woodburn (The Woodburn Group), Dianne Spencer (Deloitte & Touche LLP), Mike Harnish (Dickinson Wright et al), Chris Reimel (NJ Dept of Labor), and Barbara Vigilante (AICPA).

On the last day of the High Tech Task Force meeting, I gave my presentation. The meeting began at 8:00AM. By 10:00AM the High Tech Task Force was convinced that XML based financial reporting and audit schedules were important to pursue. Karen Waller who was an AICPA staffer said that what we needed to do was to put together a "Product Description" to get funding. We decided that we should build a prototype. We knew that Barry Melancon, president of the AICPA, had authority to approve projects up to $50,000. So, we decided that our prototype would cost no more than $49,000 (but really had no idea what we were getting into). Wayne Harding already had a meeting with Barry Melancon in two weeks, he would present to product description and try to get it approved. Two weeks later, Barry approved the project.

Next, I convinced Mark Williams, the CEO of Knight, Vale and Gregory, that I could do the prototype and to agree to accept any cost overruns. I had built a small prototype for an IBM financial statement and I knew what we had to do. I knew we needed someone to help us with some aspects of the project but it was hard to find people with XML expertise. After a few false starts, I was lucky to stumble across Mark Jewett who had started a business that did work with XML, he had recently left Microsoft. Mark Jewett and his company helped to use XSL (the first version of what was to become XSLT) to create the ability to render. We decided that the first financial statement we would create in XML was Great Plains Software, a public company, the company for which Wayne Harding worked.

In early January of 1999, Wayne Harding, Mark Jewett, and I went to New York City to present the XML Prototype to the AICPA. The prototype included the XML financial statement, the beautifully rendering of the statement in a web browser which looked literally identical to their financial statement section of the Great Plains annual report, and a demo which extracted data from the XML document on a web server in the basement of my home in Tacoma, Washington into an Excel spreadsheet on a laptop at the AICPA. I forget all who was at the meeting, but they were very impressed with what could be done with XML-based financial reporting. I still have a copy of the original XML based financial statement prototype, the style sheet, and the Excel spreadsheet.

Our question: What next?

I flew back to Tacoma and early that next week I met with Mark Williams, the CEO of KVG. I told him that everything went great and that we were within our budget. He told me that was great. Mark said that clearly the CPA firm could not fund taking this any further. I told him that I realized that and gave my two weeks notice, I was going to pursue this. I had no idea how.

I proposed to the AICPA that the next step was to put together a business plan. The AICPA agreed and they agreed to fund the business plan, so now I had a little bit of income. The AICPA assigned the project to Louis Matherne. Wayne Harding said he could help out when he had time, but he had a full time job with Great Plains. I forget if it was Wayne or Louis who asked me if I had heard of this other person who was talking about XML also. He as a CPA who had a small practice in Rochester, New York and his name was Eric Cohen.

The chair of the AICPA became aware of and interested in the XML project. His name was Bob Elliott. I think the chair of the AICPA serves a one year term, Bob was a partner with KPMG.

Over the next several months, I wrote the business plan with the help of Louis Matherne, Wayne Harding and Eric Cohen.

In May of 1999, I presented the business plan to the AICPA. I still have a copy of the business plan. It is interesting to see what we thought then, and how things turned out. The title of the business plan said, “Extensible Financial Reporting Markup Language – XFRML”. Bob Elliott, chair of the AICPA, was at the meeting. I had presented the plan focusing on financial reporting. Bob had the foresight to understand that the scope should be not financial reporting, but business reporting in general. So, our focus changed to all of business reporting.

I was given a contract (funded by the AICPA) to create 10 additional prototype XML-based financial statements to continue exploring concept.

Bob Elliott, who worked with KPMG, gets his assistant, Zack Coffin involved with XML-based business reporting project. Zack was the first non-CPA involved with the project. Zack had experience in standards with the entertainment industry.

During the time I was writing the business plan, I became aware that the SEC was modernizing the EDGAR system. They were seeking feedback on their plan to use HTML and PDF. I sent a letter to the SEC suggesting that they consider using XML as an unofficial format and mentioned that the accounting profession was working on creating a standard for XML based financial statements.

In early July or so I called up Tim Bray, author of the XML Specification. I learned that Tim lived in Vancouver, British Columbia, Canada ... just up the street. I asked him what his consulting fees were and asked if I could spend a day with him and discuss XML. He agreed and I spent the day with Tim Bray. Some of the best money I have ever spent.

Sometime in July, I received an email from Tom Howland of PricewaterhouseCoopers. Tom indicated that he read an email send by Charlie Hoffman to the US Securities and Exchange Commission relating to considering the use of XML as a reporting format, rather than considering only HTML and PDF. He wandered if I was that "Charlie Hoffman". I had mentioned that a consortium was being set up to build XML based financial reporting. Tom Howland called me and I explained what the AICPA was doing to create XML-based financial reporting. Tom mentioned this discussion to his boss, Walter Hamscher. Walter mentioned this to his boss, Mike Willis.

Walter invited me to come down to the PWC technology center and spend the day with him. Walter spend the entire day with me, showing me around, talking about what the technology center did and this impressive book they published summarizing trends in technology. At the end of the day, Walter told me that PWC wanted to join the consortium creating this XML standard for business reporting, Walter wanted to know who to make the check out to and for how much.

I told Walter that I would get back to him with that information the next day. I called Louis and told him the story and asked Louis what we should do. Somehow we decided that the fee to join the consortium was $10,000. I called Walter back, told him that the check should be made out to the AICPA for $10,000 and that congratulations, PWC was the second member of the consortium.

After Walter told me he was sending the check, I immediately told Zack Coffin that PWC was the first member of the consortium knowing full well that he would be livid. I did this to motivate KPMG to cut the second check. Zack got his check to the AICPA and we now had three members.

One of the people we wanted to join the consortium was Edgar Online. I had heard that FreeEdgar of Bellevue, Washington was being acquired by Edgar Online. Somehow, I got the name Mark Schnitzer. I went up to Bellevue to meet with Mark and he said he would do what he could to get Edgar Online to join the consortium, but his company could not join because it was being acquired.

I finished the 10 prototypes with the help of a Starbucks bistro. Literally. I had been talking to this Starbucks bistro, Mitch Dombrausky, about things I was doing. I had graduated from Pacific Lutheran University and Mitch was a religion major but was taking some time off. He said he wanted to learn programming. To make a long story short, Mitch helped create the XSL (again, still not XSLT) to render the prototypes while I created the prototypes. Mitch eventually quit his job at Starbucks and now works for a little software company in Redmond, Washington called Microsoft. I don't know if Mitch finished his religion degree, but I hope he went back and finished that.

Other things happened. Feel free if there are other tidbits which fill out this story. I do know there were lots of things going on that I was not even aware of. (What I still don't know to this day was how the original members were encouraged to sign on.) Then, we were ready…

In September 1999, the first meeting of what was to become the XBRL International Consortium was held in New York City at the offices of the American Institute of Certified Public Accountants.

People call me the "father of XBRL". My response is usually that I am the guy who did the obvious. And I also tell them that it took a lot of people with a lot of different skills. That is all you great people of XBRL International. Technical skills, business skills, marketing skills, political skills, administrative skills, and lots of other skills and sub skills. If any one person was missing, XBRL and XBRL International would be slightly different. Frankly, I don't even realize a lot of what it takes because I focus on the stuff I know. But others are saying things like, "The results are impressive." And they are right. I have met a lot of great people over the last ten years and hope to meet a lot more over the next ten years.

Again, thank you everyone for the experience of a lifetime. Not a lot of people get an opportunity to do the kind of work we do. Everyone should be quite proud of what we as a group have been able to achieve, each playing our own little role.

Charlie Hoffman

Charles Hoffman, CPA

UBmatrix

1 Introduction

```
<PLAY>
<TITLE>The Second Part of Henry the Fourth</TITLE>
<FM>
<P>XML version by Jon Bosak, 1996-1998.</P>
<TITLE>SCENE III. York. The Archbishop's palace.</TITLE>
<STAGEDIR>
Enter the ARCHBISHOP OF YORK, the Lords HASTINGS, MOWBRAY, and
BARDOLPH
</STAGEDIR>
<SPEECH>
<SPEAKER>ARCHBISHOP OF YORK</SPEAKER>
<LINE>Thus have you heard our cause and known our
means;</LINE>
<LINE>And, my most noble friends, I pray you all,</LINE>
<LINE>Speak plainly your opinions of our hopes:</LINE>
<LINE>And first, lord marshal, what say you to it?</LINE>
</SPEECH>
```

William Shakespeare could not have known of computers or that his plays would end up encoded in XML. Yet the Gutenberg movable press was little more than a century old when he wrote his first plays in the late 16th century and only a few decades before the *father* of double entry bookkeeping, Luca Pacioli, published his masterpiece *Summa de Arithmetica, Geometria, Proportioni et Proportionalita* in Venice in 1494. The Gutenberg press with its movable type, had revolutionized the production and distribution of knowledge. From illustrated manuscripts handwritten by monks, read and owned by only a tiny proportion of the population, society adopted printed books with gusto. Technology constantly affects the production, distribution and consumption of knowledge broadly and business reports more specifically. From the Gutenberg press to the telegraph to the Internet, we have seen how changes in technology bring about rapid movement in the production and use of knowledge. The eXtensible Business Reporting Language (XBRL) is an important foundation for the high quality exchange of business and other reports on the Internet. XBRL provides the opportunity to make significant changes in the distribution and use of information in a variety of information value chains. In this chapter, we discuss the nature of business reporting on the Internet. We set out the requirements for high quality information transfer of business reporting data. At a conceptual level, we then describe the functioning of XBRL. This sets the scene for the more detailed technical analysis in later chapters.

The Internet and the Web have dramatically changed the method for the distribution of business information over the last decade. No corporation of any size is without a Web site. The investor relations functions of companies listed on stock exchanges have taken to the Web with enthusiasm. The Web is ideal for the one-to-many relationships that characterize investor relations. Earlier in the lifecycle of the Web, securities regulators and other government agencies were less active in their adoption of the Internet and the Web for the collection and subsequent transfer of information with other interested parties. This comes from the more typically many-to-one relationships that we see in business entities reporting to regulators and agencies and perhaps from the inherent resistance to change in the regulator community. Regulators around the world are, however, now adopting XBRL in a variety of settings. Regulatory needs are instrumental in the adoption of XBRL in many countries and settings. They see benefits in speed, data quality enhancement, cost reduction and the ability to meet the needs of a wide variety of stakeholders within the regulator community and beyond.

1.1 Metadata

In most adoptions of the Internet for the distribution of business reports, we see the equivalent of *electronic paper.* On corporate investor relations Websites, financial reports are formatted in HTML; published in Adobe Acrobat, Microsoft Word, Excel or PowerPoint or embedded in an Adobe Flash movie. Internet search engines can usually index the data within these reports. The search engine potentially allows a user to locate a particular report. These search engines do not, however, allow a human or a software application to reliably acquire the data in the report and bring the data into their analytical software at an acceptable level of reliability and quality. Even in a clearly defined relationship between an organization and a consumer of their business reports, such as a regulator, *electronic paper* is not sufficiently reliable for information extraction and transformation.

The essential problem is that electronic paper formats are weak in their representation of metadata. The underlying logic of XBRL is to resolve this problem and provide high quality metadata about the facts in business reports on the Internet or on intranets. Business facts are meaningless unless seen in context. Metadata provides that context. Metadata is information *about* a set of data. It allows us to understand the meaning of facts and put them into context and we see metadata in everyday life. For example, the International Standard Book Number (ISBN) provides simple metadata on the publisher of books and book-like products. The thirteen digits of the ISBN has data on the country, publisher and title together with a check digit. From the ISBN we can navigate to much more information about the product. The ISBN is included on bar codes and elsewhere.

Similarly, each time a consumer plays music or watches a video on their MP3 player or phone they see the name of the track, artist, time of the track, picture and album data. The ID3 metadata standard provides many buckets of data for publishers of music, audiobooks, videos and podcasts. The standard includes data on the original format, even including the wax cylinders of the 19th century, original artist, composer, recording date, copyright information and many other items of information about the recording. From this information encoded with each track, the MP3 player or software can represent the metadata as the audio or video is played on the device.

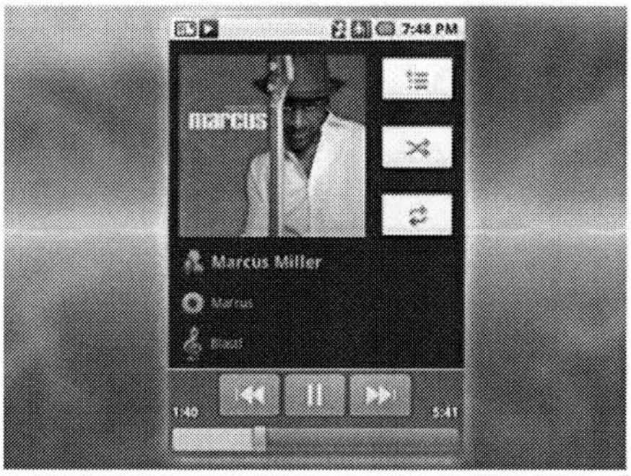

Fig. 1.1: MP3 Metadata at Work on Android Platform

In the private and public sectors, a great deal of performance information moves within and between organizations. Within firms, data on production, sales, logistics, human relations, quality, purchase and sales transactions and many other aspects that allow managers to co-ordinate, measure and control the functions of the enterprise. Then, organizations make a wide variety of information available to an array of stakeholders, government agencies and regulators. This release of data from organizations includes items as diverse as carbon consumption for compliance with national laws because of the Kyoto convention, census data, value added and income taxation and solvency data for financial institutions. Some of this information is released voluntarily by the organization. An example of voluntary disclosure is the many releases made by corporations under the ambit of the Sustainability Reporting Guidelines published by the Global Reporting Initiative (GRI). Much of the disclosure is mandated by governmental regulation. Some of the regulator-inspired data is in the public domain and some flows confidentially from a corporation to the regulator.

All of this information flow has associated metadata. Some of the metadata can be relatively simple. Some can be as complex as the ID3 metadata standard for music and video. There are many metadata standards that range from domain specific such as ID3 to general purpose tools such as the Dublin Core metadata set. The eXtensible Business Reporting Language (XBRL) came into existence to meet a broad range of needs for adding formal and computable metadata to a variety of information transfers in the business and related domain. As a product of the accounting profession, XBRL has had a primary focus on metadata associated with financial reporting. Because of its flexible design, however, XBRL has had acceptance beyond the bounds of financial reporting to a variety of other information value chains. In later chapters, we will traverse the details of the specification and point to many issues that come with the design and production of metadata in an XBRL world. First, however, let us consider the metadata that comes with typical financial reports Then, at a relatively high level of abstraction, we will show how this metadata is implemented in XBRL.

1.2 Metadata in business reports

Figure 1.2 shows the Statement of Financial Position (Balance Sheet) for the Air New Zealand group, which is headquartered in Auckland, New Zealand and listed on both the New Zealand (NZX) and Australian (ASX) stock exchanges. This statement comes from Air New Zealand's printed report, indeed one that after more than a half millennium, Fr. Luca Pacioli could easily recognize.

There is much metadata embedded in the report that the producer expects the user to understand implicitly. This is perhaps acceptable when a human is the consumer of information, who can disambiguate the embedded and implicit metadata. It is not acceptable when a computerized information system will be the consumer of the report. Metadata standards such as XBRL are necessary to conduct this disambiguation. There are 37 rows of facts in this report each with four time periods, for a total of 148 facts. So, what metadata is associated with these 148 facts?

Entity: First, this report is for a particular entity, in this case a limited liability corporation. It is not good enough, of course, to know only the name of the company. We would like to know something about this company. In which country and which corporate law is it registered? Where is it principal place of business? Where is it register of shares kept? On which stock exchanges is it listed? Who are its principal officers? The list of metadata about the company potentially is long and complex. Interestingly, however, we can see that this report has information not just about the group of companies that makes up the Air New Zealand group but also about the parent company, Air New Zealand Limited. We differentiate between the legal entity and the economic group. As we can see this report has data for both the group and the company. When presenting the 148 facts, we must differentiate between the 74 that relate to the economic group and the 74 that are for the legal entity.

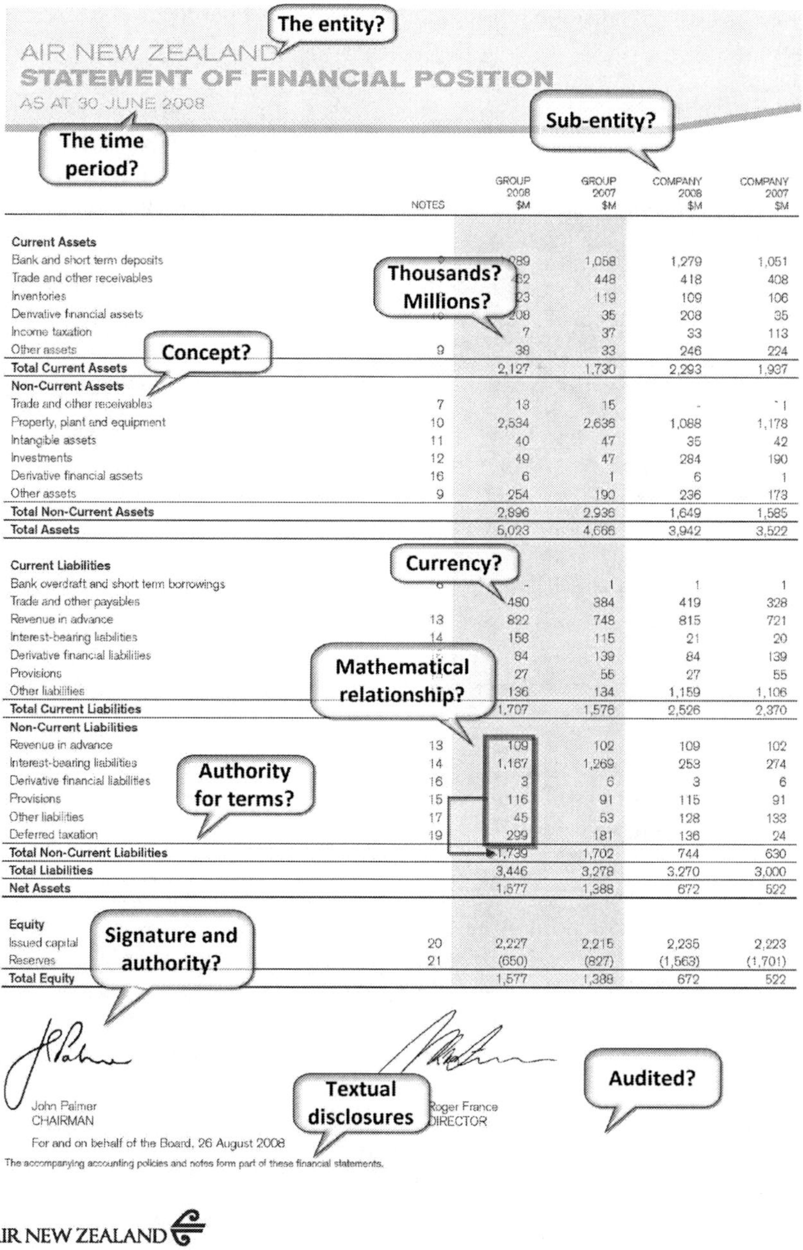

AIR NEW ZEALAND
STATEMENT OF FINANCIAL POSITION
AS AT 30 JUNE 2008

	NOTES	GROUP 2008 $M	GROUP 2007 $M	COMPANY 2008 $M	COMPANY 2007 $M
Current Assets					
Bank and short term deposits	[illegible]	[illegible]	1,058	1,279	1,051
Trade and other receivables	[illegible]	[illegible]	448	418	408
Inventories	[illegible]	[illegible]	119	109	106
Derivative financial assets	[illegible]	[illegible]	35	208	35
Income taxation		7	37	33	113
Other assets	9	38	33	246	224
Total Current Assets		2,127	1,730	2,293	1,937
Non-Current Assets					
Trade and other receivables	7	13	15	-	1
Property, plant and equipment	10	2,534	2,636	1,088	1,178
Intangible assets	11	40	47	35	42
Investments	12	49	47	284	190
Derivative financial assets	16	6	1	6	1
Other assets	9	254	190	236	173
Total Non-Current Assets		2,896	2,936	1,649	1,585
Total Assets		5,023	4,666	3,942	3,522
Current Liabilities					
Bank overdraft and short term borrowings	[illegible]	-	1	1	1
Trade and other payables	[illegible]	480	384	419	328
Revenue in advance	13	822	748	815	721
Interest-bearing liabilities	14	158	115	21	20
Derivative financial liabilities	[illegible]	84	139	84	139
Provisions	[illegible]	27	55	27	55
Other liabilities	[illegible]	136	134	1,159	1,106
Total Current Liabilities		1,707	1,576	2,526	2,370
Non-Current Liabilities					
Revenue in advance	13	109	102	109	102
Interest-bearing liabilities	14	1,167	1,269	253	274
Derivative financial liabilities	16	3	6	3	6
Provisions	15	116	91	115	91
Other liabilities	17	45	53	128	133
Deferred taxation	19	299	181	136	24
Total Non-Current Liabilities		1,739	1,702	744	630
Total Liabilities		3,446	3,278	3,270	3,000
Net Assets		1,577	1,388	672	522
Equity					
Issued capital	20	2,227	2,215	2,235	2,223
Reserves	21	(650)	(827)	(1,563)	(1,701)
Total Equity		1,577	1,388	672	522

John Palmer
CHAIRMAN

Roger France
DIRECTOR

For and on behalf of the Board, 26 August 2008

The accompanying accounting policies and notes form part of these financial statements.

4 AIR NEW ZEALAND

Fig. 1.2: Embedded Metadata in Financial Report

Time period: This report is for two time periods, for the years ended 30 June 2007 and 2008. We must potentially distinguish between many time concepts. These include the concepts of an instant in time be it for a particular day or time and the flows of time. These flows are particularly problematic. They include concepts of days, weeks, quarters, the 4/5 week quarters that are common in the retailing section and years. Even the concept of a year is difficult to define, as we may need to differentiate between a calendar year and a fiscal year. Some companies have fiscal years that end on different calendar days from year to year. Additional complexity comes with time zone, daylight saving times and other aspects that arise with geographic diversity.

Scaling and management: The facts in the report are in millions. We must alert the consumer of the data that we must multiply by a factor of 1m. There is also the question of the level of reliability that we attach to this data. As we scale data, there is a question of how much precision we signal to the information consumer.

Concept: Each of the facts in a business report has a foundation in some measurement system. We can differentiate between a general measurement system that applies to all of the facts in a report and measurement that may apply to a single fact. The essence of business reporting is to compare and contrast. A measurement system that has a single member is as useful as the very first cell phone with no-one to call. As a result, we must build a metadata system that includes standard concepts so that we can compare and contrast disparate organizations. Therefore, whether an entity *calls* a line item *Bank and short-term deposits* or *Cash and cash equivalents* these are synonyms and should link to the same metadata concept.

Authority: An important metadata attribute is the authority for a particular concept. Users of business reports will likely place greater value in a measure by a reputable standards setter, such as the International Organization for Standardization (ISO) or International Accounting Standards Board (IASB) than a concept described by a single company. For Air New Zealand, the *basis of preparation* section of the Annual Report advises that Air New Zealand *"prepares its financial statements in accordance with New Zealand Generally Accepted Accounting Practice (NZ GAAP). NZ GAAP consists of New Zealand equivalents to International Financial Reporting Standards (NZ IFRS)."* Therefore, this is the measurement system that applies to the totality of this report. There are particular concepts and facts that are specified explicitly within this particular measurement system. These facts are consistently reported across all the entities and organizations using this measurement system. The measurement system sets out the various concepts. In this case, the various IFRS standards (the so-called *Bound Volume*) include each of the concepts, albeit in a way that was not intended for computer based disclosure. Other facts within the measurement system are commonly observed within the reporting community. By coding of the standards and observation of the real world of business reporting within the domain of the particular measurement system, we can relatively easily build a reference list of metadata concepts. Then, in business reporting there is a great deal of variation in key performance indicators from industry to industry. For example, in the airline industry we often see separate disclosure of assets such as aircraft, airframes and engines. There are also performance metrics, distinct from the financial statements that are the focus of this example. Key airline performance metrics include Cost per Available Seat Mile (CASM) and Revenue per Available Seat Mile (RASM). Finally, there are facts that are applicable to the particular entity or organization. These facts are material for the entity but not typically observed for the industry or the complete measurement system. A business reporting system of metadata must accommodate all of this variation in concepts.

Currency and other quantitative measures: All of the quantitative facts in this report are financial in nature. They are set out in a particular currency. The accounting policies notes that *"The financial statements .. are presented New Zealand Dollars which is the Company's functional currency."* When information from the report is packaged up and transmitted in digital form to other computer systems, external reference to a textual statement of accounting policies is not a feasible option. The metadata system for business reporting must distinguish between different types of data including textual and quantitative data. When considering quantitative data we must be able to differentiate between count (integer, float, decimal etc.), length (miles, meters etc.), weight (ounces, kilograms etc.), volume (liters, cubic inches etc.) and other measures and monetary data that represent a store of value. When we consider monetary data, we must be able to differentiate between a million New Zealand dollars, as is the case of Air New Zealand, US dollars, Estonian kroons, Polish zlotys or Euros.

Mathematical relationships: Many business reports have mathematical relationships between concepts. These relationships may be straightforward, as in the summation of each of the non-current liability concepts to *Total non-current liabilities*. Other relationships are complex, and take on the form of business rules (*if-then*, *if-then-else* etc.). For example, where *Total non-current liabilities* is more than twice the level of *Total non-current assets*, the level of financial stress is likely to be high. This simple rule links two concepts (*Total non-current liabilities* and *Total non-current assets*) to a third (*Financial stress*). In business reporting, metadata must allow resolution of each of these simple and more complex relationships.

Authority and signing: This report has the names of the Chair and Deputy Chair of the board and replicas of their signatures. These artifacts do not readily translate to a digital world. Metadata coupled with various security mechanisms are necessary to couple facts in digital form with document authority.

Context: There is a variety of contextual metadata that we can associate with business reports. We point to just one of these contexts in Figure 1.2: is this report audited? This is, of course, an important quality attribute of business reports. There are many other potential contexts: Is this report preliminary? Final? Restated? Forecast? Actual? Budgeted? Interim? All of these various contexts can be included on a single report. Metadata must accommodate these different classes of reports.

Presentation: Users of financial reports, such as a Statement of Financial Position, have a particular mental representation of how the report appears on paper. The order, indenting and other aspects of presentation are all important for human consumption of the information.

In the previous discussion, we provide a flavor of the difficulty of defining, expressing and interrelating metadata. We also point to the wide variety of possible information value chains in which we can insert metadata defined in XBRL. Now we consider the way in which information flows in business reports. Business reporting is markedly different from other information flows. The metadata for MP3 audio and video that we discuss above is relatively complex. However, once designed, the metadata is generic and unchanging. In every genre, country and market, music and video share essentially common metadata. Once defined, the same metadata can apply to modern electronic reproductions of wax cylinders from the 19th century to the latest news podcast and from court music of Barbod the Great in 7th century Persia to current rock videos.

1.3 Use cases for metadata and business reporting

In business reporting, we must define use-case specific metadata. Consider the following use cases. In the first use case (Fig 1.3), financial information flows from division to headquarters. This data may take very different formats. There will be rules for balanced scorecard data that will be set by headquarters and apply equally to each division. Some of those balanced scorecard data elements may be drawn from external sources. For example, in the airlines industry a customer-focused balanced scorecard data element might be on-time arrival data from a national airline regulator. Others will apply only to the particular division. In essence, the metadata for balanced scorecard data information flows will vary widely from industry to industry and from firm to firm.

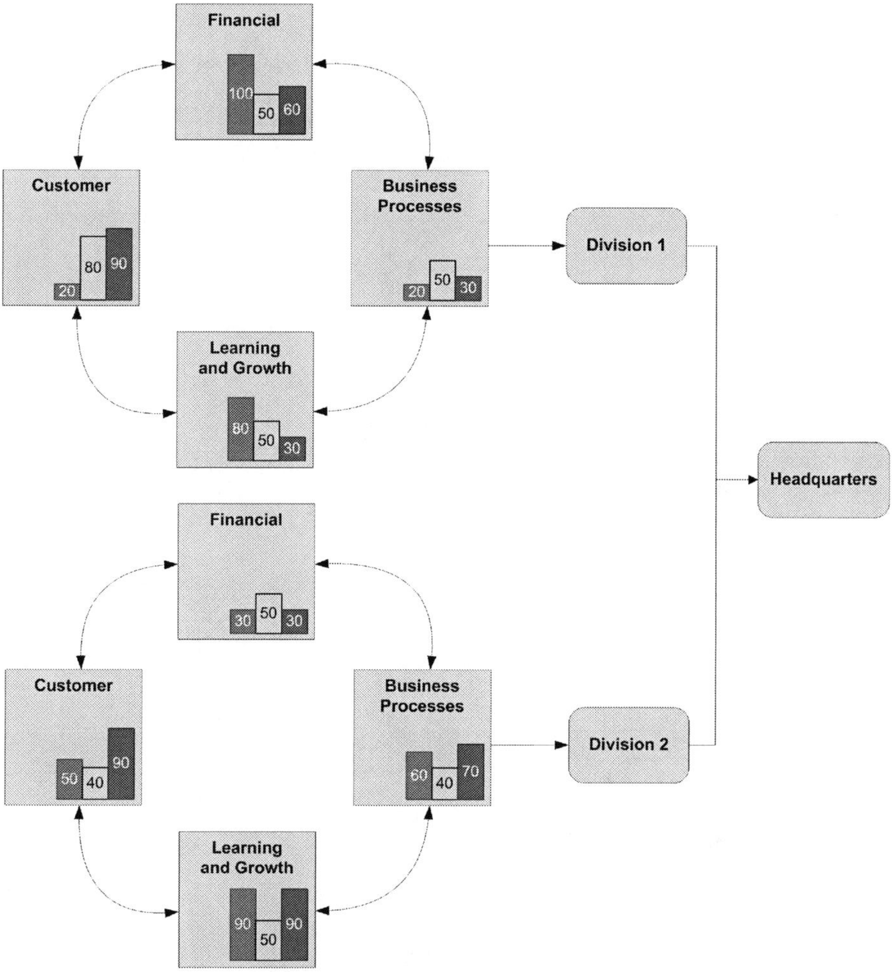

Fig. 1.3: Multi-dimensional information

The second use case, shown in Figure 1.4, is a more typical flow of information across an information value chain. Mandated corporate performance reports including financial statements and reports of the board of directors flow from the corporation to a securities regulator. The financial statements accord with the standards set by accounting standards setters. They are subject to audit by an external auditor. In turn, the securities regulator exports the information, transformed, aggregated and consolidated to a national statistics office and to the central bank. The corporate financial statements go in their raw format to the Internet and to information aggregators. The information aggregators again transform and standardize the financial statement data. The aggregators output their data to their financial institution clients and in a different form to the Internet.

The use case involves many parties each with their own objectives and interests. Data is subject to a variety of transformations. The data may be aggregated or *chunked* into smaller components. The financial statement report data may come to the Internet directly from the corporation, indirectly from the securities regulator or in raw or some transformed form from information intermediaries.

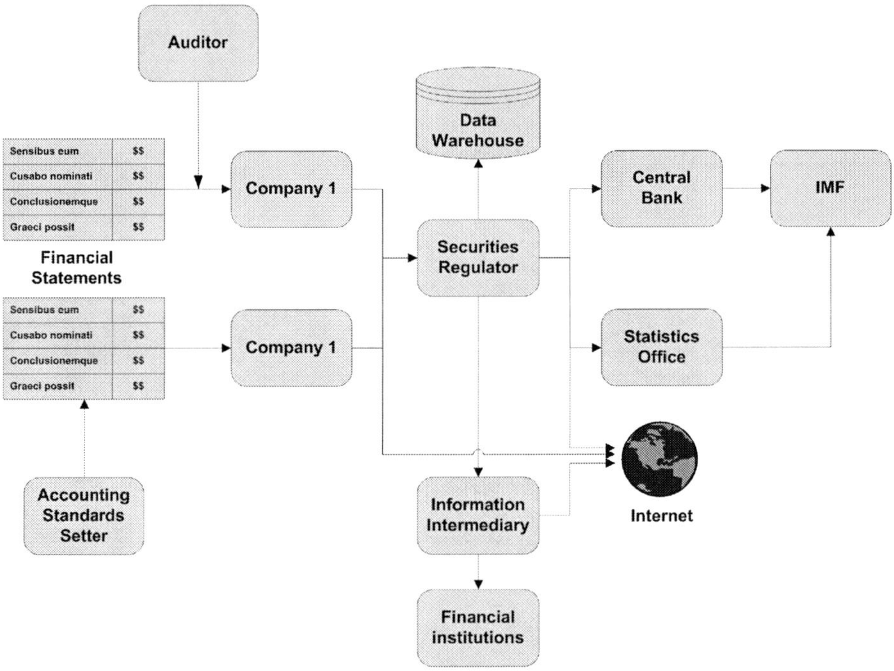

Fig. 1.4: Information Value Chain

The accounting standards setter defines the measurement principles under which reporting takes place. They may also define many of the concepts included in the financial statements. The corporations take on the responsibility of applying these standards to their own unique business case. The auditor expresses an opinion of the relationship between these reports and the requisite accounting standards. Each of the parties must accord to the same underlying measurement and disclosure standards, while at the same time allowing construction of additional concepts. For example, there may be a requirement on the auditor to produce a report in electronic form. They may need to make quite different reports from client to client, when required to report on the quality of internal controls as in the case of the Sarbanes-Oxley Act, Section 404. The auditor must adjust their reports for the particular circumstances of the client.

These two use cases illustrate that a different approach to metadata was necessary for business reporting. At every stage in the information value chains we show below, data is drawn into a variety of databases. These databases may be as simple as a spreadsheet or as complex as a data warehouse to support automated business intelligence. At every stage, data is transformed and analyzed by software programs. While humans are, of course, the ultimate consumer of this information, computer programs support their analysis. The primary design for XBRL was to construct a framework that would allow information consumers, intermediaries and regulators to construct systems of metadata for their own particular use. The XBRL specification is that framework. It is implemented in XML and a core set of XML standards including XML Schema and XLink. The specification, currently Version 2.1, sets out *how* metadata is to be defined in a *taxonomy*. The taxonomy implements the actual metadata for the particular information transfer solution. When producers of information generate their reports (*instance documents*) they *tag* or link facts represented in the instance document against concepts defined in the taxonomy. This process couples the metadata in the taxonomy with the facts in the instance document. In addition, there is some metadata that is resident in the instance document, rather than in the taxonomy. For example, metadata about the entity or time period, as we discussed in the worked example earlier in the chapter, is set out in the instance document. The information consumer in the information value chain must work with both the instance document and the taxonomy to extract all the requisite metadata.

1.4 Instance documents and taxonomies

Earlier in the chapter, we saw some of the complexities in the metadata for a business report. The XBRL specification supports a number of metadata concepts. As there is a wide variety of potential business reporting solutions, the specification does not pre-define concepts. Instead, taxonomy builders place all their concepts in a XML *schema*. The XML schema standard allows developers to construct their schemas similarly to the development of relational or object-oriented database schemas. These data structures are not sufficiently flexible, however, for the business-reporting environment. Instead, the schema is merely a simple list of all the concepts in the taxonomy. Structure in the taxonomy is provided in so-called *linkbases*. These are implemented in the XLink language. Figure 1.5 illustrates the interaction between schema and linkbases. The linkbases add all the richness of metadata to the concepts listed in the schema. We illustrate four of the linkbases in this example. The first linkbase adds human readable labels to the concepts (label linkbase). The XML technology allows taxonomy builders to provide a variety of labels (e.g. terse labels, verbose labels, standard labels). Labels may also be contextual in nature with, for example, a different label for positive values and negative values for quantitative concepts. A second linkbase provides relatively straightforward mathematical relationships between concepts (*calculation linkbase*). While the XBRL specification does not aim to provide a full rendering of XBRL tagged data, the *presentation linkbase* provides simple instructions on the ordering and indenting of concepts in the taxonomy. Finally, the genus of the information concepts is set out in the definition linkbase. Collectively, we refer to the concepts in the *schema* and the metadata representations in the linkbases as a *taxonomy set*.

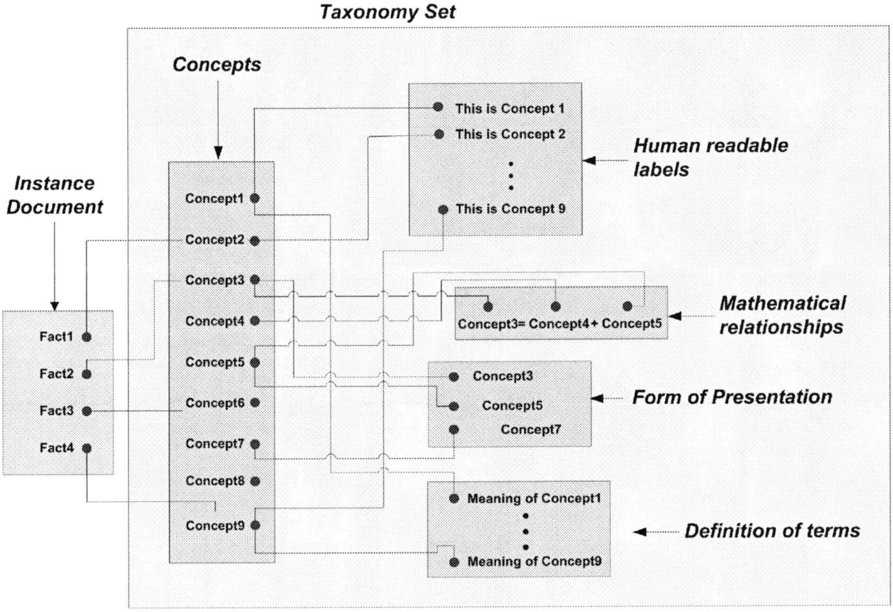

Fig. 1.5: Multi-dimensional information

The business facts in this reporting environment are in an *instance document*. In the example in Figure 1.5, we see that the facts in *instance document* are tagged with the concepts in the schema. Software then follows those tags across the Internet to the taxonomy suite, known technically as a *Discoverable Taxonomy Set* (DTS). Then we can retrieve the metadata in the various linkbases. We can see the label, any calculation relationships and understand the definition and meaning of the concept.

1.5 Multidimensionality

Thus far, we have considered relatively simple reports. The Statement of Financial Position for Air New Zealand that we reproduce in Figure 1.2 is a simple table with just two dimensions. These dimensions are concepts, in this case financial statement facts, and time periods. There are many business reports, however, that can only be represented in multi-dimensional tables. A simple three dimensional table is shown in the cube in Fig 1.6. Here there are concepts that apply to several divisions and across a number of periods.

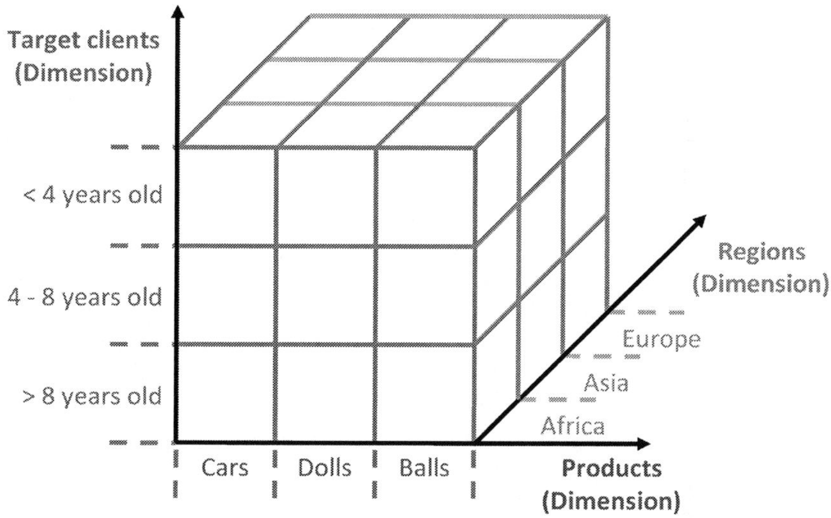

Fig. 1.6: Multi-dimensional information

In an important addition to the XBRL suite of standards, the XBRL community added a Dimensions specification in 2007. The dimensional specification allows taxonomy builders to construct n-dimensional tables (cubes) for the delivery of data such as that set out in the figure. The dimensional specification was a particularly important addition to the toolkit of the taxonomy developer as so many important use cases for business reporting involve multidimensional data.

1.6 What comes next ...

Having set out the background to business reporting on the Internet, we now go on to provide a detailed analysis of XML as a foundation technology, XBRL taxonomies and instance documents the role of multidimensional taxonomies. We complete our discussion with a review of recent and forthcoming XBRL technologies.

2 Handling Semantics in Information Exchange – An Introduction to XML

Good information is hard to get.
It is even more difficult, to use it.
[Sir Arthur Conan Doyle (1859 – 1930)]

This citation is even more valid for the information age with many billions of Web page and in these times of the semantic web. The main issue for Web users is not getting information. Rather the principal task for the user of the Web is to separate relevant from irrelevant information. Humans can use their knowledge and subtle clues when they face a long list of results from a search engine. Conversely, when there is automated processing of information, large numbers of unreliable search results are often a serious problem.

Opening Vignette: Will XML be the ultimate platform? Or will it be the next EDI?[1]

I hear it's going to cure cancer," says Tim Bray, its co-creator. "It's going to do my dishes, I hear," says Anne-Marie Keane, Staples' vice president of B2B e-commerce. Behind the flip jokes lies XML - a syntax that underpins a growing list of more than 300 nascent data standards. MathML, for instance, will make it possible to manipulate advanced mathematical equations on a Web page. Spacecraft Markup Language standardizes databases that operate telemetry and mission control. And then there's MeatXML, a comical name for a serious effort to create a universal meat and poultry supply chain standard. With XML going in so many directions at once, you can't blame CIOs for being confused. The hyperbole often makes XML sound like a salve for all pain. Finding the truth behind the tales takes some digging. Technologically, XML is a giant leap for IT. It can drastically reduce development time while making data transfer over the Internet simple. If nurtured properly, it may even become the ASCII text of online business - ubiquitous and assumed. Or it could become the next EDI, fractured under the pressure of vendor self-interest. One thing is certain: for XML to reach its full potential, CIOs will have to take an active role in forcing their partners, their vendors and even their competitors toward a radically more open computing model than what existed before.

This chapter deals with enhancing the understanding of an electronic document and information exchange. The eXtensible Markup Language (XML) and

---

[1] Excerpted from Scott Berinato, "XML: The Hype Stuff", CIO Magazine, available at http://www.cio.com.au/index.php/id;212673785.

derivatives are nothing other than an approach to realize the understanding of an electronic document. XML is a foundation of the semantic web. In recent years, discussion is not just on markup languages. Increasingly the dialog about exchange of information includes also the term ontology. This term is rather scary for a number of people who are not intimately involved in the field. The task of ontologies is merely to describe things and the relationships between things. This increased emphasis on ontologies has come into focus by the semantic web.

Over many years, organizations and public agencies have come forward to develop standards to solve communication hurdles. These standards exist to establish and disseminate communication methods to allow smooth understanding in information flows. For example, SWIFT is an important communication standard that supports automated money transfer between banks. Some communication standards are already accepted. For example, the SWIFT codes to facilitate money transfers are encoded in an International Standards Organisation (ISO) standard (ISO 9362). There is even an XML wrapper for SWIFT codes (swiftML). There are also emerging or *de facto* standards. The XML recommendations from the World Wide Web Consortium (W3C) are good examples of such *de facto* standards. They only have the force of the consortium behind them. Yet a wide array of important standards rest on these *de facto* standards.

XML is a basis for several communication standards. The reasons for development of XML were many problems with the HyperText Markup Language (HTML). These issues are seen in the so-called HTML dilemma. To understand this dilemma, the following Code example 2.1 shows the structure of a typical HTML document.

```
<html>
    <head>
    <title >Skeleton of a HTML document</title>
    </head>
    <body>
    <h1>HTML documents</h1>
    <p>This is a simple <strong>HTML document
    </strong>without navigation<p>.
    </body>
</html>
```

Code example 2.1: Document structure using HTML

HTML is a markup language for the standardized display of information. Web browsers take tags such as <h1> (highest heading level) and <p> (paragraph) as clues to represent information on the screen for a human user. Different browsers have a different understanding about the document structure information. Seeking a more positive user experience, websites will often use HTML tags for other than their intended purposes. As a result the content (or better the semantics) of a HTML document remains unclear for information exchanges purposes.

The dilemma of HTML is that it is on the one hand very easy to structure documents for Web presentations - which is positive. On the other hand, HTML does not allow a machine understandable structuring of documents. Search engines such as Google, allows ready access to a wide variety of documents on the Internet. Unfortunately, that variety of search results is often a major impediment to finding a desired value. All search engine users have the experience of a result list with a million or more web pages. Most of these pages are not relevant for the user. The result list is at the level of the relevance of the complete content in each document, which is inappropriate in the realm of intra- or inter-enterprise communications of designated values such as *Revenue* or *Qualified Carbon Credit*. Automated document retrieval by search engine cannot ensure document or value validation - which is negative. The construction of XML plays an important role in resolution of these existing problems.

2.1 What is XML?

The eXtensible Markup Language (XML) is a World Wide Web Consortium (W3C) defined open standard. Its task is to contain, name, structure, and secure information. Thereby XML is not a programming language. The task of XML is to describe the content of an electronic document. This means to clarify the meaning of *name*, *address* and so on and then to structure it in an appropriate format (the first row of a document is *name*, second row is *street* etc.). XML is a text-based meta-language to exchange, visualize and manipulate structured data to support heterogeneous applications.

The following example (Fig. 2.1) shows textual information, typed in a text-processing program such as Microsoft Word. A human reader can read and understand the text, which is nothing else than first name and surname. If a user wishes to store this information, the application stores it as a single document with a number of characters without knowing the meaning of these characters. XML manages information in an entirely different way. First, XML defines the structure of a document. Second, XML fills the information structure with appropriate values. This leads to human- and machine-readable documents. XML has a similar appearance to those structured in the HTML. HTML is only able to define the presentation of the stored information. XML defines content. As a result, XML is an important foundation of the semantic web.

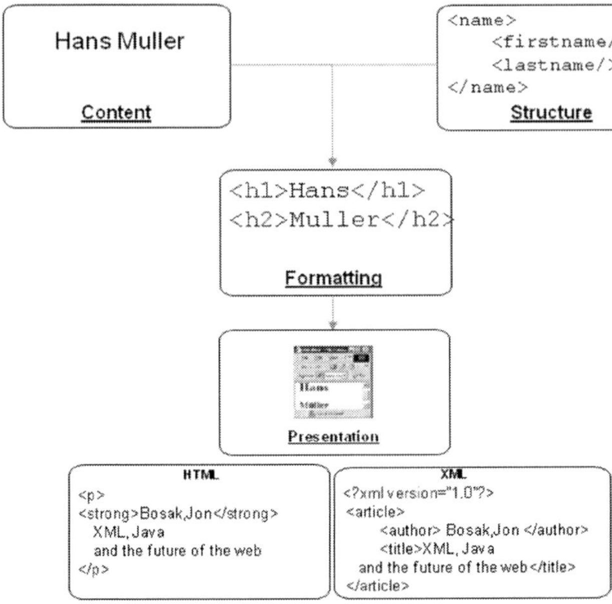

Fig. 2.1: XML task, HTML and XML

Importantly, XML is an open standard. It is an information container and a toolset for other more specific markup languages, such as XBRL. XML documents are machine- and human-readable, although the level of readability varies with the level of their complexity. They are also structured like a tree, which is a very common pattern in computer science. The following ten aspects characterize XML:

1. XML represent structured data.
2. XML looks a bit like HTML.
3. XML is text, but not for reading.
4. XML has a full design.
5. XML is a family of techniques[2].
6. XML is new, but not that new.
7. XML transfers HTML to XHTML.
8. XML is modular.
9. XML is the basis for the Semantic Web.
10. XML is freely licensed, platform- and company independent and well supported.

Besides the structuring of documents, data can be stored and retrieved by using XML standards and tools. Additionally, the output can be formatted by using

[2] XML is a collection of a number of languages, rule collections and data structures. It contains e.g. XSLT, XPath, XLink and XML schema.

XML together with style sheets (CSS). They can be transformed into an HTML document (XML and XSLT), a PDF document (XML and XSL-FO) and many other formats. As already stated, XML describes data. The following Code example 2.2 shows an email described by XML.

```
<?xml version="1.0" encoding="ISO-8859-1"?>
<email>
    <from>jenny</from>
    <to>benny</to>
    <subject>Hi</subject>
    <message>Hello Benny! How are you doing?</message>
</email>
```

Code example 2.2: Email as an XML file

This example is easy to understand, because the tags are readable and context oriented. There is no limit about the complexity or the hierarchy depth of an XML document. The logical structure works in a hierarchical order, where the stored information is represented as concepts. As the concepts are interrelated, we model the interdependencies in a hierarchical tree structure. As far as the physical data structure is concerned, the XML document is nothing more than a string of characters.

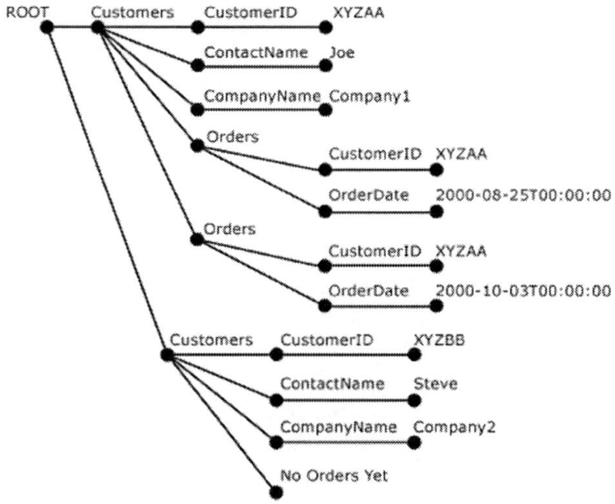

Fig. 2.2: Tree of an XML document

XML is a standardized language that includes the capability to define the markup language syntax. Since the definition of XML in 1998, many more initiatives have come from the XML community. The following shows the most important XML language family members.

- **XLink** (Recommendation, 27 June 2001)
- **XPointer** (Recommendation, 25 March 2003)
- **XML Namespaces** (Recommendation, 14 January 1999)
- **XSL** (Recommendation 15 October 2001)
- **XSLT 1.0** (Recommendation, 16 November 1999),
- **XSLT 2.0** (Recommendation, 23 January 2007)
- **XPath 1.0** (Recommendation, 11 November 1999),
- **XPath 2.0** (Recommendation, 23 January 2007),
- **XQuery 1.0** (Recommendation, 23 January 2007).

XML document: The following figure shows the construction of an XML message.

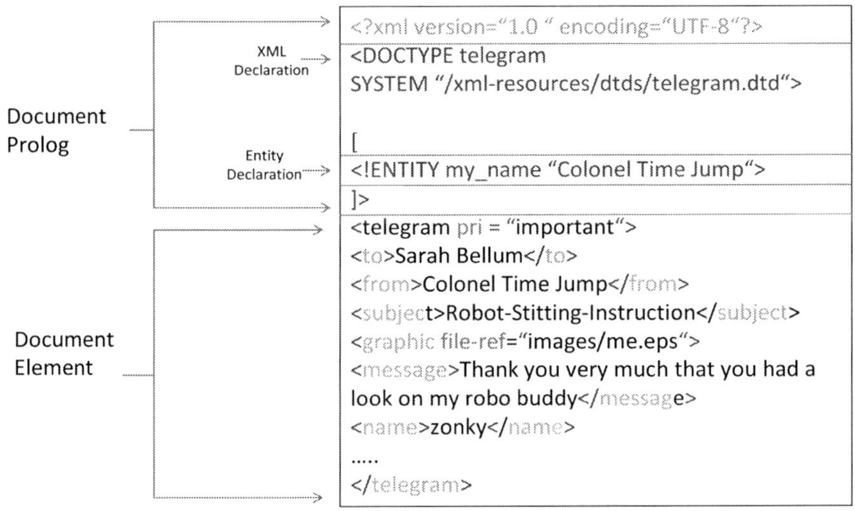

Fig. 2.3: Construction of an XML document

The XML declaration is a collection of information to prepare software processors for use of the information stored in an XML document. The declaration is always the first row of the XML document.

A container tag, or just tag or element, is a markup symbol which is symbolized by < > brackets. There must be a closing tag for each open tag. Tags symbolize that there is information about the semantics of the document structure. The following example shows the syntax of a container tag.

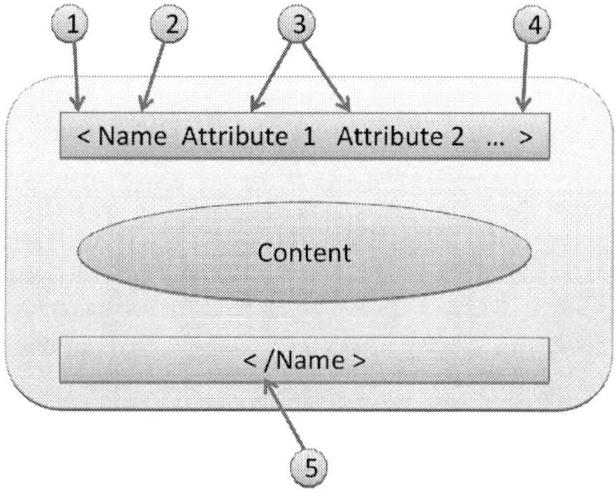

Fig. 2.4: Syntax of a container element

The figure above shows an (1) opening bracket, an (2) element name, (3) optional attributes of the initial tag, a (4) closing bracket and a (5) closing tag with forward slash after its opening bracket. The following syntax rules apply:

→ Tags cannot be overwritten (comparable to brackets in mathematic formulas)

```
Wrong:     <b>This text is bold <i>and italic</b></i>
Correct:   <b>This text is bold <i>and italic</i></b>
```

Code example 2.3: Example of nesting of tags

→ Capitalization matters (because the computer differentiates according to the case of text)

```
Wrong:     <Text>This text is bold and italic</text>
Correct:   <text>This text is bold and italic</text>
```

Code example 2.4: Example of capital case use in XML

→ Correct structure (each element can have subelements but they need to be properly nested as presented in the Examples 2.3 and 2.5)

```
<root>
  <child>
    <subchild>....</subchild>
  </child>
</root>
```

Code example 2.5: Example of proper nesting in XML

→ Valid characters for element names are 0-9, a-z, A-Z, dot (.), hyphen (-) and underline (_). The initial character of an XML name must be a letter. The element name must not start with a hyphen, number, punctuation character or string *xml* (XML, Xml, xml, etc,). The length of an element name is not limited.

```
Correct    <_-_>allowed</_-_>
Wrong      <-_>not allowed</-_>
Wrong      <2nd-phone-number>13</2nd-phone-number>
Wrong      <advise+question>Bla</advise+question>
```

Code example 2.6: Example allowed and disallowed characters for tags

The content of an XML document comes through information within the tagged element, attributes of the tag, and sub-elements of the tag in an information structure. Attributes characterize things of the reality we want to describe in our document. Each attribute is as a container storing appropriate information. Technically, an attribute is a pair of a name and a value. For example by the means of attributes we can give an element a unique id. Attributes can provide support for differentiation of data, because the definition and amount of attributes is set up once and used several times. We show an example in the following figure.

```
<product id="screen-15-Zoll-Sony">
       <weight>...</weight>
       <resolution>...</resolution>
       <!—More product details-->
</product>

<product id="screen-15-Zoll-IBM">
       <weight>...</weight>
       <resolution>...</resolution>
       <!—More product details-->
</product>
```

Code example 2.7: Details of data contained in attributes

The following example shows rules for expressing values of an attribute.

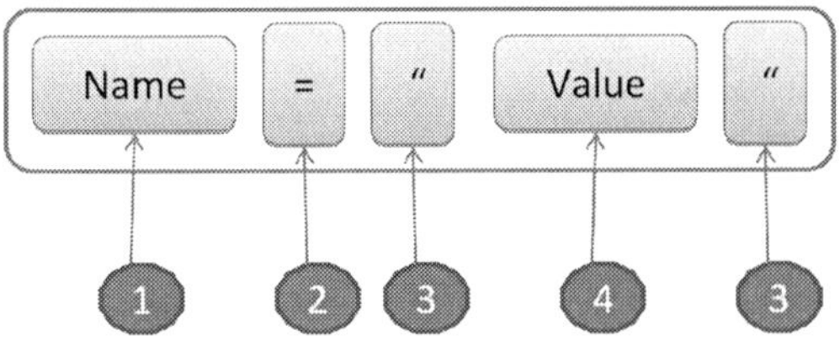

Fig. 2.5: Attribute example

The components of the Fig. 2.5 are (1) attribute name, (2) equal symbol, (3) double or single quotations, and (4) attribute value. The number of attributes of an element is not limited. The following Code example 2.8 shows a tag with four attributes.

```
<employee sex="female" age="25" height="170cm" ssn="123">
      <!—content of the tag-->
</employee>
```

Code example 2.8: Tag with four attributes

Attributes of the same element must have different names.

```
wrong: <team person="Jane" person="Joe"></team>
correct: <team person_1="Jane" person_2="Joe"></team>
```

Code example 2.9: Unifying attributes

In the previous examples, we demonstrated how data could be stored as value of an attribute. However, data can be also stored without use of attributes. The following example shows the same data stored as values of elements. In later chapters, we will explain how elements and attributes are used to capture certain financial reporting data.

```
<team>
      <person1>Jane</person1>
      <person2>Joe</person2>
</team>
```

Code example 2.10: Content without using attributes

Attributes can be used to describe values. Other possibilities to get machine-readable semantics are elements. Attributes were introduced to describe information that is contained in the element itself as its value.

```
<from name="Maria Lara" email="ml@xyz.com">I am coming
soon!</from>
```

Code example 2.11: Information container

The final table summarizes the tag types in XML.

Tab. 2.1: Tag types in XML

Object	Reason	Example
Empty element	Represents information at a specific point within the document.	<xref linkend="abx"/>
Container element	Groups elements and character set data.	<p>This is a new section. </p>
		<!ENTITY Author “John Doe”>
Declaration	Enhances the parsing environment with new	<?print formatter create new row?>

	parameters, entities or grammar definitions.	
Comment	Enhances the document with a comment which is ignored by the XML processor.	<!--I stopped here-->
CDATA section	Creates a section with character set data that are not parsed (to keep all specific elements within the document).	<![CDATA[AND-CASCADE!&&&&&&]]>
Entity reference	Informs the parser to fill in textual parts that are stored at a different location.	&companyname;

2.2 *XML namespaces*

When we draw data from a variety of different sources, identical names can have different meanings. For example, the term *article* can mean an article of a book club, an article in a magazine or an article within the articles of incorporation of a company. To solve this problem, we can use namespaces coupled with element names to give truly unique combinations.

Fig. 2.6: Namespaces

Namespaces are parts of the XML family in general and of XBRL in particular. XML namespaces are a mechanism to link elements and attributes into groups.

We are going to take a closer look into XML applications that use attributes and elements within a single XML document (markup vocabulary). Such XML documents are used and understood by different software modules. It is more appropriate to reuse markup vocabulary as defined in the XML document. Such reuse of markup vocabulary is hindered when recognition and collision problems occur[3] in XML applications. Thus as a rule, tags and attributes must be unique. Collisions, where we have identical attribute names or element types, should not then cause errors during processing. XML namespaces exactly satisfy this requirement.

[3] The usage of identical terms with different meaning can lead to problems. For example, *Orange* can be a fruit or can also be a European mobile phone company.

Recommended XML Namespace for Government Organizations[4]

The US federal government is actively engaged in developing and deploying XML. It is critical that the government establishes a cohesive, coordinated namespace approach to support its various XML efforts. This namespace approach must define a standardized structure for federal namespace as well as establish a standardized naming convention for those namespaces. Without such a coordinated approach, individual government organizations will create a proliferation of disparate XML namespace structures and names resulting in chaotic management of XML components.

To summarize, we define the term namespace as follows: An XML namespace is a collection of names, identified by URI links that are in use as element types and attribute names within XML documents. URIs are necessary to be able to identify namespaces. To make it clear - URIs are part of the set of URLs. The syntax is of a namespace declaration is:

```
xmlns:prefix="URI"
```

The following example shows a code part of an XML document that uses namespaces to demonstrate the unique identification of attributes.

```
<order
   xmlns:bo="http://www.book.com/"
   xmlns="http://www.magazine.com/">
  <bo:article number="1234">
      <bo:description>XML and XBRL</bo:description>
  </bo:article>
  <article id="111">
      <name>Information Systems<name>
  </article>
</order>
```

Code example 2.12: Namespaces

The example contains namespaces with the attribute declaration *xmlns:bo* and *xmlns*[5]. The elements of the shown order belong to the first or the second category.

---

4 Excerpted from J. L. Glace and M. R. Crawford: Recommended XML Namespace for Government Organizations, August 2003, available at http://xml.gov/documents/completed/lmi/GS301L1_namespace.pdf.

5 *xmlns="http://www.magazine.com/"* is treated as default namespace and therefore is not assigned a prefix.

2.3 XML schema

The W3C developed XML schema as a language for the description of XML documents. An XML schema contains the necessary element types, attributes and entities to align with XML instance documents. XML schema is similar to a database schema for a database such as Microsoft Access or Oracle. An instance document contains information that aligns with the schema. The instance document includes processable information encoded by the tags from the schema. The XML schema defines syntactical rules and the structure of a class of XML documents.

A corresponding XML schema assures the validity of an XML instance document. XML parsers or validators will validate whether an instance document is a well formed XML document. Additionally the schema is an explicit coding of rules which contain information about what is valid and necessary and what is unnecessary.

Besides the already existing XML-based languages, XSD (XML schema description language) has the highest practical recognition. XBRL uses XSD as we describe later in the book. An XML schema can ensure a number of validation quality checks:

- It defines the elements that can be used within a document.
- It defines the attributes that can be used in a document.
- It defines the child elements of an element.
- It defines the order of child elements of an element.
- It defines the number of child elements.
- It defines if an empty element is allowed.
- It defines data types.
- It defines fixed and default values.

An XML schema supports differentiation of namespaces that go hand in hand with the structure of well-formed constraints on the content of an instance document.

An XSD document is organized as a tree of schema elements. The root of the schema file is always *<xsd:schema>*. The root element includes other elements *<xsd:complexType>* or *<xsd:simpleType>*. The prefix *xsd* shows that all elements belong to the XML schema family. The XML schema namespace declaration is:

`xmlns:xsd=http://www.w3.org/2001/XMLSchema`.

A typical XSD schema documents has several different components. Primary components are simple or complex type definitions, element or attribute declarations. We explain the roles of these components using a number of examples in this section. As shown in the following example, simple type definitions contain just a single value such as a number, a date or text. The XML schema means that an XML document created upon such a schema is supposed to provide a value for the element *name*.

```
<xsd:element name="name">
  <xsd:simpleType>
    <xsd:restriction base="xsd:string"/>
  </xsd:simpleType>
</xsd:element>
```

Code example 2.13: Simple data type

Complex type definitions are elements that contain subelements or attributes. This means that an XML document based on the following schema should provide values for *projectMember*, *projectBudget* and *projectGoal*. All these three exist within the element *projectDescription*.

```
<xsd:element name="projectDescription">
<xsd:complexType>
  <xsd:sequence>
    <xsd:element ref="projectMember"/>
    <xsd:element ref="projectBudget"/>
    <xsd:element ref="projectGoal"/>
  </xsd:sequence>
</xsd:complexType>
</xsd:element>
```

Code example 2.14: Complex data type

Secondary components are definitions of attribute groups, key references for uniqueness, declaration of comments and linking of names. The XML schema has additional supporting components like comment and description about using attributes.

We can use a *simple type* to express limitations such as *length, minLength, maxLength, pattern, enumeration* and *whiteSpace*. Let us look at the following examples:

```
<xsd:simpleType name="password">
  <xsd:restriction base="xsd:string">
    <xsd:minlength value="8"/>
    <xsd:maxlength value="15"/>
  </xsd:restriction>
</xsd:simpleType>
```

Code example 2.15: Password with minimum and maximum number of elements

An XML document based on the schema from Code example 2.15 can provide an alphanumeric value for the element *password* that has between 8 and 15 characters.

```
<xsd:simpleType name="dayOfWeek">
  <xsd:restriction base="xsd:string">
    <xsd:enumeration value="Monday"/>
    <xsd:enumeration value="Tuesday"/>
    <xsd:enumeration value="Wednesday"/>
    ...
  </xsd:restriction>
</xsd:simpleType>
```

Code example 2.16: Enumeration of elements

An XML document based on the schema from Code example 2.16 can provide a value for the element *dayOfWeek* that is from the restricted set (*Monday*, *Tuesday*, *Wednesday…*). One element can hold just one of these enumerated values.

```
<xsd:simpleType name="isbn">
  <xsd:restriction base="xsd:string">
    <xsd:pattern value="[0-9]{10}"/>
  </xsd:restriction>
</xsd:simpleType>
```

Code example 2.17: Fixing an example for an element

An XML document based on the schema from Code example 2.17 must provide an alphanumeric value for the element *isbn* consisting of digits between 0 and 9.

```
<xsd:simpleType name="ageGroup">
  <xsd:restriction base="xsd:integer">
    <xsd:minInclusive value="18"/>
    <xsd:maxInclusive value="30"/>
  </xsd:restriction>
</xsd:simpleType>
```

Code example 2.18: Defining a range

XML documents based on the schema from example 2.18 can provide a value for the *ageGroup* element that is an integer with the value between 18 and 30.

```
<xsd:simpleType name="direction">
  <xsd:list itemType="xsd:string"/>
</xsd:simpleType>

XML document (instance):
<direction>North East South West</direction>
```

Code example 2.19: Defining a list

The XSD definition of the document structure provides a set of names for all possible elements and their attributes as well as links them with their respective data type. We can add additional constraints and set default values of elements. We define the element declaration with the statement *<xsd:element name="description">* (first character of a name is a letter). The XML schema allows us to define complex elements each of which have several child elements. We define this by modeling a custom data type:

```
<xsd:element name="description" type="description">
<xsd:complexType name="description">
   <xsd:sequence>
     <xsd:element name="customer" type="customer"/>
     <xsd:element name="position" type="position"/>
   </xsd:sequence>
</xsd:complexType>
```

Code example 2.20: Complex element

We can define complex data types with a so-called sequence. The term sequence[6] means that XML parsers will parse the lines in the instance document row by row.

```
<xsd:complexeType name="customer"">
   <xsd:element name="name" type="xsd:string"/>
   <xsd:element name="street" type="xsd:string"/>
   <xsd:element name="postcode" type="xsd:string"/>
   <xsd:element name="place" type="xsd:string"/>
</xsd:complexeType>

Additional fixed value:

<xsd:attribute name="currency" type="xsd:string"
fixed="Euro"></xsd:attribute>
```

Code example 2.21: Complex element defined by sequence

2.4 XLink

This section briefly explains XLink, the XML linking language. XLink is as important to XBRL as is XML namespaces. The main goal of XLink is to enable linking within and between XML documents. In order to provide this functionality, XLink allows the creation of unidirectional links as well as a complex link structures. Links in XML documents can bind elements with

6 The sequence element specifies that the child elements must appear in a sequence. Each child element can occur from 0 to any number of times. Parsers themselves unlike compilers traverse the code line by line (of any XML document or XML schema document).

individual or multiple resources[7] or with associated metadata[8]. Resources in XLink can be external websites but also other documents or sections of documents. This means that XLink is nothing else than a set of destinations (so-called resources) and a set of links between these destinations (the solution for creating links in XML documents was to put a marker on elements that should act as hyperlinks). A link contains all necessary information, to be able to decide which appropriate resources have to be linked. This does not mean that all destinations in use in a link must have a relation to another destination.

```
<?xml version="1.0"?>
<homepages xmlns:xlink="http://www.springer.com">
 <homepage xlink:type="simple"
 xlink:href="http://www.springer.com">Visit
Springer</homepage>
 <homepage xlink:type="simple"
 xlink:href="http://www.iasb.org">Visit IASB</homepage>
</homepages>
```

Code example 2.22: Linking with XLink

This example presents a way by which simple hyperlinks can exist in XML documents.

XLink has two parts: *simple* and *extended links*. *Simple links* are a connection between two resources. This is comparable to the links known in HTML. Figure 2.7 shows a *simple link* to connect a local and a remote resource. This can be for example terms in a text document that link to their definition.

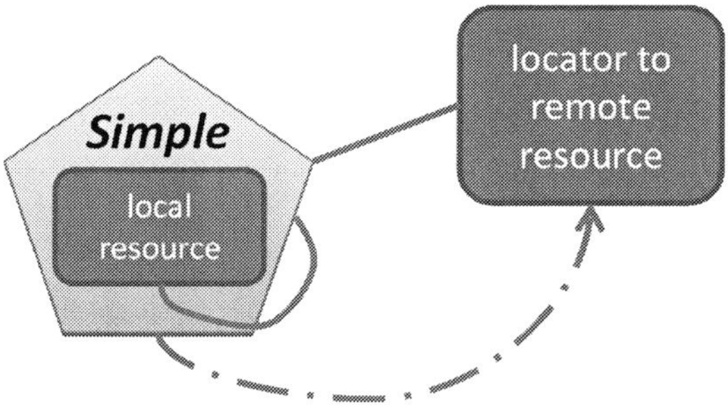

Fig. 2.7: Simple link

A *simple link* is a limited option to connect two resources. The *extended link* offers the full XLink functionalities. The *extended link* allows the association to an

7 A resource can be everything which has an own identity. The term resource has in context to the World Wide Web (WWW) different meanings. It can be an image, a file, a program or another XML document.

8 A link can contain additional semantic information.

open number of resources. The participating resources can be a free combination of local and remote destinations. The following figure 2.8 shows an example of the *extended link.*

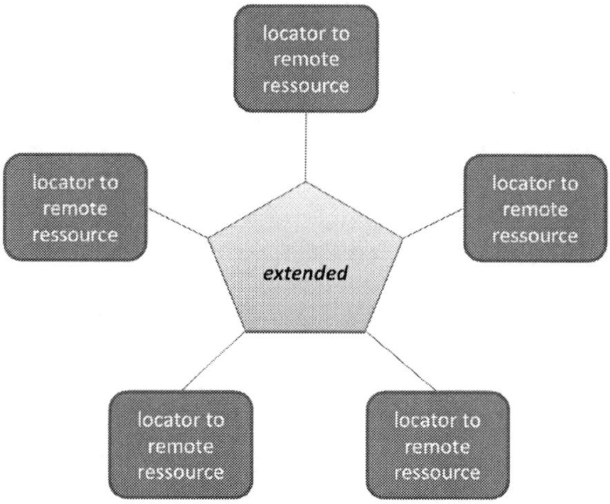

Fig. 2.8: Extended link

XLink

A language designed to allow creation of hyperlinks in XML documents. Hyperlinks may have a specific meaning (role). Using XLink allows for connecting elements and describes the nature of the connection in a computer-readable manner. XLink hyperlinks connect internal (within one XML document) and external resources (resources within the document to external and even non-XML resources). In the XBRL architecture, XLink defines the various linkbases, including presentation, calculation, definition, label and reference linkbases by using the arcs and locator methodology. The arcs can be given a specific meaning to indicate the nature of the relationship. For instance, arcs in the XBRL presentation linkbase are defined as a parent-child. This indicates the hierarchical meaning of the relationship. Arcs in the calculation linkbase are defined as summation-item indicating the aggregation nature of the relationship.

2.5 Summary

- XML is a World Wide Web Consortium (W3C) defined open standard. Its task is to contain, name, structure, and secure information. XML and derivatives are nothing other than an approach to realize the understanding of an electronic document.
- XML defines the structure of a document and fills the information structure with appropriate values. This leads to human- and machine-readable documents.
- Content of an XML-document comes through information within the tagged element, attributes of the tag, and sub-elements of the tag in an information structure.
- An XML namespace is a collection of names, identified by URI links which are used as element types and attribute names within XML documents.
- The XML schema defines syntactical rules and the structure of a class of XML documents.
- The main goal of XLink is to enable linking within and between XML documents. In order to provide this functionality, XLink allows the creation of unidirectional links as well as a complex link structure.

2.6 Key terms you should know

- XML
- XML documents
- Tags
- Elements
- Attributes
- XML namespaces
- XML schema
- XLink

2.7 *Case analysis*[9]

Improving communications between departments was one of the main reasons why governments around the world began showing early interest in XML, which emerged in 1998 as an official World Wide Web Consortium standard that built on the runaway success of its smaller cousin, the HyperText Markup Language (HTML).

Integration into all manner of products came quickly, and XML's ability to add structure and meaning to data made it a philosophical companion to efforts to open up government data storage formats. Equally popular was XML's enablement of industry or function-specific markup schemas – eXtensible Business Reporting Language (XBRL) is one, as are eBusiness XML (ebXML), Financial Products Markup Language (FpML), Math Markup Language (MathML) and myriad others with specific purposes.

Yet XML's flexibility may have muddied its message: even the official World Wide Web Consortium family of XML-based standards has grown, now including XPath, XPointer, XSLT and a host of others. With so many acronyms floating around - and specific expertise needed to take advantage of each one - it is no wonder that many organizations that might otherwise be interested in XML's benefits have put it into the too-hard basket.

Just because workers can create XML documents does not mean they will. XML is an enabler, not a destination, and will offer no real benefit without appropriate policy and framework formulation.

---

9 Excerpted from David Braue, "You Can Lead a Government to XML . . .", CIO Magazine available at http://www.cio.com.au/index.php/id;1160512555;fp;4;fpid;21.

3 Introduction to XBRL

Even now, six years into the 21st century, far too many people still think XBRL might be a new car model, or maybe a newly discovered medical condition.
[from a speech by US SEC Chairman Christopher Cox, December 5, 2006)]

Opening Vignette: Business Case for XBRL

Professional services firm Deloitte[10] announced in September 2007 the launch of a production pilot of XBRL based solutions to prepare financial reports for a number of middle market clients. The CEO of Deloitte Digital, Peter Williams, said that XBRL based solutions now in development will bring huge cost savings for business, regulators and public administration by eliminating the redundancies when reporting the same information more than once. The Deloitte pilot is a practical demonstration of the type of improvements that will be possible from Standard Business Reporting, which was recently announced in Australia. Deloitte is using the standard and has developed a suite of applications that businesses can use in future to share business and financial related information with regulators, banks and other organizations. "Deloitte's initial prototype testing of XBRL applications indicated processing time for the preparation of financial reports and regulatory returns could be reduced by up to 70 percent," Williams said. "In time, as this technology matures the interaction between business and government will be made easier by eliminating the need to report more than once and replicating tailored financial information according to reporting requirements."

Standardization of business and especially financial reporting has been an important subject for the capital markets, regulators, accounting standard setters, analysts and software companies since the late 1990s. A number of XML based solutions and standards are present, especially for transactions in the financial services industry. The use of XML for tagging financial reports has its roots in 1998 when the American Institute of Certified Public Accountants (AICPA) commenced a project to explore the possibilities opened up by XML. Eventually that project lead to the constitution of the XBRL International consortium. Today as the US SEC chairman Christopher Cox stated in a speech in 2006 “there is so much data out there that could be tagged — earnings releases, analyst research, credit ratings, mutual fund strategies and styles, and plenty of industry-specific information — that the only remaining question is not whether XBRL is good for

[10] Deloitte trials XBRL financial reporting standard Report processing times drop by up to 70 percent as reported by Sandra Rossi (Computerworld) 13 September, 2007 14:36:12.

investors, but how fast can we get this better information to them?".[11] Obviously, the focus of Chairman Cox's was on financial reporting according to US GAAP and IFRSs. The capability of XBRL goes to any environment in which there is financial reporting as well as a wide variety of business reports. For example, regulations based on the global Basel II standard for reporting of solvency ratios between banking institutions and their supervisors lies exactly within the scope of XBRL standardization initiatives.

Introduction to XBRL is the main goal of this third chapter. The chapter takes a high-level view of the major components that constitute the eXtensible Business Reporting Language. It provides a non-technical overview of the XBRL specifications. Further, the chapter also provides readers with explanations of the major terms necessary for further reading of the following chapters. This chapter starts with the definition of XBRL, followed by an introduction to the XBRL core specification that is the basis documentation for the language[12]. The next section addresses XBRL for financial reporting (XBRL FR) which most people see as the core of XBRL technology. Later in the book, we will often refer to XBRL FR with a number of examples and case studies, as it is the most common usage scenario. Although this book also analyzes XBRL for Global Ledger (XBRL GL) as well as a number of other XBRL usages, XBRL FR will dominate our examples and considerations. This is due to a number of practical implementations of the language in financial reporting scenarios as well as the roots of XBRL. The definitions and critical analysis of terms such as XBRL taxonomies, taxonomy extensions and instance documents together with the analysis of the issues concerning the current XBRL specification make up the next section of the chapter. The later discussion concerning the open and closed reporting cycles gives the reader a possibility to understand differences in recent design of XBRL taxonomies. Finally, the chapter discusses several classifications of XBRL technologies in order to organize ulterior discussions.

---

[11] For full speech of Chairman Cox see the US SEC website: http://www.sec.gov/news/speech/2006/spch120506cc.htm.

[12] XBRL is often referred to as *de facto* standard for digital business reporting so the terms language and standard are used interchangeably.

3.1 What is XBRL?

XBRL is an XML-based standard for representing business information and associated metadata. XBRL International Inc. (XII) owns and freely licenses the XBRL specification. XII recognizes themselves as:

> *"a not-for-profit consortium of approximately 550 companies and agencies worldwide working together to build the XBRL language and promote and support its adoption".*

XII defines XBRL as:

> *"a language for the electronic communication of business and financial data which is revolutionizing business reporting around the world. It provides major benefits in the preparation, analysis and communication of business information. It offers cost savings, greater efficiency and improved accuracy and reliability to all those involved in supplying or using financial data".*

The idea behind XBRL is simple. Instead of treating business reports as a block of text - as in a standard Web page, an Adobe Acrobat PDF or printed document - XBRL provides an identifying tag for each individual item of data making it computer readable. Search engines can read and index electronic documents such as HTML pages or PDF files, but only at the level of the entire document. Adding XML or XBRL to business reports brings high semantic quality to the individual "chunks" or "items" of data. For example, company's "net profit" has its own unique tag. The introduction of XBRL tags enables automated processing of business information by software, reducing laborious and costly processes of manual data entry and analysis. Software can recognize the information in an XBRL document, select it, analyze it, store it, exchange it, translate it into different formats and reproduce it automatically in a variety of ways for users. XBRL increases the speed of handling of business data, reduces the chance of error and permits automatic checking of information. The idea of XBRL is very similar to bar-coding physical products. Each reported business fact, including numbers and blocks of text, has its own barcode. Software applications can then work with this unique barcode.

Companies can use XBRL to save costs and streamline their processes for collecting and reporting financial information. Consumers of financial data, including investors, analysts, financial institutions and regulators, can receive, find, compare and analyze data much more rapidly and efficiently if it is in XBRL format. Because of its reliance on XML, XBRL can handle information in many different languages. XBRL can accommodate different reporting environments, standards or regulations.

EDGAR Online and XBRL

Today EDGAR Online, a provider of interactive business and financial data on global companies to financial, corporate and advisory professionals, needs to manually or semi-automatically transfer the data from SEC filings in ASCII or HTML format. Availability of SEC filings in XBRL format will reduce the time necessary to provide deep company and industry analysis including benchmarking, peer analysis, valuation modeling, scenario testing and contribution analysis to the stakeholders and potential investors. XBRL can flexibly be adapted to meet different requirements and uses. Data can be transformed into XBRL by suitable mapping tools or it can be generated in XBRL by appropriate software.

3.2 The XBRL base specification

XBRL is a derivative of XML for financial and business reporting. The main building blocks of XBRL technology are XBRL specifications, XBRL taxonomies and XBRL instance documents. The XBRL specifications regulate the syntax for documents created in various reporting environments. XBRL provides business-reporting specific extensions to several XML specifications that we introduced in chapter 1. These specifications include XML schema, XML documents and XLink and play a major role in an XBRL framework. XBRL taxonomies reflect business concepts in form of catalogues or thematic vocabularies. We will discuss XBRL taxonomies in detail in further chapters. The reported business facts are placed in a document (an *instance document*) and linked to a taxonomy. For example, an XBRL taxonomy can define a concept[13] *Assets* while the instance document will provide a value for *Assets* (for example €100. 00) reported for a specific company for a given date.

We present the relationship and roles of XML specifications, XBRL specifications, XBRL taxonomies and XBRL instance documents in figure 3.1.

[13] In XBRL the term concept is used when referring to XML elements defined in XBRL taxonomy. We treat both terms as synonyms in this book.

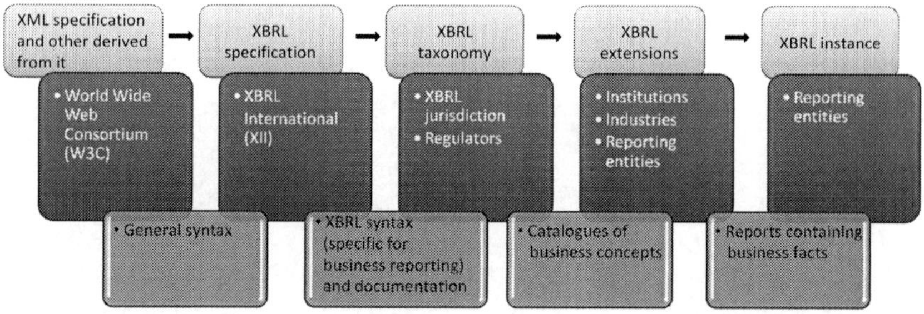

Fig. 3.1: Relationships between XML specifications, XBRL specifications, XBRL taxonomies and XBRL instances

XII and its working groups maintain the XBRL specifications[14]. The beginning of work on XBRL goes back to 1998 when Charles Hoffman started prototyping the use of XML for financial statements. The publication of the first XBRL specification occurred in July 2000[15]. It was a very experimental approach to standardization of financial reporting. This specification utilized the DTD (Document Type Definition – the predecessor of XML schema).

The next specification versioned 2.0 published in December 2001 was implementing the W3C XML schema recommendation. The XBRL 2.0 specification also brought XML Linking Languages (XLink) technology into the realm of XBRL. The inclusion of XML schema and XLink enhanced the semantic representation of XBRL and allowed for complex business reports to be conveyed by the means of the language.

With the specification 2.1, dated December 2003, XBRL reached maturity[16] and guaranteed stability over the next few years. The XBRL specification is defined as follows:

> *"XBRL is the specification for the eXtensible Business Reporting Language [which] allows software vendors, programmers, [and] intermediaries in the preparation and distribution process and end users who adopt it as a*

---

14 Apart from the XBRL specifications there are more governing documents defining the rules for XBRL vocabulary and taxonomies architecture. The most important document for creation of XBRL taxonomies is called Financial Reporting Taxonomy Architecture (FRTA). FRTA states a set of over 100 rules concerning best practices of taxonomy creation. Financial Reporting Instance Standards (FRIS) exists for the creation of instance documents and facilitates the analysis and comparison of XBRL financial reporting data by computer applications and human readers. Finally underlying principles for modeling of financial reporting taxonomy were created by Hoffman. The so called patterns are a collection of over 20 modeling examples which help to create standardized taxonomies which are FRTA valid. FRTA and FRIS, similarly to XBRL specification, are accompanied by conformance suits in order to achieve greater software compatibility.

15 The first XBRL specification was later called XBRL specification 1.0.

16 The XII assigned the recommendation status to the XBRL specification 2.1 on 31st of December 2003.

specification to enhance the creation, exchange, and comparison of business reporting[17] *information".*

We can consider an analogy to standards in the mobile telecommunication sector. Today it is possible to use a cellular telephone in most countries worldwide without concern about the underlying technical specifications. It is exactly these specifications and standards that make it possible that European cell phones can be used on every continent. In the same way, the XBRL specification creates a framework for a number of parties working with business reporting information.

IFAC on Financial Reporting Value Chain[18]

The financial reporting value chain (FRVC) refers to the people and processes involved in the preparation, approval, audit, analysis and use of financial reports. All links in the chain need to be of high quality and closely connected to supply high quality financial reporting. The cycle both starts and ends with the investors and other stakeholders, who want to make informed economic decisions about a company and, therefore, require financial information to do so. Subsequently, it is management that, under the general direction of the board of directors (supervisory board), prepares the financial information for eventual approval by the board and, in some countries, the general meeting of shareholders. The auditors interact with management and the board while auditing the financial information and provide independent opinions. The media and others distribute financial information, and analysts and credit-rating agencies evaluate it, to be used by the investors and other stakeholders. Also within the chain there are the various standard setters in the areas of corporate governance, financial reporting and auditing; the regulators, who enforce those standards and professionals, such as investment bankers and lawyers, who provide advice to the other participants.

In order to achieve a high level of standardization between XBRL software products, a conformance suite accompanies the XBRL specification. A conformance suite is a set of tests for software vendors. Passing the tests embedded in the conformance suite assures compatibility of software applications

[17] According to Engel et al. business reporting includes, but is not limited to, financial statements, financial information, non-financial information, general ledger transactions and regulatory filings, such as annual and quarterly reports. XBRL specification defines XML elements and attributes that can be used to express information used in the creation, exchange, and comparison tasks of business reporting. XBRL consists of a core language of XML elements and attributes used in XBRL instances as well as a language used to define new elements and taxonomies of elements referred to in XBRL instances, and to express constraints among the contents of elements in those XBRL instances.

[18] Excerpted from IFAC FRSC Report, http://web.ifac.org/download/FRSC-Introduction.pdf.

with the specification. The purpose of the conformance suite is to facilitate interoperable XBRL software implementations. XBRL documents produced by an XBRL application should be consumable directly by a different XBRL application without risking any loss of information.

As mentioned before XBRL specification 2.1 is the base for several adaptations of the standard. The first, which we title XBRL FR[19], deals with the creation, exchange and comparison of financial reports. The second, XBRL GL, deals with journal entries, accounting master files, and historical status reports. Another is XBRL dimensions, governed by its own XBRL Dimensions 1.0 specification (a modular extension to XBRL 2.1). XBRL dimensions deals with modeling of multidimensional information in a standardized fashion. Although XBRL dimensions are in use today in a number of financial reporting taxonomies we will follow the XBRL specifications and defer the discussions on dimensions to later chapters. In this chapter, we will use XBRL FR to explain the basic terms used in the XBRL arena. The reason for this is that financial reporting takes place all over the word between business entities, not-for-profits and governmental agencies and many different stakeholders (regulators, investors, banks, analysts, employees, news media etc.).

3.3 XBRL financial reporting

The first name of XBRL was the eXtensible Financial Reporting Markup Language (XFRML). Soon, however, the XBRL community saw that the language had broader use beyond the realm of financial reporting. The final name of XBRL indicates that it accommodates many and varied reporting aspects. Combining the XBRL definition from the XBRL specification and the definition of financial reporting we define XBRL FR as follows:

> *"XBRL for financial reporting compromises all XBRL enabled information systems oriented towards external users such as investors, creditors, customers, suppliers, competitors, regulators and the general public".*

Table 3.1 explains the basic terms in the XBRL FR arena. These include taxonomies and instance documents. XBRL taxonomies usually reflect the underlying financial reporting principles or rules in form of different accounting standards (GAAPs) encoded using standardized XBRL vocabulary. The instance documents reflect financial statements of an entity but in a digital and highly tractable format.

---

[19] The term XBRL FR is sometimes referred to as XBRL visual reporting (XBRL VR).

Tab. 3.1: Relation of XBRL financial reporting to the traditional financial reporting

	Underlying Accounting Principles	Financial Report
Traditional Reporting	GAAP	Paper, PDF or HTML financial report
XBRL FR	GAAP based XBRL taxonomy	Instance document

Figure 3.2 provides a more detailed view of the XBRL FR framework. We present the basic terms such as taxonomy, taxonomy extension, instance document or Discoverable Taxonomy Set (DTS) together along with relations among them. We will use the XBRL framework in further chapters while discussing the components of XBRL in more depth.

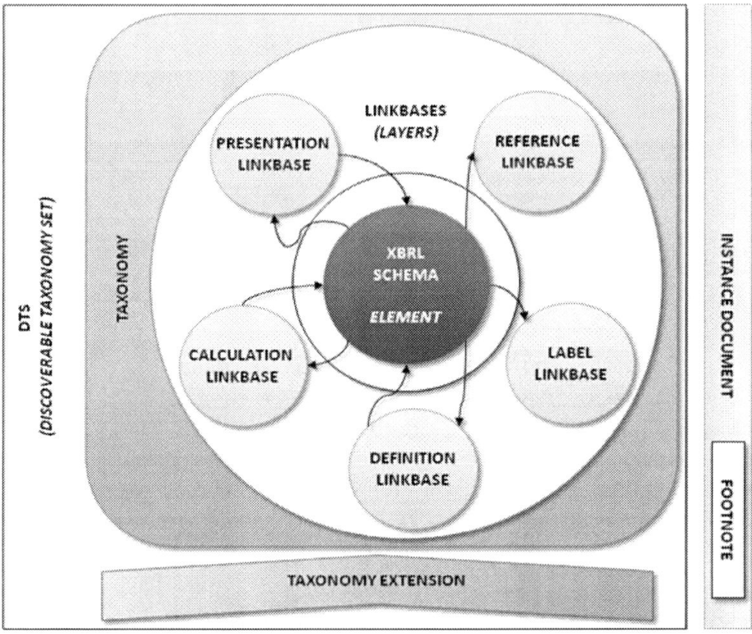

Fig. 3.2: XBRL financial reporting framework

GAAPs and XBRL Taxonomies

A number of XBRL taxonomies representing accounting standards of different countries were published beginning in 2003. Taxonomies for German GAAP, Japanese GAAP, Korean GAAP, Polish GAAP, Canadian GAAP, Irish GAAP, Chinese GAAP or US GAAP are only examples of XBRL implementations. In addition, the IFRSs are represented using an XBRL taxonomy.

A taxonomy means a catalogue or a set of rules for classification. We all recognize taxonomies of plants, animals and diseases. In XBRL, the taxonomy is a dictionary, with three principal components. First, the taxonomy contains computer-readable definitions of business reporting terms (concepts). Second, the taxonomy sets out relationships between the concepts in the dictionary. Finally, the taxonomy connects these concepts to human-readable resources. A typical taxonomy consists of a schema (or schemas) and linkbases. The role of the taxonomy schema is to define the reportable concepts - the equivalent of the words in a dictionary. The role of linkbases is to describe the relationships between the concepts and couple with human readable documentation. We will explain these terms in a more detailed fashion in the later chapters. A set of taxonomy files (schemas and linkbases) that can be discovered[20] from one entry point is called a Discoverable Taxonomy Set (DTS). The DTS term is important because taxonomies often consist of more than one taxonomy schema and several linkbases. Recent XBRL taxonomies employ several hundreds of files bound together in several DTSs for different reporting scenarios. Later, we will discuss the term DTS in more detail when we will introduce taxonomy modularization.

In many reporting environments, the core taxonomy may not meet all the needs of reporting entities. As the term *extensible* in the XBRL name suggests, XBRL supports taxonomy extensions[21] that add concepts and modify the relationships among the concepts in the core (base) taxonomies. Thus taxonomy extensions support specific reporting requirements in given accounting jurisdictions, in given industries, or for a given company. Taxonomy extensions consist of a set of taxonomy schemas and/or linkbases that augment a DTS that includes the base taxonomies.

An instance document is a business report set out in the XBRL format. It contains tagged business facts (tagged according to concepts defined in the underlying taxonomy). At the same time the instance document provides information on the context in which the facts appear and description of the measurement units. The instance document links the tagged facts to concepts specified in one or more taxonomies.

3.4 Open and close XBRL reporting cycles

We explain the use of XBRL taxonomies, taxonomy extensions and instance document using the examples of two reporting cycles. For the purpose of explanation, we differentiate between *closed* and *open* reporting cycles. We show

[20] Discovery is a technical term and means traversing over related XBRL schemas and linkbases by XBRL processor.

[21] The term taxonomy extension is used interchangeably with the term extension taxonomy.

the role that taxonomies, taxonomy extensions and instance documents play in each of these reporting cycles.

A *closed reporting cycle* relates to a situation where the reporting entity cannot adjust the data structure of the report. This particularly applies to tax and supervisory reporting scenarios. In the context of the XBRL language, it means that the receiver provides a *closed* taxonomy.[22] The receiver stipulates that the reporting entity must not extend this taxonomy. The reporting entity can only build an instance document based directly on the provided taxonomy. An important example of a closed reporting cycle is reporting by financial institutions to banking supervisors in Europe. Banking supervisors require financial institutions to send instance documents based strictly according to the published taxonomy. Figure 3.3 provides an overview of the XBRL use in the close reporting cycle.

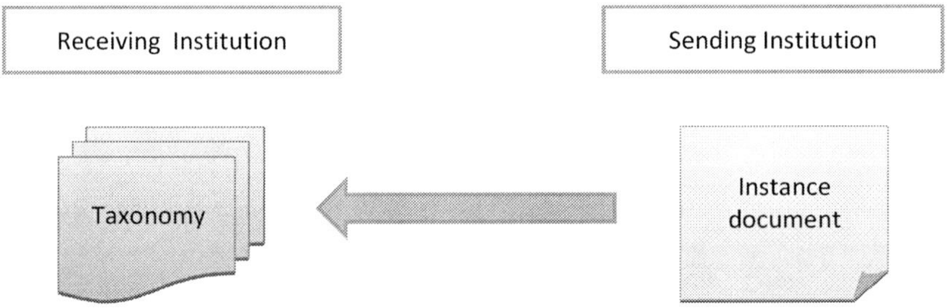

Fig. 3.3: XBRL use in the closes reporting cycle

In the *open reporting cycle*, the situation is very different. Once again, the receiver of the reports provides a taxonomy. However, in the open reporting cycle, reporting institutions or entities can extend the provided *open* taxonomy. In their instance documents, the entity reports facts aligned to both the receiver's taxonomy and the entity-specific taxonomy extension. The instance document refers to the company-specific taxonomy extension that imports the taxonomy provided by the receiving institution. An example of the open reporting scenario is reporting of companies that participated in the Voluntary Filing Program (VFP) of the US SEC. The US SEC allows companies to extend the base US GAAP taxonomy by company specific business concepts and create instance documents with the financial data based on these extended concepts. Later both taxonomy extension and instance document can be filed with the US SEC EDGAR system. Figure 3.4 provides an overview of the use of XBRL taxonomies, taxonomy extensions and instance documents in the open reporting cycle.

[22] From the technical perspective the receiving institution can also provide a taxonomy extension to international core taxonomy (such as IFRS taxonomy or European COREP taxonomy). It changes nothing for the sending institution in the close reporting cycle. The instance document created needs to refer to one (entry point) schema of the DTS indicated by the receiving institution.

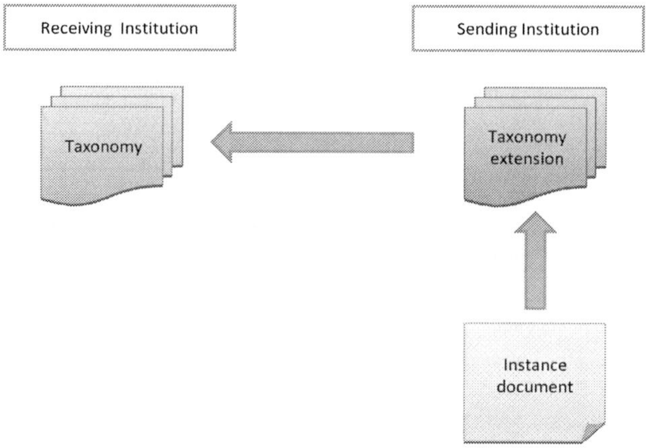

Fig. 3.4: Use of XBRL in the open reporting cycle

The differentiation between open and closed reporting cycle is common in more traditional reporting scenarios without XBRL. For example, we see closed reporting cycles in most tax reporting scenarios. The introduction of XBRL technology provides a new perspective on the choice between open and closed reporting cycles, as the use of taxonomy and taxonomy extensions more strongly impacts the information systems of both sending and receiving institutions. In addition, the issues related to mapping of data structures as well as the XBRL extensibility issues are important, especially for open reporting cycle scenarios. For example when one company extends a core taxonomy for the same concept as another company these extension concepts can be conceptually the same but will differ from technical point of view (for example an extension of class of *Cash and cash equivalents* for one company would be *Cash in bank* while for another *Cash held in bank*).

3.5 Classifications of XBRL technologies

Although development of XBRL started more than a decade ago, it is still an emerging technology. We have yet to see a solid and consistent classification for XBRL components and technologies. This section discusses different approaches to the classification of XBRL technologies and techniques. We will guide you through two different views of the classification of XBRL components. Apart from the classification provided by XII, this section presents another semantic-oriented approach to the classification of XBRL technologies. First, in figure 3.5 we present the XBRL technology stack. XII distinguishes between technology, modeling and usage of XBRL components.

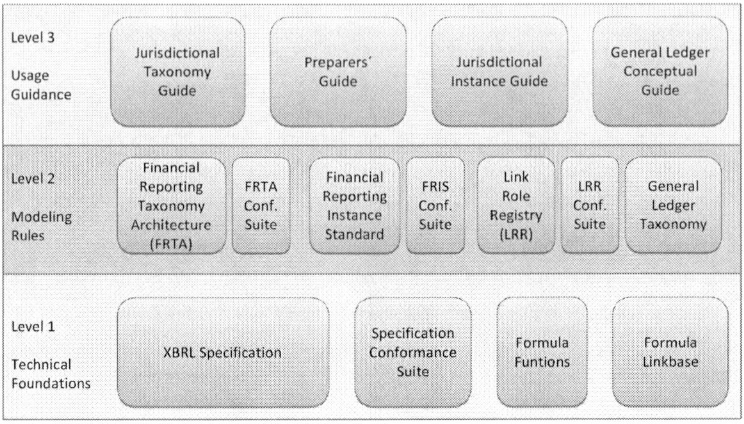

Fig. 3.5: XBRL technology stack

The technology stack classification focuses on the documentation components of XBRL. Although a number of new documentation components now exists, the technology stack view is useful as an organized approach to base XBRL. According to XII there are three layers of XBRL documentation, comprising:

- a technical foundations layer providing documentations on technical specifications and especially on XBRL 2.1 specification;
- a layer of modeling rules to guide advanced XBRL users as to how to use XBRL for applications such as financial or business reporting but also including a generic taxonomy for representation of XBRL Global Ledger;
- a usage guidance layer that enables end-users to create XBRL documents (instance documents, taxonomies and taxonomy extensions).

Within these layers, documents are aimed at different audiences. These include either strictly software developers, mainly software developers, or primarily for accountants, business process analysts or other business users and knowledge workers. The weakness of the framework is that it addresses a number of documentations that not exist yet or there is no further information from the XII that they will be finalized soon.

In addition to the official XBRL technology stack, we suggest simpler alternative classification of XBRL technologies. Building our own classification of XBRL technologies, we focus on the semantics of XBRL documents. It is important to classify the existing XBRL technologies according to their semantic importance. Figure 3.6 presents the division of XBRL technologies into three perspectives: data, document and hypercube. In so doing, we identify existing XBRL data models. We focus on those models that require integration of different XBRL taxonomies and classify them according to their level of semantic complexity.

The lowest level is the data perspective, where the main focus is on single concepts and not so much relationships among them. An indicative data model at this level is the XBRL Global Ledger (XBRL GL) taxonomy. The XBRL GL and alike taxonomies are very similar to a relational (flat table oriented) data model. Relationships between concepts are of less importance[23] with XBRL GL as the facts reported are expressed in the form of lines in flat tables. Such a data model is data oriented. It has the lowest level of semantic complexity.

The next perspective is a document orientation. The complexity is higher in case of XBRL FR taxonomies. Within this view, hierarchies of concepts represent reporting structures. These hierarchies are important as the order in which concepts are placed holds information of the semantics of the report. For example, information they inform that the concept *Assets* consists of *Current assets* and *Non-current assets*. This data model is oriented towards not only transmitting data but also expressing a complete document. These documents are typically financial reports. It is vital to ensure the reliability of semantic relationships among reported facts. Finally, XBRL dimensions (XDT) is the third and highest level of semantic complexity. The important construct at this level are hypercubes (expressing multidimensional reports). It is designed to transmit data that is multidimensional. It can be expected that XBRL formulas, which we discuss in the final chapter of this book, will introduce a new fourth level of semantic complexity.

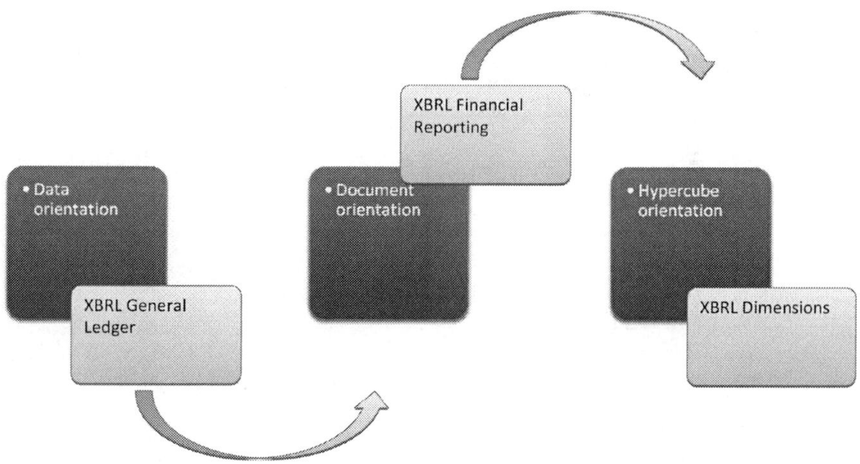

Fig. 3.6: Classification of XBRL data models according to their semantic representation

[23] But it should be stated that tables are ultimately a manner of introduction of semantics. There are relationships like contained in or parent-child within the GL taxonomy. Moreover there are relationships introduced by names and logic of the pallettes.

The above classification differs from the classification suggested by XII and presented at the beginning of this section. The semantic oriented classification does not consider the underlying documents or the level of knowledge of the users of XBRL. It focuses on the data models behind different XBRL technologies and categorizes them according to their semantic expressiveness.

3.6 Summary

- XBRL is XML-based *de facto* standard for business and especially financial reporting. XBRL is being developed and promoted by the XII, consortium of over 550 institutional members.
- A number of specifications govern XBRL. XBRL 2.1 base specification is the stable specification regulating the underlying syntax of all XBRL documents.
- XBRL taxonomies and taxonomy extensions structure data. They constitute catalogues or dictionaries of business terms that can be later reported.
- XBRL instance documents are digital reports based on a taxonomy. Instance documents consist of facts related to a business term from a taxonomy.
- Use of XBRL influences the way that the reporting is conducted in open and close reporting cycles. Mainly the use of reporting entity specific extensions by the report preparers is a challenge for information systems.
- XBRL GL is data oriented, XBRL FR document oriented while XBRL Dimensions indicate multidimensional orientation. These classification levels can be found in the semantics of the modeled taxonomies.

3.7 Key terms you should know

- XBRL International (XII)
- XBRL Specification 2.1
- XBRL FR
- Taxonomy
- Taxonomy Extension
- Instance Document
- Conformance Suites
- FRTA
- Open Reporting Cycle
- Closed Reporting Cycle

3.8 Case analysis[24]

Members of the Federal Financial Institutions Examination Council (FFIEC) – the Federal Deposit Insurance Corporation (FDIC), the Federal Reserve System (FRS), and the Office of the Comptroller of the Currency (OCC) – sought to resolve challenges in the supervisory reporting through the large-scale deployment of XBRL solutions in its quarterly bank Call Report process. In addition, through the modernization project, the FFIEC sought to improve its business processes, including:

- Securely obtaining data that can be entered automatically and seamlessly into systems without re-keying, reformatting or other "translation" effort.
- Reducing costs through automating of routine tasks.
- Quickly and automatically identifying errors and problems with filings.
- Validating, analyzing and comparing data quickly, efficiently and reliably.
- Shifting focus of effort more on analysis and decision-making with filers rather than on data manipulation.
- Promoting efficiencies and cost savings throughout the regulatory filing process.
- Moving quality assessment and error detection capabilities to the vendor supplied software.
- Embedding the capability to include the institutions' narrative explanations for valid data discrepancies and/or fluctuations in the data transmission.
- Verifying the receipt of transmissions/filings.
- Building facilities for respondents to make online corrections to their Call Report filings.
- Creating a Centralized Data Repository (CDR) where bank Call Report data can be both received from filers and delivered to users.

The new system, known as the Central Data Repository (CDR), was the first in the U.S. to employ XBRL on a large scale and represented in 2005 the largest use of the standard worldwide. The CDR uses XBRL to improve the transparency and accuracy of the financial reporting process by adding descriptive "tags" to each data concept. The overall result has been that high-quality data collected from the approximately 8,200 U.S. banks required to file Call Reports is available faster, and the collection and validation process is more efficient. Mike Bartell, Chief Information Officer of the FDIC said: "If we are truly serious about disclosure and transparency, we need to move aggressively toward the adoption of XBRL."

Improvements to the data collection process have reaped immediate benefits in the timeliness of high-quality data for the banking agencies. The CDR utilizes XBRL to enable banks to identify and correct errors before they submit their data

[24] Excerpted from FFIEC, "Improved Business Process Through XBRL: A Use Case for Business Reporting" available at http://www.xbrl.org/us/us/FFIEC%20White%20Paper%2002Feb2006.pdf

to the federal banking agencies. Consequently, initial third quarter 2005 data submissions were of a high quality received days sooner than in previous quarters, when most data validation occurred only after the initial submission to the agencies.

The main conclusions for FFIEC from XBRL implementation are the following:

- Through an open, collaborative approach to business process change, the FFIEC and its stakeholders have succeeded in achieving the improvements sought.
- XBRL helped the FFIEC Call Agencies achieve both measurable improvements and qualitative enhancements to its Call Report process.
- The XBRL implementation had a positive incremental impact on the FFIEC's bottom line and is a viable solution – XBRL increased productivity, efficiency, accuracy and quality.

4 XBRL Taxonomies

"... the development and broader use of IFRS XBRL taxonomies will strongly complement the IASB's objective to enable investors to allocate capital more efficiently across borders by providing greater comparability of financial data"
[Chairman of the IASB Sir David Tweedie, Philadelphia, 2006]

Opening Vignette: US SEC and XBRL

The US Securities and Exchange Commission (SEC) will consider whether to require companies to use the XBRL programming language for their financial statements "sooner rather than later," said SEC Chairman Christopher Cox during second interactive data roundtable in October 2006. Cox said that making XBRL mandatory would be "premature," considering that the program's taxonomy is incomplete. But the SEC announced it will spend $5.5 million to complete the XBRL taxonomy—the data-labeling information needed to run the language—Cox said the SEC will consider how other countries, including China, have mandated XBRL's use. He added that once the interactive system is fully functional, companies will have no barriers for adopting XBRL. On September 29, the SEC announced a $54 million investment to update its 20-year-old EDGAR database of corporate regulatory filings and turn it into an interactive database that uses XBRL. The SEC has promoted the program as a perk for investors, who would be able to easily compare several companies' financial data on their desktops rather than retyping or printing out forms, but it only works if all those companies being compared have used XBRL to tag their data. During the interactive data roundtable, PepsiCo CEO Indra Nooyi praised the benefits of XBRL and said the cost of initiating its use was minor. As a participant in the SEC's XBRL pilot program, Pepsi filed four regulatory forms, spending $5,000 in up-front costs for its first filing, which included outsourcing XBRL coding of its financials. For the second filing, the cost and labor hours involved "dropped dramatically", the former CFO said. "All in all, the implementation of XBRL has been relatively painless and inexpensive."[25]

The development of XBRL taxonomies is one of the most important aspects of XBRL implementation. Users of data in XBRL format must understand the scope of the taxonomies they apply. Equally, preparers need to be familiar with taxonomies in order to prepare XBRL instance documents, extend taxonomies or adjust their reporting systems. In this chapter, we will deal with the principal component of the XBRL framework – taxonomies.

---

25 Excerpted from Johnson S. "The Good and Bad About XBRL's Future", CFO October 4, 2006.

The word taxonomy derives from the Greek verb *tassain* which means to classify and the noun *nomos* that translates into English as law or science. Combined and interpreted taxonomy means classification of a kind of knowledge. Initially, it referred to the science of classifying living things, but later it received wider meaning and currently applies to either classification of things in general or rules governing this classification. Frequently taxonomies have hierarchical structures or form networks. As such, taxonomies represent concepts in a classification and the relationships between them.

Virtually everything could be a subject of classification under some taxonomy. The most common example of a taxonomy is classification of living creatures. The root concept, which is the most general one, is organism since all living things are of this group. Its first child is domain, which in turn is a parent of kingdom whose subgroup is division that is divided into classes and so on. One important characteristic of taxonomies is that children (lower level concepts) may have many parents (upper level concepts) and the so-called unique location issue arises[26]. Accounting literature recognizes the chart of accounts as a very common taxonomy in the accounting domain. A chart of accounts classifies business and accounting entries into categories of assets, liabilities, revenues and expenses so that stakeholders can better control business activity.

Analyzing an XBRL taxonomy in the context of our general taxonomy definition[27], the taxonomy schema (which is technically nothing else than an XML schema) is the part that contains declarations of concepts (such as assets, equity or liabilities) whereas taxonomy linkbases provide relationships between them. In the example of living things the explanation of what is an organism, kingdom, division and class would be placed in the schema while the hierarchical relationships between them would appear in the linkbases. Taking accounting vocabulary into consideration the linkbases would provide the relationships between assets, equity and liabilities in form of balance sheet presentation and its calculation structure.

[26] In some classifications, spiders could be categorised as insects, in others as eight-legged arthropods and in another as non-flying organisms.

[27] Close correlation can be found between ontology and XBRL taxonomy. Nevertheless the XBRL framework is based on taxonomies as metadata and instance documents as data of the reports. The domain of ontologies does not put such emphasis on this distinction.

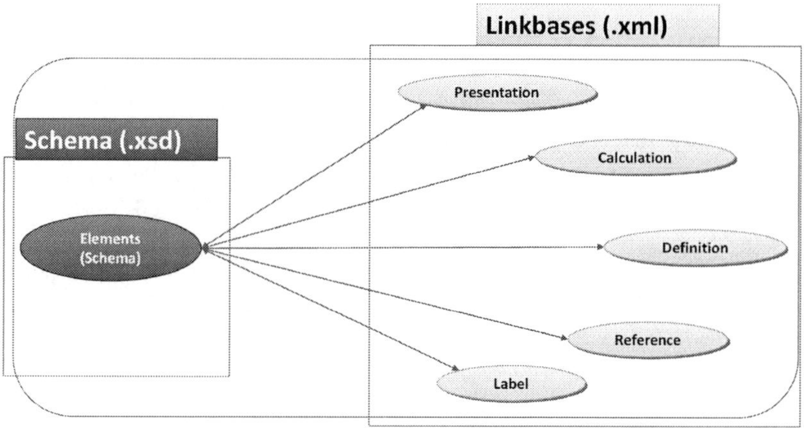

Fig. 4.1: XBRL taxonomy architecture in form of a DTS

Figure 4.1 provides an overview of an XBRL taxonomy *DTS* (Discoverable Taxonomy Set). The set includes, then, one or more schemas together with linkbases related to them. The term DTS came into use as taxonomies became more complicated and more closely interrelated[28]. The *schema*, in the form of an *.xsd* file, connects to one or more linkbases in form of *.xml* files. Standard XBRL linkbases defined by XBRL specification are *presentation*, *calculation*, *definition*, *label* and *reference* linkbase.

4.1 Taxonomy schema

An XBRL schema stores information about taxonomy concepts such as their names, identifiers (ids) and various other characteristics. The XBRL schema is a container that describes a list of unrelated concepts and references appropriate linkbase files. From a technical perspective, the XBRL schema is an XML schema tailored to particular business or financial reporting needs. The use of schema allows reporting of facts in instance documents and later their validation against corresponding concept definitions in the schema.

In any XBRL DTS, all concepts must be unique. However, a concept with the same name (e.g. *CashAndCashEquivalents*, *IndirectEconomicImpacts*) can exist in many schemas. Each of these schemas would assign a different meaning[29]. We need a method to distinguish between *IndirectEconomicImpacts* in one schema

[28] A complete DTS of the IFRS taxonomy released in 2005 consisted of 47 files (including three schemas). Modular taxonomies are often approached using another entry schema. This so-called shell schema imports core DTS schema that defines all elements and refers to selected linkbases. The new shell schema importing core DTS creates a new DTS.

[29] For example under various GAAPs the accounting concept *Assets* may be defined differently.

and *IndirectEconomicImpacts* in another. XBRL uses XML namespaces to differentiate these different concepts which we discussed in the second chapter. Defining, for example,

```
xmlns:ifrs="http://xbrl.iasb.org/ifrs/"
```

allows an instance document to simply use prefix ifrs (for example *<ifrs:Assets/>*) instead of quoting the whole URI before a concept name.

The main purpose of XBRL schemas is to provide an application that consumes XBRL data with information on the representation and processing of reporting concepts. To achieve this, definitions of concepts that appear in schemas are constructed according to a specific set of rules. The example below describes simplified (prefixes are omitted) definition of the concept *Assets*.

```
<element
name="Assets"
id="Assets"
periodType="instant"
balance="debit"
abstract="false"30
substitutionGroup="item"
type="monetaryItemType"/>
```

Code example 4.1: Concept declaration in XBRL taxonomy

The basic attributes provided in Code example 4.1 and most important from the business perspective are *name*, *type*, *balance* and *periodType*. The first component assigns a concept a unique name. As explained in the previous chapters a concept name (as an XML element) must meet several criteria and cannot contain spaces and other characters that operate differently in various operating systems[31]. XML distinguishes between upper and lower case so *assets* and *Assets* are different concepts. The *periodType* attribute relates to the accounting distinction between flows and stocks. Since it is natural to provide a value of assets on a particular date and time[32], the value of the attribute is set to *instant*. Flows such as payments, proceeds, revenues, costs or profit have *duration* assigned as the *periodType* attribute value.

Another accounting characteristic that an application needs to recognize is the balance nature of a concept. According to the essential T-rule of double entry

---

30 Abstract attribute determines if an element can appear in an instance document. Elements with the value "true" for the abstract attribute are used for hierarchical ordering of the taxonomy structure for the presentation purposes.

31 The list below provide an overview of special characters: ( ) * + [ ] ? \ / ^ { } | @ # % ^ = ~ ` “ ‘ ; : , < > & $ ▯ €.

32 The stocks are usually reported at the end of the reporting period.

accounting, assets and expenses have standard balances in debit while equity, liabilities and revenues have balances in credit. Therefore, to increase an asset or expense, the account is debited and to decrease them the account is credited. To reflect the rule in XBRL, each concept carrying a monetary value may contain in its definition an indication of whether it normally has a debit or credit balance. This requirement meets the need to have comparable data and to perform accounting calculations. It also enables creators of instance documents to assign proper positive or negative value to the reported fact[33]. For example, the concept *cost of sales* as an expense could have a negative value and *add* to revenue (credit) in order to calculate gross profit. Alternatively, it could be a positive figure, which by subtraction from revenue would give the desired result. Table 4.1 explains the use of the balance attribute values and their relation to reported facts as well as calculation relationships[34].

Tab. 4.1: Sign of reported fact in an instance documents in correspondence to the balance attribute of a concept

Concept	No balance attribute assigned				Balance attribute assigned	
Revenues	+	1,000	+	1,000	+	1,000 (Cr)
Cost of Sales	-	1,200	+	-1,200	-	1,200 (Dt)
Gross Profit (Loss)	=	-200	=	-200	=	-200 (Cr)

Application of a balance attribute is useful and straightforward in case of balance sheet or income statement. However, it creates difficulties in calculating some cash flows statement concepts. The issue with cash flow concepts is that they do not necessarily follow credit or debit rules[35].

Another important characteristic of a concept is the *type*. In financial reports companies include information that are in the form of figures with monetary units (e.g. £100), numbers (e.g. number of employees), percents (interest rates), strings (regular text) and others. To help applications recognize each of these, the XBRL

[33] For example assigning *credit* to the attribute for an element *Profit/Loss* means a positive number reported is a profit while a negative number reported is a loss.

[34] The use of a balance attribute is also related to the sign of a reported fact in a broader sense. The negative debit is treated as a credit in a debit element and a negative credit as a debit in a credit element which ensures more flexibility while defining the taxonomy elements.

[35] Treating a positive cash flow (inflow of cash) as an increase in cash and cash equivalents, that is a component of assets, the natural balance attribute would be debit. But calculating cash flows in indirect method, net profit or loss is a credit as part of equity and as a result of subtraction of debit expenses from credit revenues. In operating cash flows the adjustment concerns position for non-cash items and items from income statement related to investing or financing activities. A problem occurs while subtracting change in receivables or change in inventories (increase of both is debit) and adding change in payables (increase of which is credit). So the operating cash flow, as stated above, could have debit balance attribute as an increase of cash and on the same time credit as the excess of revenues over expenses.

specification uses, with minor adjustments, the built-in datatypes of the XML schema. By doing so, applications can check the validity of data entered according to the type as well as perform calculations. The most common types that appear in financial statements are *monetaryItemType*, *stringItemType* and *decimalItemType*.

There are circumstances when taxonomy developers wish to ensure that values entered in instance documents draw from a list of enumerated possibilities they provide. A list might include months in a year, depreciation rates or stock exchange symbols. The enumerated list is a concept well known from programming languages. It is a helpful feature that restricts and allows validating user entries[36]. XML and related technologies provide several solutions to model enumerations. XBRL, by extending XML with XML schema and XLink imposes constraints and at the same time reduces the number to fewer possibilities.

An enumerated list is a list where all (or at least some) values are known. It could refer to values of concepts or their attributes. In particular, a concept from an enumerated list may be associated with other concepts that must be present when a fact for this particular concept appears in an instance document.

Code example 4.2 provides definition of an enumerated list of values for measurement base. The alternatives are historical cost, current cost, realizable settlement value, present value and fair value.

```
<complexType name="measurementBaseItemType">
 <simpleContent>
  <restriction base="xbrli:tokenItemType">
   <enumeration value="Historical Cost"/>
   <enumeration value="Current Cost"/>
   <enumeration value="Realizable Settlement Value"/>
   <enumeration value="Present Value"/>
   <enumeration value="Fair Value"/>
  </restriction>
 </simpleContent>
</complexType>
```

Code example 4.2: Enumerated list declaration

Code example 4.3 demonstrates the use of enumerated list defined in Code example 4.2 for a concept *MeasurementBaseForGoodwill*. The predefined enumerated list is recognized as a type for the defined concept.

[36] Enumerations of data type values are known from the HTML as well as programming languages such as C#.

```
<element
name="MeasurementBaseForGoodwill"
id="MeasurementBaseForGoodwill"
type="measurementBaseItemType"
substitutionGroup="item"
nillable="true"
periodType="duration"/>
```

Code example 4.3: Use of enumerated list for type attribute[37]

The business concepts described above appear in taxonomies as items. One important characteristic is the *substitutionGroup* attribute. In Code example 4.1 as well in Code example 4.3 *substitutionGroup* is set to *item*. Items are not associated in schema with any other items. Nor are they grouped in any way. Facts in instance documents referring to items are unique in any one context and within the same unit of measure. However there are some concepts in business reporting domain that are expressed in XBRL using concepts whose definitions and constructions differ significantly from those presented above. They have *substitutionGroup* attribute value assigned to *tuple*. Tuples express concepts connected in order to create compound or complex concept structures in the schema. Tuples may contain items or other tuples[38]. Code example 4.4 provided below demonstrates concept definition with the *substitutionGroup* set to *tuple* for *deposits*. The tuple *deposit* contains three items to *describe* the deposit, its *amount* as well as the *effective interest rate*. Tuples do not have the same constraint as items concerning uniqueness of the facts in instance documents. Facts reported for tuples can appear more than once in the same context and having the same unit in an instance document[39].

The definition of the content of a tuple includes additional information concerning the order of concepts and their minimum number of occurrences (*minOccurs*) and maximum number of occurrences (*maxOccurs*)[40]. In Code example 4.4 the minimum number of occurrences equals one or zero which means that for each set of values expressed as a tuple in an instance document at least *DepositDescription* must be reported.

---

[37] In a number of examples prefixes are omitted in order to simplify the code.

[38] Tuples contained within other tuples are referred to as nested tuples.

[39] Tuples have no *periodType* attribute. It means that for a tuple in an instance document no context will be assigned. Contexts are assigned only for single facts referring to items within the tuple.

[40] Attributes *minOccurs* and *maxOccurs* determinate how many times an item element can appear within one tuple element in an instance document. Default values (1;1) can be omitted.

```
<element id="Deposit" name="Deposit"
substitutionGroup="tuple" nillable="true">
 <complexType>
  <complexContent>
   <restriction base="anyType">
    <sequence>
     <element ref="DepositDescription" minOccurs="1"/>
     <element ref="DepositAmount minOccurs="0""/>
     <element ref="EffectiveInterestRate" minOccurs="0"/>
    </sequence>
   </restriction>
  </complexContent>
 </complexType>
</element>
```

Code example 4.4: Tuple declaration

Once concepts and their characteristics are set out in the schema, taxonomy developers face the task of providing applications with knowledge on relations between concepts and their links with descriptive resources. These constitute components of five linkbases that we describe in the later section.

4.2 Taxonomy linkbases

Figure 4.1 provided an overview of five linkbases[41] that fall in one of the three categories:

- *relation* linkbases (calculation, definition and presentation) that manage the relations between taxonomy concepts;
- *label* linkbases that associate taxonomy concepts with text labels defined in various languages;
- *reference* linkbases that connect concepts with authoritative literature.

Linkbases use two XML technologies. The first, which we introduced in chapter 2, is known as XLink. This technology provides a framework for creating both basic unidirectional links and more complex linking structures in XML documents. The second is the XML Pointer Language (XPointer). This helps to express fragment identifiers for any URI reference (for example concepts definitions in XBRL schema). In order to create a relationship between two concepts from the schema, a linkbase needs to point to these concepts or resources

[41] Taxonomy linkbases are often referred to as taxonomy layers.

and define the type of relationship between them. A simplified example of a hierarchical relation from a presentation linkbase is:

```
<loc type="locator"
href="schema.xsd#Assets"
label="Assets_Locator"/>

<loc xlink:type="locator"
href="schema.xsd#CurrentAssets"
label="CurrentAssets_Locator"/>

<presentationArc
type="arc"
arcrole="http://www.xbrl.org/2003/arcrole/parent-child"
from="Assets_Locator"
to="CurrentAssets_Locator"
order="2"/>
```

Code example 4.5: Locators and arcs

A locator labeled *Assets_Locator* points to the concept that is defined in the schema file schema.xsd with *id* attribute value *Assets*. Similarly, the second locator points to the concept *CurrentAssets*. The *presentationArc* describes the relation between located concepts by describing the type of relationship using *arcrole* attribute. An arcrole defines the type of relation that in this particular case is *parent-child*[42]. The arc attributes *to* and *from* point to locators. In the example, the relation defines that *CurrentAssets* is a child of Assets.

The relation linkbases as presented in Code example 4.5 operate on the locator-arc-locator principle. In other words by means of two locators and a single arc a relationship between two concepts from taxonomy schema is constructed. Figure 4.2 demonstrates the linkbase operating mode graphically.

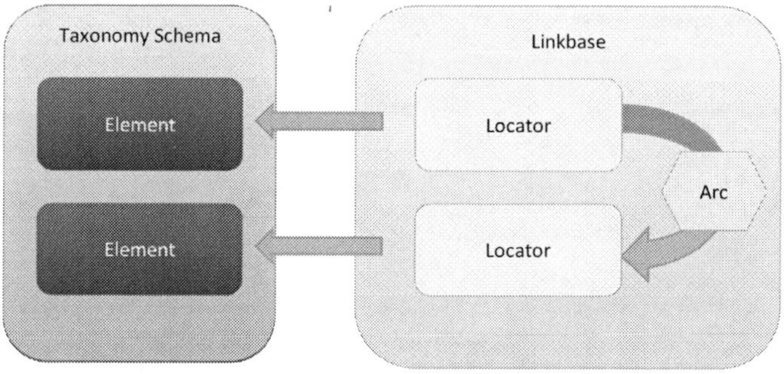

Fig. 4.2: Operating mode of relational linkbases

[42] *Parent-child* arcrole together with the *order* attribute defines a hierarchical relationship between elements.

Linkbases provide descriptions of connections between concepts by localizing them (by means of locators) and defining the type of relationships (by means of attributes of an arc and especially by utilization of the arcrole attribute). Each of the five linkbases (presentation, calculation, definition, reference and label) contains definitions of different types of relations. Table 4.2 provides an overview of arcroles available in each of the five linkbases.

Tab. 4.2: Overview of the linkbases in regards to the corresponding arcroles

Linkbase	Arcrole
Presentation	parent-child
Calculation	summation-item
Definition[43]	general-special
	essence-alias
	similar-tuple
	requires-element
Label	concept-label
Reference	concept-reference

Most data structures that exist in financial reports employ hierarchical trees or tables. The presentation linkbase stores information about relationships between concepts in order to organize the taxonomy content. This allows arrangement of concepts in a structure according to the hierarchical relationships in particular domain. The groupings can be performed in many ways. For example, a typical balance sheet contains assets, equity and liabilities. The concept *Assets* has two children concepts, *Current assets* and *Non-current assets*. *Current assets* are split in *Inventories*, *Receivables,* etc. The presentation linkbase, using *parent-child* relations supported by the order attribute organizes concepts in this way and helps users find concepts they are interested in. Figure 4.3 presents the hierarchical structure of the presentation linkbase.

[43] Together with introduction of the specification for XBRL Dimension 1.0 new arcroles are defined for the definition linkbase.

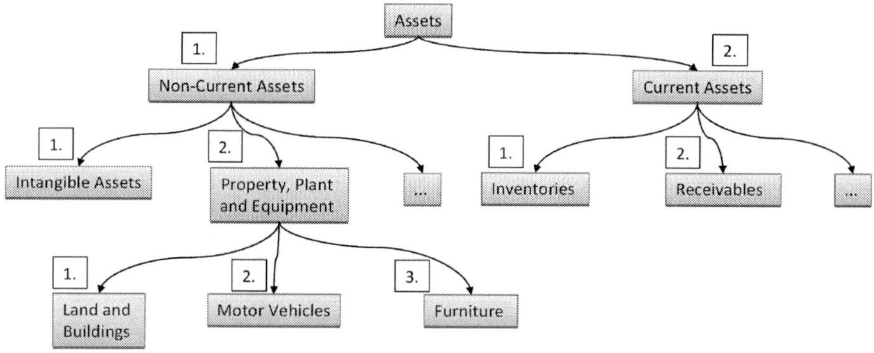

Fig. 4.3: Hierarchical view of presentation linkbase

The main drawback of a hierarchical structure in a presentation linkbase is that it only allows the presentation of flat lists of concepts, while financial statements also contain more sophisticated reports such as changes in equity or movements in property, plant and equipment that are presented in form of tables. Hoffman provides a set of patterns enabling and standardizing modeling of report data structures in XBRL taxonomies. Nevertheless, due to difficulties with later rendering of such taxonomies the solution still raises many questions[44].

The underlying idea of the calculation linkbase is to improve the quality of data reported in an XBRL instance document. It contains definitions of basic validation rules, which apply to all instance documents referring to a particular taxonomy. Calculation linkbase sorts all monetary concepts in a hierarchical way, so that the lower level concepts sum up to or are subtracted from one another. The upper level concept is the result of these operations. It needs to be stressed that calculation linkbase does not compute anything and that the resulting value (from calculation rules) is compared to the values provided in the report.

Tab. 4.3: Calculation structure

Calculation		
Gross Profit		
	Revenue Total	+1
	Cost of Sales	-1

The sign and multiplication factor of the relationship depend on the weight attribute assigned to the arc connecting two concepts. Table 4.3 and Code example 4.6 show two calculation arcs providing details concerning relations between *gross profit*, *revenue* and *cost of sales*. *Gross profit* is a difference between the other two concepts. Therefore, the *weight* attribute assigned to the value is 1 on the arc connecting *gross profit* and *revenue* and -1 between *gross profit* and *cost of*

[44] The XII is currently working on rendering solution that provides help for the automatic creation of tabular reports and is addressed in the later section.

sales[45]. The calculation linkbase utilizes the arcrole *summation-item* to express the type of relationship between concepts.

```
<calculationArc xlink:type="arc"
xlink:arcrole="http://www.xbrl.org/2003/arcrole/summation-
item"
xlink:from="GrossProfit" xlink:to="RevenueTotal"
order="1" weight="1"/>

<calculationArc xlink:type="arc"
xlink:arcrole="http://www.xbrl.org/2003/arcrole/summation-
item"
xlink:from="GrossProfit" xlink:to="CostOfSales"
order="2" weight="-1"/>
```

Code example 4.6: Calculation linkbase arcs

The reason for the difference between calculation and presentation linkbases is that the total concept that stands for the summation of all concepts often appears at the bottom in the financial statements whereas in the calculation linkbase it must be placed as the parent concept. Table 4.4 demonstrates the difference between the presentation and calculation structure of the balance sheet section assets.

Tab. 4.4: Differences between presentation and calculation structures

	Presentation	**Calculation**	
Assets	Assets, Total	Assets, Total	
	Assets, Non-Current	Assets, Non-Current	+1
	Assets, Current	Assets, Current	+1
	Assets, Total		

There are two major rules concerning calculation relations in XBRL. The first rule is that it is not possible to conduct calculations on concepts with different values of the *periodType* attribute assigned in the schema. We often refer to this as the cross-context calculation rule. This relates to the definition of some concepts (representing flows) as *duration* and others (stocks) as an *instant*. For example, concepts that appear on balance sheet are instant which means that their value is presented as a stock as of a specified day, while concepts in the income statement are duration because they represent flows that took place over a period. The problem emerges for example in the statement of changes in equity or movements

[45] The value of either -1 or 1 is usually assigned to the *weight* attribute

in property, plant and equipment where instant concepts are mixed with duration concepts. It is impossible in these circumstances to perform calculation checks[46].

The second rule is the double entry accounting rule that requires definition of the credit/debit nature of monetary concepts. As a basic accounting rule, it does not allow the addition of concepts with opposite balance attributes or subtraction of concepts with identical balance attributes[47]. Calculation linkbase enables additions or subtractions of multiplied concept values (facts) according to the formula:

$$X = (+/-)\ A \times Y$$

where X and Y are reported and A the value of the weight attribute. The allowed operation complying with accounting rules are:

- credit concept + credit concept,
- credit concept – debit concept,
- debit concept + debit concept,
- debit concept – credit concept.

There are no limits on calculation of concepts that do not have assigned the balance attribute from the credit/debit attribute perspective.

The definition linkbase provides taxonomy developers with the opportunity to define various other kinds of relationships between concepts. There are four standard types of relationships supported by the definition linkbase.

The first example is of the *general-special* type. It distinguishes between concepts that have generic or more specific meaning. For example, ZIP code is the US representation of postal code, which is in use worldwide. Therefore, to indicate that connection, taxonomy developers define postal code as a general term to which there is more specialized concept zip code (usually also by restricting its data type to a specific pattern or enumeration).

The second available type of relationship is *essence-alias*. By utilizing it, taxonomy developers are able to indicate that two concepts have similar meaning. For example, some airlines may want to use the term *planes* to describe their main component of their property, plant and equipment while other would prefer *aircraft*. To state that meaning of these two is the same and that they can be used interchangeably, taxonomy developers may connect them using *essence-alias* arcrole[48]. Such relationship is often utilized when combining two DTSs for

---

[46] The solution to this issue is provided by the formula linkbase. Formula linkbase provides taxonomy developers with various functions more advanced than just simple addition or subtraction available in the calculation linkbase. Formula linkbase is addressed in the further chapters in more detailed way.

[47] Elements with the opposite *balance* attribute must be subtracted.

[48] The use of *essence-alias* type of relationship is not recommended since it intorduces redundancy of concepts in a taxonomy.

analytical purposes (for example indicating equivalence between *ifrs:Assets* and *us-gaap:Assets*).

The third standard type of relationship is *requires-element*. Taxonomy developers use it to force instance creators to enter the value of one concept, if they provide the value of another. For instance, a regulator may want to require disclosures in the notes on a particular component of assets if it appears on the balance sheet. In order to achieve that, the definition linkbase defines *requires-element* relationship between two concepts (for example between concepts *Property, plant and equipment* and *Disclosures for property, plant and equipment*).

The fourth relationship is *similar-tuple*. It resembles the *essence-alias* relation but applies explicitly to tuples. It connects two tuples that are equivalent in terms of definition (documentation from label linkbase or reference in reference linkbase) but are diverse from the XML perspective (e.g. the tuples do not have identical content models). One of the reasons that this type of relation came about is the impossibility of schema redefinition in XBRL. It implies that no changes are allowed in the base schema for the content of the tuples when creating taxonomy extensions. An example of the use of similar tuple could be extending our tuple from Code example 4.4 by concept *DepositHoldingPeriod.* Such extended tuple would also conceptually reflect disclosures about deposits but would differ on XML syntax level. In such a case, the relationship *similar-tuple* indicates tuples equivalence.

The difference between relation linkbases and reference or label linkbase is the use of resources. Code example 4.7 presents a locator on a concept *CurrentAssets*. There is also a label resource for the concept with an English label *Current Assets*. The label arc connects the locator with the resource and not, as in the case of relational linkbases, with another locator.

```
<loc xlink:type="locator"
xlink:href="schema.xsd#CurrentAssets"
xlink:label="CurrentAssets_Locator"/>

<label xlink:type="resource"
xlink:role="http://www.xbrl.org/2003/role/label"
xlink:label="CurrentAssets_lbl"
xml:lang="en">Current Assets</label>

<labelArc xlink:type="arc"
xlink:arcrole="http://www.xbrl.org/2003/arcrole/concept-
label"
xlink:from="CurrentAssets_Locator"
xlink:to="CurrentAssets_lbl"/>
```

Code example 4.7: Resources, locators and arcs

We show the difference in the operating mode of the label and reference linkbases in figure 4.4. The operating mode is different for relation linkbases and works on the principle locator-arc-resource.

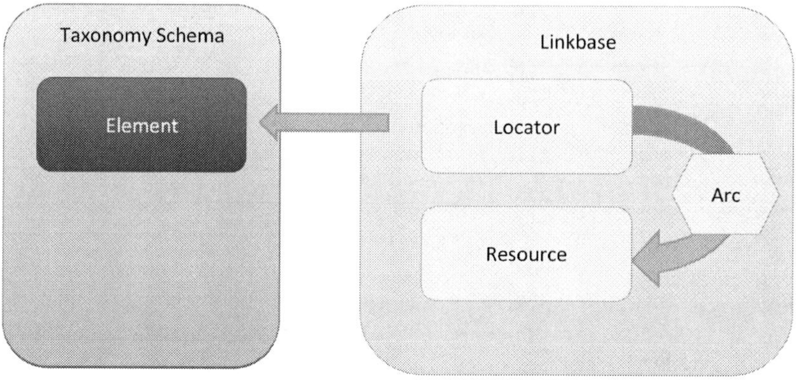

Fig. 4.4: Operating mode of resource type linkbases

Financial concepts appearing reported in financial statements often stem from regulatory documents issued by various authorities. For example, the IFRS taxonomy describes financial reports prepared based on the so-called IFRSs Bound Volume[49]. Concepts defined in the taxonomy refer to the specific terms and concepts explained in the IFRSs. For this reason, the taxonomy often contains a reference linkbase to present relationships between concepts and external regulations or standards. Reference linkbase helps users understand the intended meaning of each concept defined in the schema. The reference linkbase does not contain the full text of the regulations or standards. Instead, it points to source documents by identifying their name and indicating the relevant paragraphs and clauses[50]. This connection is created using the *concept-reference* arcrole.

There are several types of references that could be provided for each concept. Table 4.5 demonstrates the most commonly used types of references defined using role attribute in the reference resource. XBRL allows a concept to be linked to various types of references containing examples, commentaries, etc.

Tab. 4.5: Reference role attribute values and their meaning

Reference Role	Meaning
reference	Standard reference for a concept
definitionRef	Reference to documentation that details a precise definition of the concept
disclosureRef	Reference to documentation that details an explanation of the disclosure requirements relating to the concept

[49] The IFRS Bound Volume is the common term used for the book annual publication of IFRSs.

[50] The other solution is to enclose documentation in the label linkbase under a special defined label resource role (*documentationRef*).

presentationRef	Reference to documentation which details an explanation of the presentation, placement or labeling of this concept in the context of other concepts in one or more specific types of business reports
measurementRef	Reference concerning the method(s) required to be used when measuring values associated with this concept in business reports
commentaryRef	Any other general commentary on the concept that assists in determining appropriate usage
exampleRef	Reference to documentation that illustrates by example the application of the concept that assists in determining appropriate usage

Code example 4.8 defines references for *CashFlowFromUsedInOperations*. First, it provides a reference to a text that explains how and where the concept should be presented in terms of its placement and labeling (role *presentationRef*). IAS 7, paragraph 14 describes the presentation of the concept *Cash Flows from Operating Activities*. Secondly, measurement reference provides explanations about what determines the value of the concept and how it should be calculated (role *measurementRef*). This can be found in IAS 7 but in paragraph 18 and subparagraph a.

```
<reference xlink:type="resource"
  xlink:role="http://www.xbrl.org/2003/role/presentationRef
"
  xlink:label="CashFlowsFromUsedInOperationsTotal_ref">
       <ref:Name>IAS</ref:Name>

       <ref:Number>7</ref:Number>

       <ref:Paragraph>14</ref:Paragraph>

</reference>

<reference xlink:type="resource"
  xlink:role="http://www.xbrl.org/2003/role/measurementRef"
  xlink:label="CashFlowsFromUsedInOperationsTotal_ref">
      <ref:Name>IAS</ref:Name>

      <ref:Number>7</ref:Number>

      <ref:Paragraph>18</ref:Paragraph>

      <ref:Subparagraph>a</ref:Subparagraph>

</reference>
```

Code example 4.8: Reference resources[51]

[51] Locators and arcs are omitted in this example.

Concepts defined in a taxonomy schema convey accounting meaning to applications. In order to make it easier for applications to process their names, they have to obey a number of rules[52]. Additionally, taxonomies such as the IFRS taxonomy obey specific rules of naming and labeling to ensure consistency within the schema. For example, there could be a list of words that are excluded from the names (e.g. and, of) or words that appear only in a particular order (i.e. "current" or "gross" at the beginning of the concept name).

In the label linkbase, concepts connect to human readable labels using the *concept-label* arcrole. Concepts have labels assigned in different languages. Code example 4.9 describes definitions of labels of the IFRS taxonomy concept *AssetsTotal* in *English*, *German* and *Polish*.

```
<label xlink:type="resource"
xlink:role=http://www.xbrl.org/2003/role/label
xlink:label="ifrs_AssetsTotal_lbl"
xml:lang="en">Assets, Total</label>

<label xlink:type="resource"
xlink:role="http://www.xbrl.org/2003/role/label"
xlink:label="ifrs_AssetsTotal_lbl"
xml:lang="de">Vermögenswerte, Gesamt</label>

<label xlink:type="resource"
xlink:role="http://www.xbrl.org/2003/role/label"
xlink:label="ifrs_AssetsTotal_lbl"
xml:lang="pl">Aktywa, Razem</label>
```

Code example 4.9: Label resources in different languages

To distinguish between languages, XBRL uses the XML attribute *lang* in label linkbases. Taxonomy creators may also define different types of labels for a single concept.

One of the ideas of XBRL is that information about the period and unit for which the concept reports is not contained within a concept definition but comes as a context in instance documents. In financial reporting, many terms express the date for which they are being reported, for instance *Property, plant and equipment at the beginning of the period* or *Property, plant and equipment at the end of the period.* XBRL allows creation of different labels depending on the context in which a concept is in use.

---

[52] For example, the use of spaces is not allowed so *Cash and Cash Equivalents* would be named *CashAndCashEquivalents* in the IFRS taxonomy. Other taxonomies such as German Accounting Principles taxonomy may provide own sets of rules for the naming patterns for element.

Similar to reference linkbase the label linkbase utilizes a role attribute on resources. Table 4.6 provides an overview of the most important values for the role attribute on the label resource.

Tab. 4.6: Meaning of the label role attribute values

Label Role	Meaning
label	Standard label for a concept.
terseLabel	Short label for a concept, often omitting text that should be inferable when the concept is reported in the context of other related concepts
verboseLabel	Extended label for a concept, making sure not to omit text that is required to enable the label to be understood on a standalone basis
totalLabel	The label for a concept for use in presenting values associated with the concept when it is being reported as the total of a set of other values
periodStartLabel periodEndLabel	The label for a concept with *periodType="instant"* for use in presenting values associated with the concept when it is being reported as a start (end) of period value
documentation	Documentation of a concept, providing an explanation of its meaning and its appropriate usage and any other documentation deemed necessary

Code example 4.10 presents three different labels assigned to one concept by applying different values of role attributes on label resources. The concept *PropertyPlantAndEquipement* is associated with three different label resources using three different roles. The concept can be later reported in two different contexts for the beginning or ending balance.

```
<label xlink:type="resource"
xlink:role="http://www.xbrl.org/2003/role/label"
xlink:label="ifrs_PPE_lbl"
xml:lang="en">Property, Plant and Equipment, Net</label>

<label xlink:type="resource"
xlink:role="http://www.xbrl.org/2003/role/periodStartLabel"
xlink:label="ifrs_PPEBB_lbl"
xml:lang="en">Property, Plant and Equipment, Net, Beginning
Balance</label>

<label xlink:type="resource"
xlink:role="http://www.xbrl.org/2003/role/periodEndLabel"
xlink:label="ifrs_PPEEB_lbl"
xml:lang="en">Property, Plant and Equipment, Net, Ending
Balance</label>
```

Code example 4.10: Label resources with different roles

The approach of labeling one concept with the use of different roles allows for higher flexibility when rendering financial information on the basis of the presentation linkbase[53] and thus greater reporting consistency. All three labels from Code example 4.10 refer to the same concept *PropertyPlantAndEquipement* that can be reported in the instance document in three different contexts[54].

Finally, we introduce the concept of an ELR (Extended Link Role). An ELR is set of relations representing particular piece of a report (e.g. statement or disclosure) indicated by a role. Extended link roles are used in taxonomies to separate linkbases (mostly presentation, calculation and definition linkbases) into smaller, logical *chunks* (each statement and each note separately). This allows for different classifications of concepts (necessary when one concept may have different subconcepts in different *trees*) as we present in Figure 4.5.

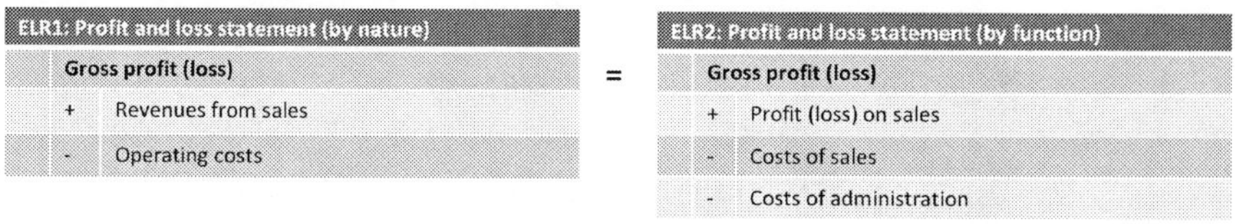

Fig. 4.5: Different sets of relationships in different ELRs

The same extended link role may be reused in many files (extensions and modular frameworks). The XBRL 2.1 specification provides a predefined ELR *http://www.xbrl.org/2003/role/link*. It is also possible to define custom ELRs in XBRL schema file as presented in Code example 4.11. The purpose of *roleURI* and *id* attributes is to enable unique identification and linking. The definition element provides container for human readable label (but ELRs lack of mechanism for translation by extension taxonomies as we explained for the taxonomy concepts in form of label linkbase). The element *usedOn* indicates linkbase where the role can be applied.

```
<link:roleType roleURI="http://www.br-
ag.eu/role/StatementOfFinancialPosition"
id="StatementOfFinancialPosition">
  <link:definition>Statement of financial
position</link:definition>
  <link:usedOn>link:presentationLink</link:usedOn>
```

[53] The attribute *preferredRole* on the presentation arc enables setting the appropriate label for the presentation tree. It is possible for example to display only terse (short) labels for a given concept in the presentation linkbase view.

[54] XBRL does not handle well the mapping between reported facts in different contexts with the proper presentation according to presentation linkbase *preferredRole* attributes. So for example it is difficult to create the movements-oriented view of the cash flow with the beginning balance element at the top and ending balance element at the bottom in an automatic way since they are reported in different contexts.

```
  <link:usedOn>link:calculationLink</link:usedOn>
  <link:usedOn>link:definitionLink</link:usedOn>
 </link:roleType>
 <link:roleType roleURI="http://www.br-
ag.eu/role/ProfitAndLossStatement"
id="ProfitAndLossStatement">
  <link:definition>Profit and loss
statement</link:definition>
  <link:usedOn>link:presentationLink</link:usedOn>
  <link:usedOn>link:calculationLink</link:usedOn>
  <link:usedOn>link:definitionLink</link:usedOn>
 </link:roleType>
```

Code example 4.11: Definition of ELR in the XBRL schema file

ELRs shall be referenced and used in linkbase files as presented in Code example 4.12.

```
<link:roleRef roleURI="http://www.br-
ag.eu/role/StatementOfFinancialPosition"
xlink:type="simple"
xlink:href="schema.xsd#StatementOfFinancialPosition"/>

<link:roleRef roleURI="http://www.br-
ag.eu/role/ProfitAndLossStatement" xlink:type="simple"
xlink:href="schema.xsd#ProfitAndLossStatement"/>

<link:presentationLink xlink:type="extended"
xlink:role="http://www.br-
ag.eu/role/StatementOfFinancialPosition">

<!-- Definitions of presentation relationships in statement
of financial position-->

</link:presentationLink>

<link:presentationLink xlink:type="extended"
xlink:role="http://www.br-
ag.eu/role/ProfitAndLossStatement">

<!-- Definitions of presentation relationships in profit
and loss statement -->

</link:presentationLink>
```

Code example 4.12: Use of the ELR in the presentation linkbase

4.3 XBRL Global Ledger (GL)

This section discusses the XBRL GL[55] taxonomy. Although this book focuses on the XBRL FR approaches, we find it useful to provide background information for this specific taxonomy developed by XII. The GL taxonomy provides an interface to transactional standards and a common model for moving data through an ERP system. It may contain links to end-reporting schemas and XBRL taxonomies. This section commences with the discussion of the XBRL GL taxonomy and follows with the aspects of the instance document modeling. Finally, we discuss the enhancement to the XBRL GL taxonomy, the Summary Reporting Contextual Data (SRCD) module, at the end of this section.

XBRL GL was developed by XII as an interface for exchange of disaggregated financial data. It enables encoding of such data while being accounting system neutral. In order to do so XBRL GL specifies a framework for encoding the accounting field. Additional fields enable linkage to the summary reporting.

The XBRL GL taxonomy provides a standardized format for representing the data fields found in accounting and operation systems and transactional reports. The GL taxonomy allows organizations to tag journal entries, accounting master files and status reports in XBRL. It has ability to provide the underlying detail for financial reporting taxonomies and instance documents. XBRL GL is an adaptation of XBRL, implemented via a taxonomy. It is not a separate specification, but a taxonomy based on the XBRL specification 2.1. However, XBRL GL is not governed by the FRTA and FRIS, which we mentioned earlier. The XII published as drafts the XBRL GL Instance Standards (GLIS) to facilitate analysis and comparison of XBRL GL data by computer applications and human readers and the GL Taxonomy Framework Technical Architecture (GLFTA). This later architecture will establish rules and conventions to assist in comprehension, usage and performance among different ledger-focused taxonomies. From a technical viewpoint XBRL GL is a stand-alone taxonomy, suitable for representing basic accounting databases and transactions. The most important features of the XBRL GL taxonomy are:

- possibility to perform multi-GAAP drill-ups to XBRL reporting taxonomies;
- providing a standard format to move non posted and posted GL information to consolidating systems, budgeting and forecasting tools and reporting tools;
- providing a standard format to move information from client systems to auditor system;
- providing a tool for representing detail drill-down for performance measurement reporting items;
- creating possibilities for any type of mandatory audit trial.

[55] XBRL GL refers to either XBRL General Ledger or XBRL Global Ledger.

From our perspective, the most important point is the first that addresses the linkage between XBRL FR and XBRL GL in the form of drill-ups. We discuss this in a later section. We first make a general analysis of the XBRL GL taxonomy and GL instance documents.

We illustrate the modular structure of the XBLR GL taxonomy in Figure 4.6. The modular set consists of the COR (Core), the BUS (Advanced Business Concepts), MUC (Multi Currency), USK (concepts for the US, UK, etc.) and TAF (Tax Audit File) modules.

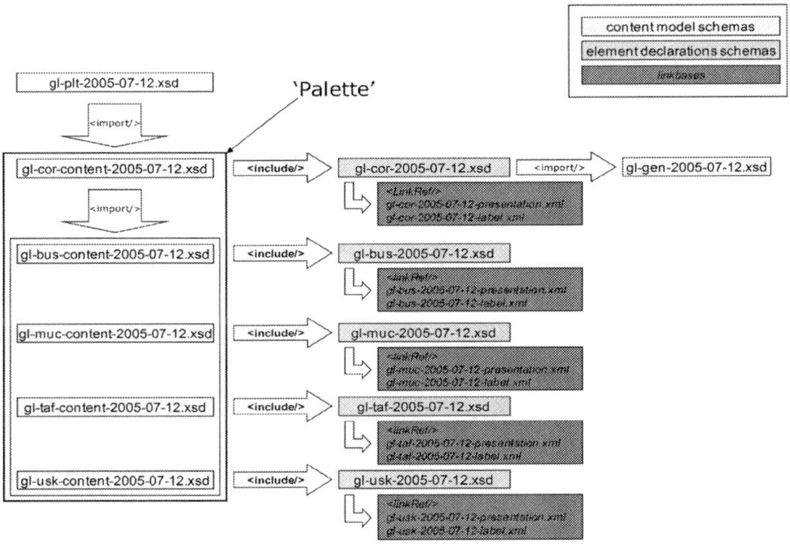

Fig. 4.6: XBRL GL taxonomy framework

The COR module is the foundational schema with document information, entity information and the entry header/entry detail data structure. This is in a package with elemental concepts for representing accounting data.

The BUS module extends the COR with business facts less common in the general ledger itself. It represents concepts such as inventory along with business metrics, organizational detail and the entity information section and other common items to supplement the resources, agents and events that represent the customer, vendor and employee related transactional details. The BUS module contains approximately 80 unique, individually identified, pieces of information related to the data found in an accounting system.

The third, USK, module extends the XBRL GL COR with accounting and business concepts more prevalent to accounting conducted in continental Europe. The USK module provides data fields found in accounting and operation systems that will allow organizations to tag journal entries, accounting master files and historical status reports with additional information necessary for accounting needs common to Saxon accounting model[56]. The USK module concepts represent job costing information and repetitive and repeating journal entries to supplement the resources, agents and events that represent the customer, vendor and employee related transactional detail that feed from operational systems. In turn, these are summarized and aggregated into financial reporting taxonomies. It contains approximately 15 unique, individually identified pieces of information related to the data found in an accounting system. In the general ledger module of many accounting systems, there are means for creating a library of journal entries for reuse and especially templates of journal entries that can be tracked, recalled and reused. Systems of this type, especially those that lead to automated creation of journal entries, would raise problems with governmental audit. As a result, these items are not considered as a component of COR. The USK accounting module standardizes data fields for creating libraries of standard, recurring and repeating entries for archival, backup and migration purposes.

The MUC module extends the XBRL GL COR with additional fields necessary for multicurrency tracking of transactions. In addition, it provides XBRL GL with the ability to collect multi-currency information to supplement data fields underlying detailed entries required for accounting, business operations and other data found in accounting systems. Specifically, the MUC module represents local and home currencies and exchange rates. It contains seven unique, individually identified pieces of information related to the data found in an accounting system.

The next described module is TAF[57] which adds data fields needed for a tax audit.

The last presented module is GEN. It contains type definitions (content models) that are in use in different modules. This module is not subject to extension.

The structure of the taxonomies within the GL family is such that we build a complete taxonomy by assembling a set of schemas via a palette schema[58]. Since the content models of many concepts vary depending on the combination of modules in use any application, the taxonomy schemas are separated into multiple physical files. These connect by means of include and import XBRL mechanisms. Each module's own schema is divided into two main parts – the concept declarations and the content model declarations that combine to form a complete schema.

XBRL GL taxonomy is heavily tuple oriented. Thus, most of the semantics (meaning relationships between reported facts here) is expressed with the use of instance documents and not contained in the taxonomy as in case of XBRL FR.

---

56 Data fields representing specifically the needs of other accounting models are not referred to as XBRL GL modules.

57 The addition of TAF fields enables XBRL GL to be used by the international tax agencies and was developed with the input of groups such as the OECD SAF-T group and the OASIS tax XML group.

58 *Palette schema* is always in the file named *gl-plt-2005-11-07.xsd*.

Basic structure of instance documents for XBRL GL following entry type documents can be described using instance documents:

- account - information to fill in a chart of accounts file;
- balance - the results of accumulation of a complete and validated list of entries for an account (or a list of account) in a specific;
- entries - a list of individual accounting entries, which might be posted/validated or non-posted/validated;
- journal - a self-balancing (debit equals credit) list of entries for a specific period including beginning balance for that period;
- ledger - a complete list of entries for a specific account (or list of accounts) for a specific period (debits do not have to equal credits);
- assets - a listing of open receivables, payables, inventory, fixed assets or other information that can be extracted from but are not necessarily included as part of a journal entry;
- trial balance - the self-balancing (debit equals credit) result of accumulation of a complete and validated list of entries for the entity in a complete list of accounts in a specific period.

XBRL GL uses a journal entry metaphor as a framework to characterize accounting master files, asset listings and journal entries themselves. It is through a combination of the appropriate fields that master files, transactional files, status listings and other files can be properly accomplished. XBRL GL relies substantially on enumerated values directly associated with a certain representation. Analyzing journal entry structures is important to understand how to model XBRL GL instances. XBRL GL instance documents have one or multiple *accountingEntries* structures within an instance document. This allows one physical XBRL GL instance document to convey several different types of information/entries. This is especially helpful in reducing redundant entries in a transactional/journal entry file. There is a separate listing of account with the related information once per account, rather than repeating all of the related information (such as description or mapped taxonomies) for every line item. The most important concept at this level is the *entriesType*. This concept has enumerated values to communicate that the information with *accountingEntries* relates to a list of accounts, an asset listing and a set of journal entries, a complete ledger and other options. There is one or more *entryHeader* structure within an *accountingEntries* structure. This is primarily important for representing multiple entries or groupings of entries. There is one or more *entryDetail* structure within an *entryHeader* structure. Multiple *entryDetail* lines are in use for many different reasons and especially using the repetitive structures that are contained with *entryDetail*. This includes:

- account and within account, *accountSub*, so the subaccounts;
- *xbrlInfo*;
- *identifierReference*.

By the judicious and consistent repetition of these structures within the *entryDetail* structure, XBRL can achieve most of the important representations of accounting. For example, we can use XBRL GL to associate a company specific chart of accounts with a standard chart of accounts. This by use of *entryDetail* structures that contain multiple account structures. Each structure has an associated *accountPurposeCode* such as standardized and company specific. Using *xbrlInfo*, different concepts from XBRL taxonomies (or other schemas) can also be associated. This can represent a link between a standard and internal taxonomy. Combining account and *xbrlInfo*, we can accomplish a complete set of mappings as well as the ability to drill down from a report and on to other reporting taxonomies. Figure 4.7 presents the relationships between XBRL GL and XBRL FR.

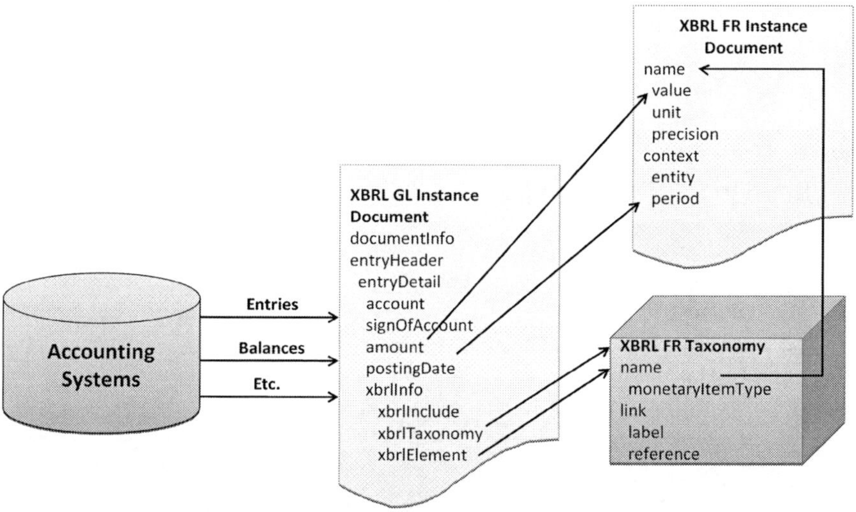

Fig. 4.7: Relationships between the XBRL GL and XBRL FR

In this section, we introduce briefly the *xbrlInfo* concept of the XBRL GL taxonomy responsible for the linkage with XBRL FR taxonomies. This section discusses how XBRL International deals with the other ways to drive the creation of end financial reports. It also discusses the linkages to specific reports, representing sophisticated ways to drive XBRL FR creation and alternative way of annotating the exact content in an original XBRL FR instance document that XBRL GL represents. This is realized with the introduction of the Summary

Reporting Contextual Data (SRCD) module[59], which helps XBRL GL concepts drive linkages to the contextual data (contexts, units and other attributes) found in summary reporting (especially XBRL FR reporting). This section discusses also the relationships between XBRL GL and XBRL FR from the business perspective.

Code example 4.13 presents a part of a trial balance where the amount *232042.26 USD* from the account *1001 SunTrustOperating* is linked to the closing balance of the *US GAAP* XBRL taxonomy concept *Unrestricted Cash*.

```
<entryDetail>
 <lineNumber contextRef="now">2</lineNumber>
 <account>
  <accountMainID contextRef="now">1001</accountMainID>
  <accountMainDescription contextRef="now">SunTrust
Operating</accountMainDescription>
  <accountPurposeCode
contextRef="now">usgaap</accountPurposeCode>
  <accountType contextRef="now">account</accountType>
 </account>
 <debitCreditCode contextRef="now">D</debitCreditCode>
 <amount contextRef="now" decimals="2"
unitRef="USD">232042.26</amount>
 <postingDate contextRef="now">2005-06-30</postingDate>
 <xbrlInfo>
  <xbrlInclude
contextRef="now">ending_balance</xbrlInclude>
  <summaryReportingElement contextRef="now">usfr-
pte_UnrestrictedCash</summaryReportingElement>
 </xbrlInfo>
</entryDetail>
```

Code example 4.13: Journal entry in the XBRL GL instance document

Figure 4.7 provided the overview of the relationships between single components of the XBRL GL instance document and XBRL FR taxonomy and instance document. For example, the amount from XBRL GL instance document is linked to the value of the fact from the XBRL FR instance document. XBRL FR does not include agreed-upon tools for drilling down from summary information to more detailed information. According to XBRL GL principles in the linkage from XBRL FR to XBRL GL (or vice versa), the weight falls upon XBRL GL to provide any explicit links from detail to summary information. The COR module described in the section above on XBRL GL includes the *xbrlInfo* structure, which identifies the link to the concept within an FR taxonomy. Using logic and content

[59] The SRCD module works with the existing XBRL GL framework and is currently available in a palette that includes all of the current modules.

from an XBRL GL instance, retrieval of information necessary to create (or link to) FR instance is possible. The linkage between GL and FR is especially important from this perspective. The high level of sophistication of the transfer from trial balance to the financial statements addressed in chapter three opens perspectives for the use of standardized and linked financial information there.

The primary reason for the development of the SRCD module was to unambiguously associate details in XBRL GL with summarized information found in XBRL FR instance. Before SRCD, XBRL GL had the representational capability to store all of the necessary information at a detailed level, but possibility to conduct simple transformations, rather than transformations requiring additional programming logic, was necessary. In addition to being able to encode explicit representation of the summary reporting contextual information, users interested in having XBRL GL meet with XBRL FR stated their need to communicate conditional selection and filtering rules to move from GL detail to FR summary information[60].

4.4 Summary

In this chapter, we address the major component of the XBRL framework that is the XBRL taxonomy. We analyzed the role of the XBRL taxonomy schema as a container for the definitions of concepts and the role of taxonomy linkbases for creating relationships between concepts as well as between concepts and resources. Further, we analyzed the XBRL GL and especially the link between XBRL GL and XBRL FR taxonomies. Major outcomes of this chapter are:

- XBRL taxonomy schema is the part that contains declarations of concepts whereas taxonomy linkbases provide relationships between them.
- The basic attributes for concept declared in taxonomy schema and valid from the business perspective are *name*, *type*, *balance* and *periodType*.
- XBRL taxonomies can contain up to five linkbases that fall in one of the three categories: relation linkbases (calculation, definition and presentation) that manage the relations between taxonomy concepts; label linkbases that associate taxonomy concepts with text labels defined in various languages and reference linkbases that connect concepts with authoritative literature.
- XBRL GL taxonomy provides an interface to transactional standards and a common model for moving data through an ERP system. XBRL GL was developed as an interface for exchange of disaggregated financial data. It enables encoding of such data being accounting system neutral.

---

[60] SRCD is able to represent the exact dates found in an FR instance. It also provides a rule on which of a number of GL dates might provide conditions that trigger certain details to be summarised.

4.5 Key terms you should know

- Taxonomy schema
- Presentation linkbase
- Calculation linkbase
- Definition linkbase
- Reference linkbase
- Label linkbase
- XBRL FR
- XBRL GL

4.6 Case analysis[61]

The main reason for following the *Standard Approach* is for ease of maintenance of the IFRS taxonomy. The *Standard Approach* allows IFRS Taxonomy development to be aligned with the International Accounting Standards Board[62] agenda, thus creating a stable long-term platform for XBRL and IFRSs. The *Standard Approach* organizes IFRS taxonomy in a way that is familiar to many preparers, and provides for increased readability and usability of the taxonomy. The *Standard Approach* followed by the *IASC Foundation XBRL Team* is based on modeling the IFRS taxonomy standard by standard. The content of the folder for each modeled standard is organized in statements (including notes to financial statements) while dimensions is a single separated folder.

The IFRS taxonomy uses a single schema approach for the definition of reporting concepts (*ifrs-cor_YYYY-MM-DD.xsd*). Dimensions, domains and domain members are placed in separate schema (*ifrs-dim_YYYY-MM-DD.xsd*).

As organizing the folder structure of the IFRS taxonomy follows the *Standard Approach*, linkbases corresponding for example to the IFRS 1 can be found in the folder *../ifrs/ifrs_1_2008-03-01*. Modeling the IFRSs the taxonomy 2008 utilizes three main techniques – hierarchies, intersection tables and dimensions. The most common technique is the use of hierarchies/lists in the presentation and calculation linkbases (or presentation linkbase only). An example of hierarchy modeling is the *ELR [520000] Consolidated statement of cash flows, indirect method*. Hierarchical modeling is in use for most statements and notes in the IFRS Taxonomy.

---

61 Excerpted from IASC Foundation XBRL Team, "IFRS Taxonomy Guide", London 2008, available at http://www.iasb.org/NR/rdonlyres/95D8BAE9-24A1-40D1-A6B1-46F1B9F32436/0/IFRSTaxonomyGuide100080828.pdf.

62 The IASB is responsible for the release of the IFRSs while the development of the IFRS taxonomy is in scope of activities of the IASC Foundation (governing body of the IASB).

5 XBRL Taxonomy Extensions

The nice thing about standards is that there are so many of them to choose from.
[Andrew Stuart Tanenbaum]

Paraphrasing Tannenbaum we could say: *the nice thing about XBRL specifications and taxonomies is that there are so many of them to choose from.* The variety of financial, supervisory and tax reporting domains, together with the XBRL, resulted during last few years in numerous international and local taxonomies and even greater number of extensions. This abundance is described by some as an advantage of the XBRL standard, proving its adaptability to diverse requirements. Those indicate the flexibility as a key factor allowing reflecting contemporary, dynamic business environment. However, others point out the increasing intricacy for end-users and software vendors to comply with often disparate taxonomies. Those bring also up the confusion of the primary role of a standard: a unique and consistent expression of rules and concepts – a point of reference. Although it is difficult to assess whether variety is a contemporary requirement, or a handicap of consistent and standardized business reporting, it is undoubtedly a primary result of the extensibility concept. In this chapter, we will discuss the concept of XBRL extensibility and analyze various approaches and techniques utilized to achieve it.

When discussing the XBRL extensibility we will focus on the three areas we present in figure 5.1.

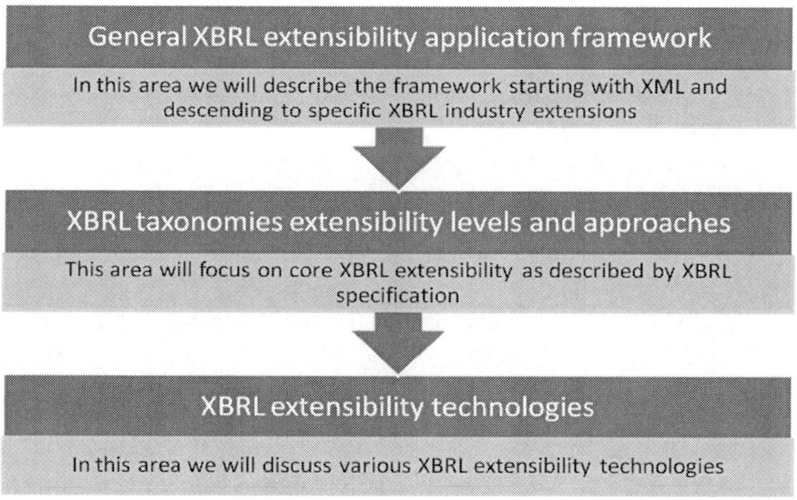

Fig. 5.1: A roadmap for understanding XBRL extensibility

Some rules for extension developers

Before we discuss the XBRL extensibility technologies it is important to note a general issue of extensibility related to XBRL. The taxonomies are often perceived by end-users and software vendors as standards or in other words points of reference. Therefore, to avoid users' confusion with multiple *standards to choose from* as the introductory citation says, we may define general hints for creation of XBRL extensions:

- Use non-confusing namespaces to resolve domain identification;
- Verify if there is no taxonomy suiting your purposes already available;
- Avoid creating concepts in the extension taxonomy that are duplicates of concepts defined in the base taxonomy;
- If possible try to follow the base taxonomy design rules and conventions;
- If you know that there is an identical concept in the base taxonomy, but you still need to create a new one, try to identify relationship between these concepts by using essence-alias arcrole in the definition linkbase.

5.1 Extensibility

The word *extensibility* originates from Latin *extendere* and the Medieval Latin *extensibilis* with the primary meaning of *to stretch*. The word is now in use primarily in the computer science discipline, and particularly for systems, platforms and languages design. The inherently related word *extension* means:

Logic: *The class of objects designated by a specific term or concept; denotation.*

Mathematics: *A set that includes a given and similar set as a subset.*

According to the logical meaning of the word extension, we could say that extension details the base concept or class of concepts by adding some supplementary or other information and therefore *expands* the base class. From the mathematical point of view, extension contains the base set as a subset and, as we presume, adds other sets or concepts. Both definitions apply to extensions from the perspective of XBRL taxonomies.

In the software engineering domain, extensibility is a principle according to which software design should consider future, potential growth of solutions. Extensions are implemented sequentially by modifying current functionality or as incremental functionality. Changes should have minimal impact on existing implementations. A similar definition is in use in the systems design domain. In addition, XML and XBRL were designed specifically with the extensibility concept as their core feature.

5.2 General XBRL extensibility framework

The XBRL standard, as a dialect of XML, addresses the business-reporting domain. A fundamental design characteristic of the standard was the capability to adjust and adapt to a very wide variety of reporting demands. In this section, we provide a framework for that extensibility.

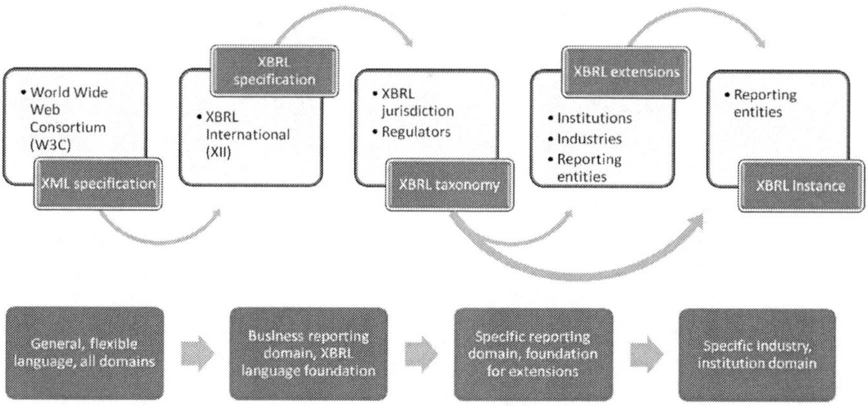

Fig. 5.2: Extensions and other XBRL components

Figure 5.2 presents XML, XBRL, taxonomy and extensions in graphical way. This extends the view that we provided in chapter 3 by adding extensions perspective. XML specifications in a sense provide foundation for further extensions like XBRL, BIOML, MathML and other languages. The XML specification allows experts who specialize in a particular domain to use XML for their particular purposes. For instance, the XBRL founders envisaged that business-reporting domain would require specific common attributes (such as *balance* or *periodType*) and data types (such as *monetaryItemType*) for definition of concepts in XBRL taxonomies. The design of the XBRL specification explicitly enabled further application at different domain levels by creation of domain-related XBRL taxonomies, such as the IFRS or US GAAP taxonomies. In turn, these taxonomies may receive further adjustment for specific industry or institution domain requirements by XBRL taxonomy extensions. An important example of such extension is the FINREP (Financial Reporting) taxonomy by the CEBS (Committee of European Banking Supervisors). This taxonomy extends the IFRS taxonomy explicitly to meet banking supervision requirements.

The intention of this chapter is to focus on extensibility within XBRL. In particular, we review how extensibility influences XBRL taxonomies, extensions thereto and the resulting instance documents.

5.3 XBRL taxonomies extensibility methods and approaches

An XBRL extension can be defined as follows:

> *Any modification of a base taxonomy that DOES NOT change the base taxonomy code.*

Financial Services Authority (FSA) Use Case

The Financial Services Authority (FSA) in one of the European Union Member Countries decided to implement a national platform for electronic reporting for public consolidated groups. The prime rationale was to streamline, enhance and speed up the supervisory processes while at the same time reducing the reporting requirements for the companies. The data gathered in the electronic way should after validation be distributed to all the government agencies analyzing it for various purposes.

The Member Country has already introduced the International Financial Reporting Standards (IFRSs) under one of the European Commission Directives. However the FSA investigated that in addition to the IFRS financial reports the public consolidated groups are required to file also environmental reports and additional management remuneration information. The key question was which standard shall the FSA use for communicating of the groups and what is the scope of information required by the FSA.

The CTO of the FSA learned, that for the purpose of electronic reporting under IFRSs the institution may use the IFRS taxonomy, developed by the IASC Foundation. During the brainstorm with the FSA team decision was made that the scope of environmental and management remuneration information should be also included in the reporting value chain. Following the IASC Foundation Intellectual Property rights the FSA team decided to extend the IFRS taxonomy. The mechanism defined by the XBRL Consortium allowed FSA to extend the base taxonomy (IFRS taxonomy) without modifying its code. The FSA successfully introduced the reporting platform based on the extended taxonomy and became one of the leaders of innovative approaches to electronic reporting in the European Union.

The ability to extend the base taxonomy without modification of its code is achieved by two rules defined in the XBRL specification. First rule sets up the *import* mechanism for inclusion of the base taxonomy within the extension. The second rule prohibits use of the *redefine*[63] XML tag. Allowing extension

[63] The prohibition of *redefine* tag will be discussed in tuple extensibility paragraph.

taxonomies to redefine concepts in a base taxonomy would rapidly lead to chaos in business reporting. The XBRL specification allows composition of "groups of existing DTSs into higher-level DTSs and [...] selectively add concepts and concept relationships via extension taxonomies". Including this information in our definition, we can now more precisely say that an XBRL extension is:

Any DTS which imports a base taxonomy and which MAY define new concepts and new relationships.

Figure 5.3 presents a sample taxonomy extension that imports base taxonomy, adds new concepts and defines new relationships in relevant linkbases. Following the XBRL specification, the diagram shows two extensibility methods allowed:

- Addition of new concepts in an extension schema,
- Addition of new relationships in an extension linkbases.

The XBRL specification also allows us to prohibit and overwrite the relationships defined by base taxonomy linkbases. The following use case illustrates the reason for introduction of *prohibition* and *overriding* of relationships.

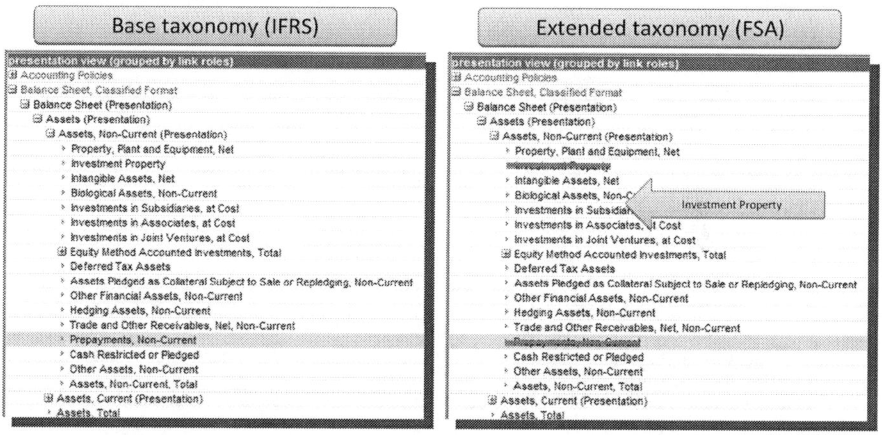

Fig. 5.3: Example of the redesign of the IFRS taxonomy presentation linkbase

The FSA team from the previous use case was asked to extend the IFRS taxonomy to meet some specific requirements. The initial analysis of the presentation linkbase of the *Balance Sheet* in the base taxonomy revealed that the order of some concepts should be changed to meet the *Member Country* rules. Particularly the financial experts from the FSA indicated that the section of *Non-current Assets* should be redesigned according to the structure presented in Figure 5.3.

The financial experts explained that *Investment Property* should appear before *Investment in Subsidiaries, at Cost* and that *Prepayments, Non-Current* should not appear on the *Balance Sheet*.

The team decided that, since they are not allowed to modify the base IFRS taxonomy presentation linkbase, in the extension taxonomy presentation linkbase they will define new relationships for the Balance Sheet:

- One prohibiting the link between *Prepayments, Non-Current* and *Assets, Non-Current (Presentation)* and;
- second, which changes the order of appearance of the *Investment Property* (new relationship overwriting the base taxonomy link between *Investment Property* and *Assets, Non-Current (Presentation)*).

In order to prohibit or overwrite a relationship, we need to employ the *use* and *priority* attributes. The Code examples and following Figures demonstrate the use of these attributes.

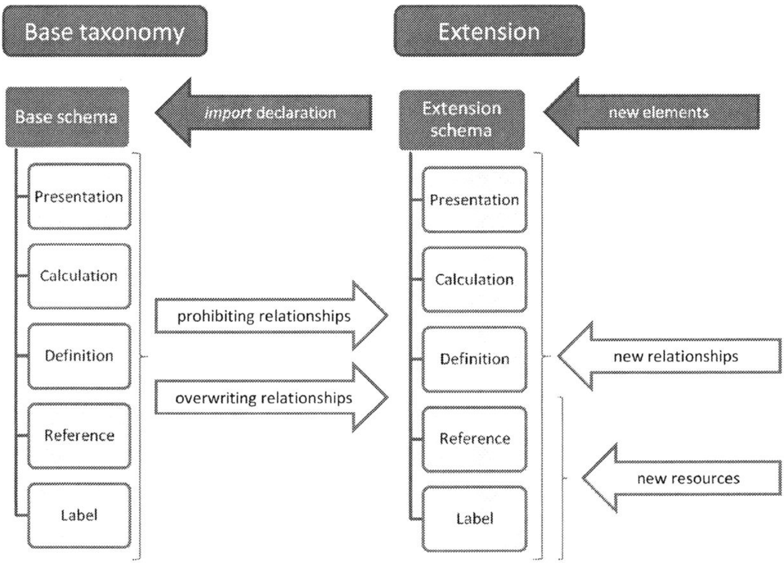

Fig. 5.4: Example of an XBRL extension

The arrows related to prohibiting and overwriting relationship point to extension taxonomy as they amend the base taxonomy relationships. These relationships are set out in the extension taxonomy linkbases. Analyzing the use case, we can see that even though the changes that the FSA team from our use case wants to introduce concern the base taxonomy, all the modifications (prohibition and overriding of relationships) are described in the extension presentation linkbase.

Table 5.1 summarizes the allowed extensibility methods, identifies their places of application and methods of application according to Figure 5.4. Importantly, none of the methods modifies the original base taxonomy code.

Tab. 5.1: Summary of XBRL extensibility methods

Extensibility method	Place of application	Method of application
Addition of concepts	Extension schema	Standard declaration of a new XBRL concept with appropriate attributes
Addition of resources	Extension label and reference linkbase	Standard declaration of label or reference resources and appropriate arcs
Addition of relationships	Linkbases of extension taxonomy	Standard declaration of locators and a respective arc
Prohibition of relationships	Linkbases of extension taxonomy	Declaration of locators and an arc with: from and to attributes equal to the one from base taxonomy and *use="prohibited"* attribute and (if required) higher priority attribute
Overwriting of relationships	Linkbases of extension taxonomy	Declaration of locators and an arc with higher priority attribute. Overwriting relationships is useful for modifying the order and use attributes.

Above, we stated that prohibition and overwriting relationships require *use* and *priority* attributes on the arcs of the linkbase. The tables below explain the nature of *use* and *priority* attributes and present their effects.

Use attribute

Tab. 5.2: Use attribute explanation

Value	**Default**	**Explanation**
Optional	Yes	If the use attribute on arc is declared as optional, then this arc is considered to take part in the network of relationships defined in the taxonomy.
Prohibited	No	If the use attribute on arc is declared as prohibited, then this arcs is considered as excluded from the network of relationships defined in the taxonomy. If an arc between the same locators existed in the network of relationships before (was defined in the base taxonomy) then this relationship should now be considered as prohibited (provided that the priority attribute on the arc is higher than the one defined in the base taxonomy).

Priority attribute

Tab. 5.3: Priority attribute explanation

Value	Default	Explanation
(integer value)	0	The importance of the relationship is indicated by the value of the priority attribute on the arc (the higher value the more important relationship).

To illustrate application of these attributes we employ the example of a calculation relationship that we show in Figure 5.5. The calculation linkbase in the base taxonomy sums the three concepts *purchaseTangibleAssets*, *purchaseIntangibleAssets* and *purchaseInventories* together to equal a fourth concept, viz: *purchase*. We wish to enter a new subtotal *purchaseIntangibleAssetsTangibleAssets* into the aggregation hierarchy. In our new structure, *purchaseTangibleAssets* and *purchaseIntangibleAssets* sum to to *purchaseIntangibleAssetsTangibleAssets*. This variable in turn adds with *purchaseInventories* to equal *purchase*.

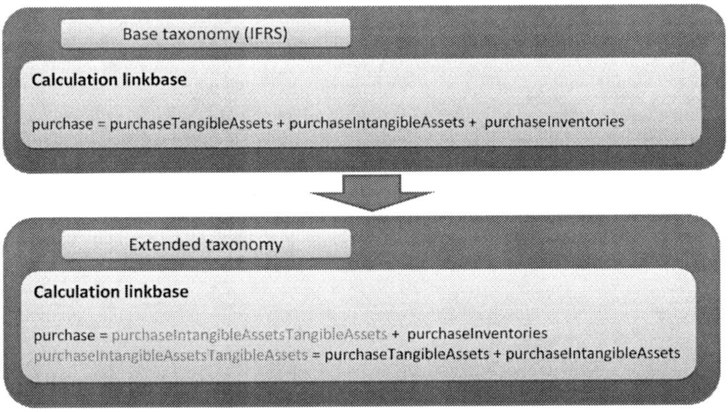

Fig. 5.5: Introduction to extension of calculations

To be precise, for the purposes of this example, we assume that:

- The base taxonomy defines four *monetaryItemType* concepts: *purchase*, *purchaseTangibleAssets*, *purchaseIntangibleAssets* and *purchaseInventories*
- In the calculation linkbase of the base taxonomy the following calculation relationship is defined:

$$purchase = purchaseTangibleAssets + purchaseIntangibleAssets + purchaseInventories$$

we will develop an extension which:

- Defines new concept *purchaseIntangibleAssetsTangibleAssets*
- Prohibits the previous calculation and in its place defines two new:

purchase = *purchaseIntangibleAssetsTangibleAssets* + *purchaseInventories*

AND

purchaseIntangibleAssetsTangibleAssets = *purchaseTangibleAssets* + *purchaseIntangibleAssets*

Figure 5.6 presents the above example in a graphical form. The example assumes that:

- We have a calculation defined which adds three components to receive the value of the *purchase;*
- We would like to change this calculation by introducing an aggregate of two of these three components and use the aggregate to receive the *purchase* value.

Explaining the above in the XBRL taxonomies context, we will use the base taxonomy with the primary calculation defined and we will create an extension to introduce the aggregate and the new calculations (Figure 5.6).
The definition of concepts flows from our assumptions. Four are in the base schema and one is in the extension schema. There are three calculation relationships (with *summation-item* arcroles) in the base taxonomy calculation linkbase, viz. relationships number 1, 2 and 3. The extension taxonomy calculation linkbase defines two relationships (1a and 2a) that prohibit relationships 1 and 2 (higher *priority="1"* and *use="prohibited").* There are also three new calculation relationships (4, 5 and 6). In the extension taxonomy, relationships 3 and 4 are the representation of the first equation. In turn, relationships 5 and 6 represent the second equation. Again, the code of the base taxonomy remained unchanged.

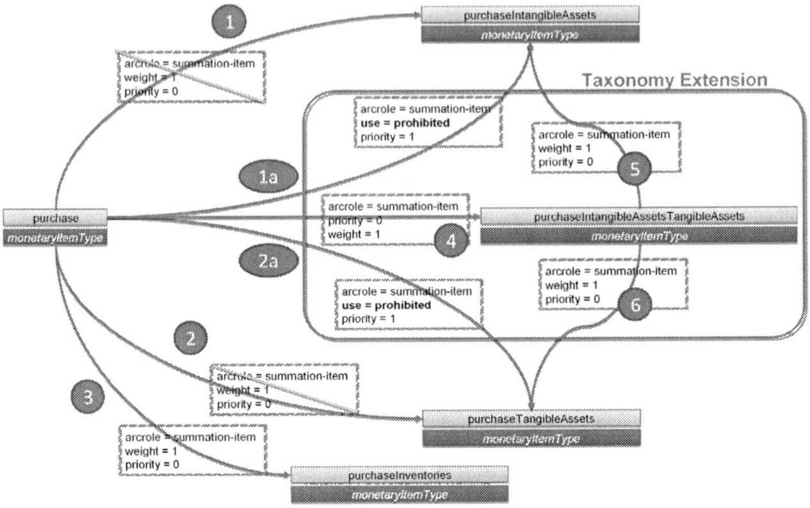

Fig. 5.6: Example for the use and priority attributes application

We now analyze how the above example appears in XBRL code. Code example 5.1 presents the code of the base taxonomy schema (*ee-bt-2008-03-09.xsd*):

```
<xsd:schema
       targetNamespace="http://www.xbrl-
examples.org/2008/extensionExample/baseTaxonomy"
       xmlns:ee-bt="http://www.xbrl-
       examples.org/2008/extensionExample/baseTaxonomy"
(...)
  <xsd:element
       name="purchase"
       id="ee-bt_purchase"
       type="xbrli:monetaryItemType"
       substitutionGroup="xbrli:item"
       nillable="true"
       xbrli:balance="debit"
       xbrli:periodType="duration"/>
  <xsd:element
       name="purchaseTangibleAssets"
       id="ee-bt_purchaseTangibleAssets"
       type="xbrli:monetaryItemType"
       substitutionGroup="xbrli:item"
       nillable="true"
       xbrli:balance="debit"
       xbrli:periodType="duration"/>
(...)
</xsd:schema>
```

Code example 5.1: Base taxonomy schema

There are two important types of declarations, which we see in bold. First, is the declaration of the base taxonomy namespace (*http://www.xbrl-examples.org/2008/extensionExample/baseTaxonomy*) and assigned prefix (*ee-bt*). The second shows the declaration of the necessary concepts. It is important to know the namespace of the base taxonomy schema to avoid creating identical namespaces for the extension taxonomy schema. We now present and analyze the code of the base taxonomy calculation linkbase.

```
<link:loc xlink:type="locator"  xlink:href="ee-bt-2008-03-
09.xsd#ee-bt_purchase" xlink:label="purchase"/>

<link:loc xlink:type="locator" xlink:href="ee-bt-2008-03-
09.xsd#ee-bt_purchaseIntangibleAssets"
xlink:label="purchaseIntangibleAssets"/>

<link:calculationArc xlink:type="arc"
xlink:arcrole="http://www.xbrl.org/2003/arcrole/summation-
item" xlink:from="purchase"
xlink:to="purchaseIntangibleAssets" order="1.0"
weight="1.0"/>
```

Code example 5.2: Base taxonomy calculation linkbase

The calculation linkbase defines three calculation arcs. We did not include two calculation arcs in the above code for the sake of brevity. We note that there are no *use* and *priority* attributes declared on the arc. As a result, XBRL software processors and parsers will assign the default values for further processing (*use="optional"* and *priority="0"*). Now we can analyze the code of the extension taxonomy.

```
<xsd:schema
      targetNamespace=http://www.xbrl-exam-
      ples.org/2008/extensionExample/extensionTaxonomy
      xmlns:ee-et="http://www.xbrl-
      examples.org/2008/extensionExample/extensionTaxonomy"
>
 <xsd:import namespace="http://www.xbrl-
      examples.org/2008/extensionExample/baseTaxonomy"
schemaLocation="ee-bt-2008-03-09.xsd"/>

<xsd:element name="purchaseIntangibleAssetsTangibleAssets"
id="ee-et_purchaseIntangibleAssetsTangibleAssets"
type="xbrli:monetaryItemType"
substitutionGroup="xbrli:item" nillable="true"
xbrli:balance="debit" xbrli:periodType="duration"/>
</xsd:schema>
```

Code example 5.3: Extension taxonomy schema (ee-et-2008-03-09.xsd)

The schema of the extension taxonomy contains two interesting sections. In the *schema* concept, the extension taxonomy declares a new namespace (*http://www.xbrl-examples.org/2008/extensionExample/extensionTaxonomy*) as a *targetNamespace* and a new *ee-et* prefix. These differentiate the extension schema from the base schema (which has the *ee-bt* prefix and *http://www.xbrl-examples.org/2008/extensionExample/baseTaxonomy* namespace). We can also see the *import* declaration that, using namespace to resolve potential domain conflicts, imports the *ee-bt-2008-03-09.xsd* (base taxonomy) schema to the extension DTS.

Import declaration

This declaration allows to indicate to the XBRL processor (parser) that some definitions of concepts, types or other XML/XBRL constructs are included in other XML/XBRL schema files. The import declaration allows to build advanced modularized XBRL taxonomy architectures and allows for development of XBRL extensions.

Note that the extension schema defines only one missing concept for our example: *purchaseIntangibleAssetsTangibleAssets*. We can now analyze the structure of the extension taxonomy calculation linkbase code.

```
<link:loc xlink:type="locator" xlink:href="ee-bt-2008-03-
09.xsd#ee-bt_purchase" xlink:label="purchase"/>

<link:loc xlink:type="locator" xlink:href="ee-bt-2008-03-
09.xsd#ee-bt_purchaseIntangibleAssets"
xlink:label="purchaseIntangibleAssets"/>

<link:calculationArc xlink:type="arc"
xlink:arcrole="http://www.xbrl.org/2003/arcrole/summation-
item" xlink:from="purchase"
xlink:to="purchaseIntangibleAssets" use="prohibited"
priority="1" order="1.0" weight="1.0"/>
```

Code example 5.4: Extension taxonomy calculation linkbase

Analyzing the above code, we can see that:

- The locators for the prohibiting arc point to the concepts defined in the base taxonomy schema – this is enabled because we imported the base taxonomy schema into the extension taxonomy DTS;
- Calculation arc defined between these two concepts has the same values for all attributes except the *use* and *priority* attributes;
- The *use* attribute has the *prohibited* value;

- The priority attribute has the *1* value (higher than arc in base taxonomy calculation linkbase).

The above example shows how XBRL achieves (1) extensibility of the scope of the taxonomy, with the addition of a concept in the *item substitutionGroup* in the extension schema, and (2) extensibility of semantic information, with the addition and prohibition of relationships in the extension linkbases. Further, there are more than a dozen technologies that we can use to achieve extensibility of other XBRL domains.

5.4 XBRL taxonomies extensibility technologies

The XBRL standard, as a derivative of XML language, offers multiple combinations of technologies, which support taxonomy extensibility. Figure 5.7 presents a summary of the most common ones[64]:

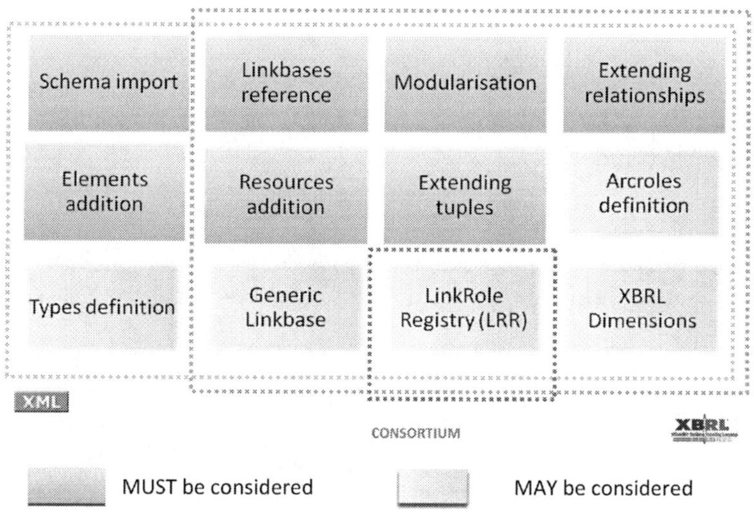

Fig. 5.7: Summary of common XBRL extensibility technologies

There are two classifications of the identified technologies:

- By importance – stating whether the technology *MUST* or *MAY* be considered while developing XBRL extensions, and;

[64] The classification of the technologies is highly subjective and we are aware of certain simplifications made for the sake of simplicity here.

- By the source of the technology – indicating whether the technology originates from the XML specification (*XML*), XBRL specification utilizing XLink specification (*XBRL*) or from XII developments (*Consortium*).

Earlier, we introduced a range of XBRL technologies including schema import, concepts addition and relationships extension or resources addition. They present some of many aspects that should be considered when discussing taxonomy extensions. In this chapter, we will focus only on the major approaches and issues for the sake of simplicity. Especially we will discuss:

- modularization,
- tuples extension.

Modularization

XBRL taxonomies are often modular in nature. This means that their components (schema and linkbases) are augmented in different physical modules or files, according to desired criteria. This, among others, allows for:

- easier management of the taxonomies;
- creation of common concepts schemas and structured DTS and;
- flexible use of required modules by users.

The extension development strategy depends on a base taxonomy modularization scheme. Figure 5.8 presents the common extension strategies depending on use of various base taxonomy modules.

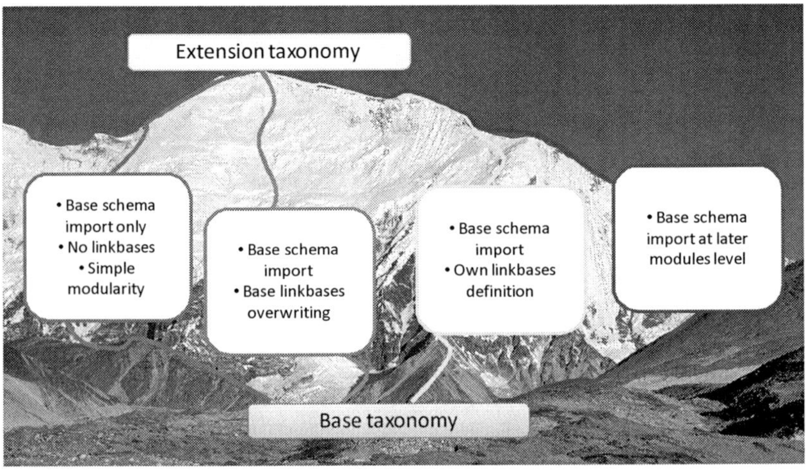

Fig. 5.8: Extension strategies and modularization

There are several paths to climb the mountain. Not all of them were listed in Figure 5.8 for the sake of simplicity. All have pros and cons depending on particular project's requirements. We now analyze the above four approaches using the example of the IFRS taxonomy architecture. Figure 5.9 presents the modularization of the IFRS 2005 taxonomy.

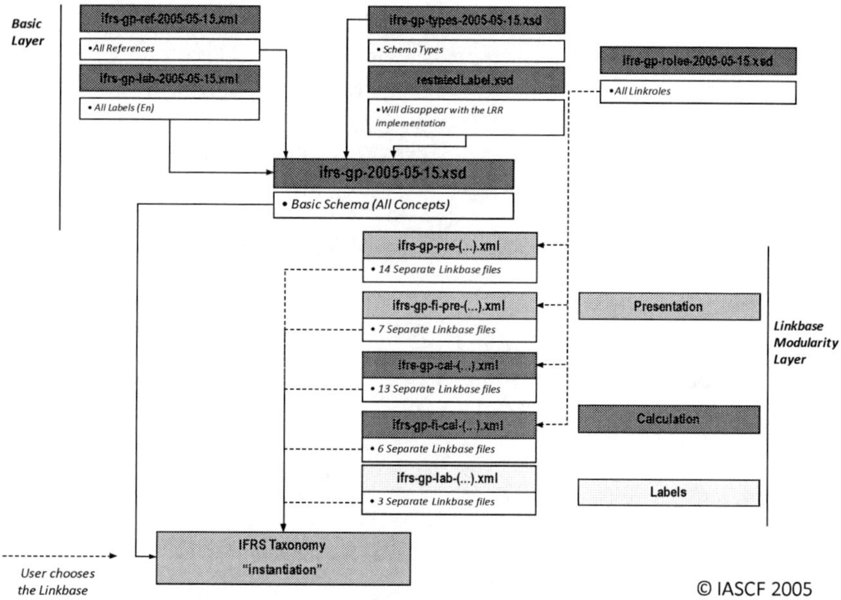

Fig. 5.9: IFRS 2005 taxonomy architecture diagram[65]

We can see that in the center of the taxonomy is *ifrs-gp-2005-05-15.xsd* schema, which defines over 4000 concepts. This schema imports two technical files (*types* definition and *restated* information concept definition) and references two linkbases (English labels linkbase and concept reference linkbase). Separately there are 43 additional presentation, calculation and label linkbases. We categorize presentation and calculation modules at two levels:

- *gp* for general purpose IFRS concepts and
- *fi* for financial IFRS concepts.

Additionally, there is another layer of modularization that splits the modules according to IFRS statements. These include *accounting policies*, *balance sheets*, *income statements*, *cash flow statements*, *statement of changes in equity* and *explanatory disclosures*. The definition of each of these components is in a separate linkbase file.

This modularization structure allows us, to select which linkbases do we want to extend. Technically, to select the linkbases we need to reference them in our schema file. We also have to import the base IFRS schema to be able to refer to

65 Source: http://www.iasb.org/xbrl.

concepts that it defines. Knowing the architecture of the base (IFRS) taxonomy, we can now discuss various approaches presented in Figure 5.8.

A first option is to import only the base schema as a simple list of concepts. We would leave behind the base presentation and calculation linkbases. We assume that we will not define our own presentation and calculation linkbases. This architecture is simple and easy to manage. This option is not necessarily user-friendly, however, as it does not provide any semantic relationships between concepts in the taxonomy. In most business reporting scenarios, there is a clear need to maintain these semantic relationships. Indeed, it is difficult to conceive of a use case where an information consumer of financial statements constructed under IFRS would be happy merely with a set of unrelated concepts.

IFRS Financial Reporting System

A Software Vendor (SV) decided they would like to allow their customers who use their Financial Reporting System to report according to the IFRS taxonomy. The financial experts explained that according to the IFRSs a company should have the flexibility to design the structure and order of the sections of their IFRS financial statement.

Analyzing the potential approaches the SV Project Team decided to follow approach number one and only refer to the core schema in the first level extension built in the product. Later the software will support the company in creation of the company-specific extension and allow definition of company specific presentation and calculation linkbases.

In the second approach, we assume that our extension schema will not only import base IFRS schema but also reference the selected linkbases and in particular the presentation and calculation linkbases.

Colombian Central Bank and XBRL

The Central Bank of Colombia decided to use the IFRS taxonomy to allow the supervised commercial banks to report their Balance Sheet in an electronic format. The financial experts indicated that they only require the Balance Sheet, Order of Liquidity Format section from the presentation linkbase. The experts also explained that no changes are required in the order and structure of the Balance Sheet.

As a result, the Taxonomy Team decided to import the base schema into the extension taxonomy and reference the presentation linkbase that defines the structure of the Balance Sheet, Order of Liquidity Format. This approach allowed the Bank to minimize the work required to adjust the structure and use the authoritative IFRS taxonomy.

Under this option, we can use all the semantic information provided in the relationships of a base taxonomy. At the same time, we significantly increase the dependency with the base taxonomy. We will need to align our development plans with the base taxonomy releases. This may create substantial management effort. Since we do not define our own linkbases, we will need to depend fully on the base taxonomy design.

The third approach allows us to import the base schema and selected linkbases and also define our custom linkbases.

Government Agency in France

A Government Agency in France decided to build a national reporting framework based on the IFRS taxonomy. The business experts indicated the requirement to extension the IFRS taxonomy however explained that although original presentation and calculation linkbases may be used to save time required for project conduction the Agency decided to implement own set of linkbases.

Based on the experts' advice the Taxonomy Development Team decided to extend the base taxonomy, modify its scope with the allowed extensibility techniques, primarily by providing custom linkbases and deliver a flexible customizable reporting framework for French companies.

This is the most common approach, which is efficient from the taxonomy design point of view. However the outcome DTS (Deliverable Taxonomy Suite) becomes increasingly sophisticated for end-users. It is an interesting solution from the presentation and calculation re-design point of view as we can create any relationship we need. However, it requires substantial effort if we were to recreate all relationships of the IFRS statements and disclosures. It also requires certain domain knowledge and detailed investigation of concepts available in the base taxonomy.

In the fourth approach, we can assume that our target taxonomy is an extensive DTS that should incorporate not only the IFRS but also other domains of reporting.

Government in New Zealand

The Government in New Zealand decided to implement a national business-reporting framework. The framework should enable to report, financial, tax, statistical, environmental and other information required by legal regulations. Since New Zealand companies have already been filing financial reports according to IFRSs but the scope of the required information exceeded the scope of the IFRS taxonomy the Taxonomy Development Team decided to develop customized New Zealand Taxonomy which will import and extend several other taxonomies (among them the IFRS taxonomy). This approach allowed the Government to address all reporting domains and at the same time use international standards like the IFRS taxonomy.

In this case, we may need to import the IFRS taxonomy into the New Zealand DTS. This approach requires us to consider the impact on end-users and software developers. Important here is the fact that XBRL implementation cost may increase with growing sophistication and number of concepts. This can lead to issues with taxonomy acceptance in the market. In addition, management of large DTS requires certain planning and possibly additional advanced tools.

There could be more approaches to the modularization strategies, which have different impact on the extensibility. Additionally the technical modularization approaches may be driven by two orientations:

- technical architectural orientation and/or,
- business domain requirements orientation.

Business domain may require the taxonomy to be designed in a specific manner. For instance, regulatory agencies in the tax domain require taxonomies to reflect certain forms-driven structures. These regulators require standardized and relatively inflexible reports. Conversely, the IFRS financial domain, being more flexible, must allow end-users to structure required disclosures in customized way. In the design of extensions, we should consider both orientations.

Tuple extension

In previous paragraphs, we focused on extension of concepts from the *item substitutionGroup*. We showed how to add concepts in extension schema and relate them to the base taxonomy schema. We also identified technologies such as relationships addition, prohibition and overwriting. However, in Figure 5.7 we separately identified extensibility of tuples as an important concept.
There are three reasons for that:

- prohibition of redefine construct;
- construction of a tuple as a complex content;
- extensibility via *similar-tuples* arc.

As we mentioned earlier the XBRL specification prohibits the use of *redefine* tag in XBRL taxonomies schemas. This means that we cannot redefine concepts defined in base schema and modify their type, attributes or their complex content (*tuples*). However, the above prohibition does not support situations where the redefinition is correct from the business reporting perspective. Therefore, in order to allow users to extend tuples defined in a base taxonomy, XBRL specification employs a special *similar-tuples* arcrole in use in the definition linkbase. This arcrole identifies two tuples from different schemas as identical (also refer to chapter 4 and *Deposits* example). The following example presents the use of this arcrole.

We will assume that in the base schema (prefix: *bs*) there is an *AddressTuple* tuple defined with the *Street, BuildingNumber, Postcode* and *TownCity* items in the content model. In an extension schema (prefix: *es*) we would like to have additionally *Region* item available in the content model. Fig 5.10 presents the above example.

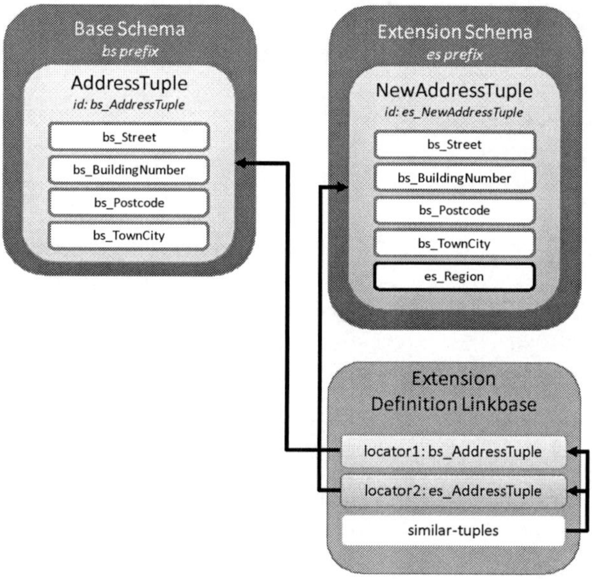

Fig. 5.10: Example of similar-tuples arcrole use

As we can see, the *NewAddressTuple* content model includes new item *es_Region* defined in the extension schema (es prefix). The extension definition linkbase locates the two tuples from base and extension schemas and relates them by *similar-tuples* arc. Code example 5.5 presents the code of the base schema with the original tuple and its content defined.

```
<xsd:element name="Street" id="bt_Street"
type="xbrli:stringItemType" substitutionGroup="xbrli:item"
nillable="true" xbrli:periodType="duration"/>
<xsd:element name="BuildingNumber" id="bt_BuildingNumber"
type="xbrli:stringItemType" substitutionGroup="xbrli:item"
nillable="true" xbrli:periodType="duration"/>
<xsd:element name="Postcode" id="bt_Postcode"
type="xbrli:stringItemType" substitutionGroup="xbrli:item"
nillable="true" xbrli:periodType="duration"/>
<xsd:element name="TownCity" id="bt_TownCity"
```

```
type="xbrli:stringItemType" substitutionGroup="xbrli:item"
nillable="true" xbrli:periodType="duration"/>
<xsd:element name="AddressTuple" id="bt_AddressTuple"
substitutionGroup="xbrli:tuple">
 <xsd:complexType>
  <xsd:sequence>
   <xsd:element ref="bt:Street"/>
   <xsd:element ref="bt:BuildingNumber"/>
   <xsd:element ref="bt:Postcode"/>
   <xsd:element ref="bt:TownCity"/>
  </xsd:sequence>
 </xsd:complexType>
</xsd:element>
```

Code example 5.5: Tuple extension example - base schema

As we can see, the tuple content model is referring by *qname* (qualified name - prefix:name) to the item concepts defined earlier. In Figure 5.10, this code we illustrate this as the *AddressTuple* content container. Once we know what the base tuple structure is we can analyze the extension schema presented on Code example 5.6.

```
<xsd:import namespace="http://www.xbrl-
examples.org/2008/tupleExtension/baseTaxonomy"
schemaLocation="te-bt-2008-03-14.xsd"/>

<xsd:element name="Region" id="es_Region"
type="xbrli:stringItemType" substitutionGroup="xbrli:item"
nillable="true" xbrli:periodType="duration"/>

<xsd:element name="NewAddressTuple" id="es_NewAddressTuple"
substitutionGroup="xbrli:tuple">
 <xsd:complexType>
  <xsd:sequence>
   <xsd:element ref="bt:Street"/>
   <xsd:element ref="bt:BuildingNumber"/>
   <xsd:element ref="bt:Postcode"/>
   <xsd:element ref="bt:TownCity"/>
   <xsd:element ref="es:Region"/>
  </xsd:sequence>
 </xsd:complexType>
</xsd:element>
```

Code example 5.6: Tuple extension example - extension schema

The definition linkbase allows us to indicate the relationship between the *old* and the *new* tuples and define this relationship as *similar-tuple*. The extension schema defines the *Region* item and the new tuple with its content model (items from base and extension schemas). The definition of the new tuple content follows the same code pattern as the old tuple definition. Since we have already defined the new tuple content model, we will analyze the definition linkbase code that explicitly indicates the similarity between them.

```
<link:loc xlink:type="locator" xlink:href="es-2008-03-
14.xsd#es_NewAddressTuple" xlink:label="NewAddressTuple"/>

<link:loc xlink:type="locator" xlink:href="te-bt-2008-03-
14.xsd#bt_AddressTuple" xlink:label="AddressTuple"/>

<link:definitionArc xlink:type="arc"
xlink:arcrole="http://www.xbrl.org/2003/arcrole/similar-
tuple" xlink:from="NewAddressTuple" xlink:to="AddressTuple"
order="1.0"/>
```

Code example 5.7: Tuple extension example - extension definition linkbase

The above code presents an arc defined by the two tuples that semantically identifies them as similar. In this way, we extend the tuple without changing the base taxonomy code and without using the XML *redefine* tag. The XBRL-enabled software will now be able to indicate to the user that there are two versions of the *AddressTuple*.

5.5 Summary

Extensibility is inherent in the XBRL standard. It allows taxonomy builders and creators of instance documents to adjust the scope of the reported information and flexibly present it in the structure appropriate for the particular purpose of the given reporting environment. From the technical perspective, as a dialect of the XML, XBRL may employ XML extensibility technologies to support adoption for specific domains. However, with irresponsible creation of extensions taxonomy developers may contribute to the increasing number of standards, confusing the end-users and causing software-vendors to implement proprietary solutions.

Instead of standardizing the information, numerous XBRL taxonomies may confuse the audience and require them to adhere to various standards. In many cases, the market may reject using the XBRL technology primarily because of investment costs related with its implementation and workload required to create documents according to different taxonomies. Software vendors who may be required to invest upfront in implementation of the particular taxonomy may not see the business reason, which will hinder adoption of a single electronic reporting standard. Therefore, it is important to balance the requirements and take the effort to investigate available taxonomies, their content and asses their extensibility frameworks.

5.6 Key terms you should know

- Base taxonomy
- Taxonomy extension
- Prohibiting
- Overriding
- Taxonomy import
- Modularization

5.7 *Case analysis*[66]

The CFA Institute Centre for Financial Market Integrity established the XBRL Working Group of CFA Institute members in early 2007. XBRL (eXtensible Business Reporting Language) represents a new technology for delivering computer readable financial information. The objectives of the group included conducting a survey on XBRL and incorporating the survey results into a draft position paper on the topic. Through their research, discussions, and analysis of the survey results, the Working Group developed the following key principles to outline those XBRL framework attributes they believe are necessary to maximize the investors' benefits from XBRL.

1. Core taxonomy (or structure of tagging concepts) should be predefined by current financial reporting standards, including generally accepted accounting principles and other regulatory disclosure and reporting requirements.
2. Taxonomy extensibility should maintain the level of data comparability as defined by GAAP and other regulatory requirements.
3. Ultimately, companies should deliver required financial reports to regulators using the established XBRL framework.
4. The general public should have equal access to the XBRL-tagged information.
5. Regulators should develop the necessary infrastructure and protocol to ensure the timely updating of the established XBRL framework as outlined in the preceding four key principles.

[66] Excerpted from CFA Institute, "Key Principles of an XBRL Framework", available at http://www.cfainstitute.org/centre/topics/reporting/pdf/principles_for_xbrl.pdf.

XBRL Instance Documents

Creating XBRL Instance Documents (the marrying of the XBRL tag with the actual financial result)
[from xml.coverpages.org]

Opening Vignette: Edgar Online's I-Metrix for XBRL Instance Documents Analysis[67]

Extensible Business Reporting Language (XBRL) can improve the quality and efficiency of investment analysis. What has been missing is XBRL-tagged data for analysis. EDGAR Online's (EOL's) I-Metrix is overcoming this dilemma for corporate financial and operational data (referred to as fundamental data), beginning with U.S. Securities and Exchange Commission (SEC) filing data for 5,000 U.S. companies. Through application of XBRL, I-Metrix should produce a minimum of a 25 percent efficiency gain in fundamental data analysis for companies using proprietary, non-Extensible Markup Language (XML)-based fundamental data sources. Investment services companies could use I-Metrix for automating access and manipulation of fundamental data from SEC filings. I-Metrix is EOL's response to a need to automate the analysis of corporate performance data. Introduced in April 2005, I-Metrix offers online access to XBRL-tagged SEC filing instance documents, including importation into Microsoft Excel. Analytical templates are also provided. I-Metrix provides access to XBRL-tagged SEC filing data within a maximum of 24 hours, and often within minutes, of the company filing with the SEC. The data is delivered online with access through Microsoft Excel, a Web site, a visualization dashboard or a direct data feed. Users can click on individual XBRL-tagged facts in the Excel worksheet and be taken to the underlying SEC filing document for immediate verification. Standardized, customizable templates that allow analysts without explicit XBRL knowledge to work with the data are provided. There are also Excel wizards for requesting different data types and creating templates and models.

The opening vignette shows how the use of XBRL instance documents can enhance the financial analysis of corporate filings with the SEC. An XBRL instance document is a business report in an electronic format created according to the rules of XBRL. It contains facts that are defined by the concepts in the taxonomy schema it refers to, together with their values, units and an explanation of the context in which they are placed. XBRL instance documents and their

[67] Excerpted from "XBRL Reference Guide" by RR Donnelley
http://www.xbrl.org/us/us/RR%20Donnelley_XBRL_Reference_Guide.pdf

relation to XBRL taxonomy schema resembles the XML instances and their relation to XML schema discussed in chapter 1.

In this chapter, we analyze the structure of an instance document. We show how instance documents reference appropriate taxonomy schemas. We describe how instance documents set out facts. We discuss how facts connect to other characteristics of an instance document. Further, we explain the composition of the context, the meaning of *unit* as well as decimals and precision. Finally, we explore the expression of additional information about reported facts with XBRL footnotes.

5.8 *Referencing taxonomy from instance document*

Each instance document must relate to at least one XBRL taxonomy. The taxonomy defines concepts for which facts can be reported in the instance document. In order to establish the linkage taxonomy schema (or taxonomy extension schema) needs to be referenced from the instance document. Code example 5.8 presents the way how *ifrs-taxonomy-hawaii-extension.xsd* is linked to the instance document.

```
<schemaRef
type="simple"
href="ifrs-taxonomy-hawaii-extension.xsd"/>
```

Code example 5.8: Schema reference in instance document

Barcodes and XBRL instance documents[68]

Working with an XBRL instance document is similar to the work of a bar code reader. It contains the *code* for the tags and the structure that belongs to the tagged data. Instance documents are built from a combination of XML specification and XBRL, structured to produce for example financial statements. The XBRL instance document provides data while the structure can be derived from the XBRL taxonomy files for machine recognition, and human readability. Bar code readers typically scan an item for a UPS, or universal product code. The UPS is a physical tag that provides a link to information about the item. Once scanned, information about the item can be relayed to other systems such as the inventory system. The scanner contains a map from the bar code to the product definition. The list of bar

[68] Excerpted from XBRL Educational Resource Centre at Bryant University http://www.xbrleducation.com/edu/instance.htm

codes and their meanings is similar to XBRL taxonomy (the general list). The factual items tagged with a barcode resemble the instance document (the customized list). With the UPS data from the bar code reader, inventory systems can be updated, products re-ordered, management reports on sales created. Financial information, coded with XBRL tags can function similarly.

5.9 Reported single and tuple facts

The main goal of an instance document is to provide facts according to the concepts defined in the referenced taxonomy. The facts can be for a single concept or for multiple concepts within a tuple. A tuple is comparable to a table in a database.

Figure 6.1 provides an overview of the structure of an instance document. The underlying taxonomy defines two concepts *Inventories* and *Accounting policy for inventories*. The *Inventories* concept represents stock on hand. It has an instant periodType attribute assigned. Conversely, the *Accounting policy on inventories* represents narrative information. It has a duration periodType attribute. The instance document carries facts reported for these concepts *12000* and *All company inventories are measured using LIFO*. For the monetary fact (*12000*) the measurement unit is defined as *Euro*. There are two different contexts (*E2007*) and (*Y2007*). These contexts correspond to the reported facts. Both contexts refer to the same entity (*Example Inc.*) and its segment (*Aircrafts*). In addition, both state the same scenario for the reported value (*Audited*). The difference between these contexts is in the period component. The context *E2007* refers to the instant date of *31 December 2007*. Conversely, the context *Y2007* refers to a period in time from *1 January* to *31 December 2007*. The diagram also indicates that there is no relationship *between* the reported facts. A relationship can exist in the taxonomy but the facts reported in the instance document are not related[69].

---

[69] Facts in the instance document can be bound together when a number of them refer to the same context. In our example we could add fact for a element *Cash and cash equivalents* reported in the same context *E2007* and unit *Euro*.

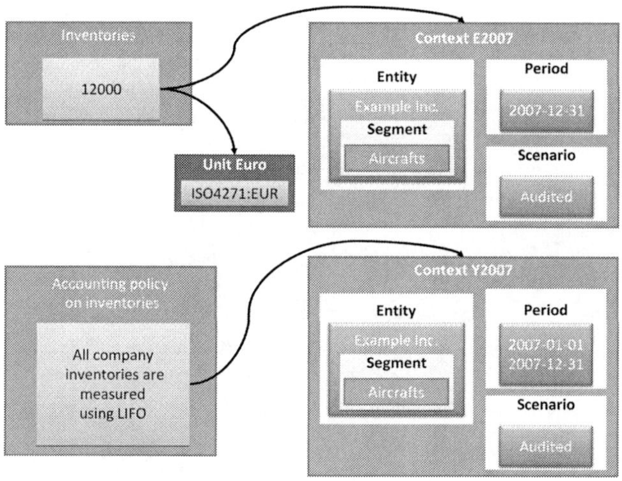

Fig. 5.11: Structure of an instance document

Code example 5.9 and Code example 5.10 provide an overview of a concept defined in the taxonomy schema and a corresponding instance document. The instance document holds a value and provides additional information about the corresponding currency. It defines the relevant period and discloses the entity to which the fact corresponds. The information metadata in the Code examples is *Profit (loss) before tax* amounting to *661,000 EUR*.

```
<element
id="ifrs_ProfitLossBeforeTax"
name="ProfitLossBeforeTax"
type="xbrli:monetaryItemType"
substitutionGroup="xbrli:item"
xbrli:periodType="duration"
xbrli:balance="credit"
nillable="true"/>
```

Code example 5.9: Concept declaration in a taxonomy

```
<ifrs:ProfitLossBeforeTax
contextRef="Current_ForPeriod"
unitRef="U-Euros"
decimals="0">661000</ifrs:ProfitLossBeforeTax>
```

Code example 5.10: Item reporting in an instance document

Apart from single facts reported for a context and entity, instance documents can carry facts for tuples defined in a taxonomy. We demonstrate the reporting on deposits based on the example previously provided in chapter four. The taxonomy defines a structure for deposits. We present an example instance document for such a tuple in Code example 5.11. The instance document consists of two set of values reported for tuple deposits. The first *Deposit A* amounts to *€ 188309.20* and the effective interest rate of *12.90* in the current period while the amount for second *Deposit B* is *€ 250000.40* (the effective interest rate is not reported).

```
<Deposit>
 <DepositDescription
contextRef="Current_ForPeriod">Deposit
A</DepositDescription>
 <DepositAmount contextRef="Current_ForPeriod"
unitRef="EUR" decimals="2">188309.20</DepositAmount>
 <EffectiveInterestRate contextRef="Current_ForPeriod"
unitRef="pure" decimals="2">12.90</EffectiveInterestRate>
</Deposit>

<Deposit>
 <DepositDescription
contextRef="Current_ForPeriod">Deposit
B</DepositDescription>
 <DepositAmount contextRef="Current_ForPeriod"
unitRef="EUR" decimals="2">250000.40</DepositAmount>
</Deposit>
```

Code example 5.11: Tuple reporting in an instance document

5.10 Context of the reported facts

Each reported fact *must* refer to a context. The context summarizes information about the reporting *entity*, any *segment* (e.g. *branch*, *division*), reporting *period* and *scenario* that relate to the reported facts. Typically, in any one instance document, a number of facts refer to a single context. For example, all the values of a balance sheet for a given period may relate to one context. In this way a context allows binding of reported information. The Code example 5.12 allows binding of the facts reported for *Sample Company Inc.* for the *2004* period.

```
<context id="Current_ForPeriod">
 <entity>
 <identifier scheme="http://www.sampleCompany.com">
  Sample Company Inc.</identifier>
 </entity>
 <period>70
  <startDate>2004-01-01</startDate>
  <endDate>2004-12-31</endDate>
 </period>
</context>
```

Code example 5.12: Context definition in an instance document

The period information is constrained by the definition of a concept provided in the taxonomy. For example, concepts with the period attribute set to duration must refer to a context with durational period information (see Code example 5.12 with *period start* and *period end* dates). For concepts with the period attribute set to instant the facts must refer to a context with contextual information provided for a certain date. Code example 5.13 provides context for *Sample Company Inc.* for the end of the reporting year *2004*.

```
<context id="Current_PeriodEnd">
 <entity>
 <identifier scheme="http://www.sampleCompany.com">
  Sample Company Inc.</identifier>
 </entity>
 <period>
 <instant>2004-12-31</instant>
 </period>
</context>
```

Code example 5.13: Context definition in an instance document

Apart from the entity and period information, the context part of an instance document provides information about entity segment for reported facts as well as the relevant scenario. Code example 5.14 demonstrates definition of the context for *Sample Company* segment *Aircrafts* and scenario *Audited.*

70 This example refers to a fact reported in the context for an element with a duration attribute value so the starting and ending date must be specified. For facts reported in the context for an element with instant attribute value only one date must be specified.

```
<context id="Current_ForPeriod">
<entity>
 <identifier scheme="http://www.sampleCompany.com">
  Sample Company Inc.</identifier>
  &lt;segment&gt;
  <my:SampleSegments>Aircrafts</my:SampleSegments>
  &lt;/segment&gt;
</entity>
<scenario>
 <my:SampleScenarios>Audited</my:SampleScenarios>
</scenario>
<period>
 <startDate>2004-01-01</startDate>
 <endDate>2004-12-31</endDate>
</period>
</context>
```

Code example 5.14: Segment and scenario definition in an instance document context

5.11 Information about units of measure

Each numeric fact link to a relevant unit of measure. These may be any formalized measurement system (currencies, weight, dimensions etc.). The Code example 5.15 has the *unitRef* attribute with the value of *U-Euros*. This unit is explained in the instance document in the unit element. We use the *unitRef* attribute to identify the unit element that is associated with the item on which the *unitRef* attribute occurs.

```
<unit id="U-Euros">
<measure>iso4217:EUR</measure>
</unit>
```

Code example 5.15: Unit definition in an instance document

The international standard ISO 4217 provides the currency codes that describe the currency for monetary amounts (for example *iso4217:EUR* for Euro in Code example 5.15).

To represent rates, percentages or ratios the measure must be set to *pure*. Rates, percentages and ratios must be reported using decimal or scientific notation rather than in percentages where the value has been multiplied by 100.

5.12 Expressing accuracy of reported numbers by means of precision and decimals

Numeric facts reported in instance documents can have different levels of accuracy. For example, financial statements may be in millions. To handle this inherent lack of exactitude, XBRL instance documents attach either the *precision* or *decimals* attributes to the reported facts. Numeric facts reported can have the decimals or precision attribute but not both. As might be expected, non-numeric facts cannot employ either attribute.

A numeric fact has a precision attribute that has the value n then it is correct to n significant figures. An application will ignore (i.e. replace with zeroes) any digits after the first n decimal digits, counting from the left. The meaning of *precision="INF"* is that the lexical representation of the number is the exact value of the fact being represented.

Tab. 5.4: Precision and lexical representation

Example	Meaning
precision="9"	Precision of nine digits. The first 9 digits, counting from the left, starting at the first non-zero digit in the lexical representation of the value of the numeric fact are known to be trustworthy for the purposes of computations to be performed using that numeric fact.

If a numeric fact has the decimals attribute with the value n then it is known to be correct to n decimal places. The meaning of *decimals="INF"*, similar as for precision attribute is that the lexical representation of the number is the exact value of the fact being represented.

Tab. 5.5: Decimals and lexical representation

Example	Meaning
decimals="2"	The value of the numeric fact is known to be correct to 2 decimal places.
decimals="-2"	The value of the numeric fact is known to be correct to –2 decimal places, i.e. all digits to the left of the hundreds digit are accurate.

5.13 Additional information about reported facts in footnotes

Footnotes appear in instance documents. They provide additional information for some of the facts[71]. If for example, in a business report, several concepts refer to the statement *For more information see Disclosures on Assets* it is possible to create a pointer between them and a footnote element containing an appropriate block of text. Code example 5.16 provides a description of the fact *Assets* reported in the current period, amounting to *€ 20,000* and defines a locator that points to this fact. The element footnote contains the text of a *footnote* and the *footnoteArc*[72] connects the element with this reference.

```
<Assets id="Assets" decimals="0" contextRef="Current_AsOf"
unitRef="EUR">20000</Assets>

<loc type="locator" href="#Assets" label="Assets"/>

<footnoteArc type="arc"
arcrole="http://www.xbrl.org/2003/arcrole/fact-footnote"
from="Assets" to="AssetsFootnote" order="1.0"/>

<footnote type="resource" label="AssetsFootnote"
role="http://www.xbrl.org/2003/role/footnote"
xml:lang="en">For more information see Disclosures on
Assets</link:footnote>
```

Code example 5.16: Using footnotes in instance documents

5.14 Summary

This chapter provides an overview of the XBRL instance documents. We analyzed the reported facts (as single facts or as multiple sets of facts for tuples), relation between facts and the context, unit and accuracy. Further, we analyzed the role of time definition in the context together with the identification of the entity and its

71 There is a difference between footnotes in the instance document and the notes to the financial statement. The footnotes provide short, additional, textual information to the reported fact value. Notes to the financial statement are a substantial part of GAAP and are modelled within a taxonomy.

72 The *footnoteArc* is similar to arcs defined in the taxonomy linkbases. The difference is that it can be used in instance documents only. The *footnoteArc* is utilising the *fact-footnote* arcrole.

segments and reporting scenario. We also provided an insight into the difference between reporting facts and disclosing information about these facts in the form of footnotes.

CPAs and instance documents[73]

A general perception is that the ability to provide third-party assurance is required for instance documents to be accepted in the marketplace. With the international growth of XBRL, CPAs have the opportunity to provide assurance on XBRL instance documents' compliance with XBRL technical specifications, and on their appropriate use of publicly available and custom taxonomies, as well as the mapping of specific data elements to the published traditional financial statements. The Auditing Standards Board (ASB) recently passed Interpretation 5, "Attest Engagements on Financial Information Included in XBRL Instance Documents," of Statement on Standards for Attestation Engagements (SSAE) 10. While many questions remain, such as how to convey instance document assurance in an electronic reporting environment, Interpretation 5 provides users of XBRL instance documents the assurance that the documents comply with rigorous technical specifications and promulgated or custom taxonomies.

5.15 Key terms you should know

- Instance document
- Context
- Entity
- Scenario
- Segment
- Unit
- Precision
- Decimals
- Footnote

[73] Excerpted from XBRL and Financial Information Assurance Services, The CPA Journal, May 2005 by Farewell, Stephanie, Pinsker, Robert http://findarticles.com/p/articles/mi_qa5346/is_200505/ai_n21372104

5.16 *Case analysis*[74]

Since mid-March 2005, the Securities and Exchange Commission (SEC) has been conducting an open-ended pilot program that invites companies that file their 10K and 8K financial reports in the required ASCII or HTML format to also submit the information in eXtensible Business Reporting Language (XBRL), an XML-based format that tags data, specifically financial data, in a way that on the surface looks like HTML tagging. This procedure, while more complex than current filing practices, promises to allow CFOs, investment analysts, SEC investigators and even average investors to compare detailed line items in a company's business reports and financial statements in an apples-to-apples way that has rarely, if ever, been seen or done in the financial community.

"You can't say to a piece of paper, 'Show me everything related to revenues, pension expenses or executive compensation,' but you can in an XBRL document," said Mike Willis, a partner at PriceWaterhouseCoopers and the founding chairman of XBRL International, the consortium that has developed the language and is the prime mover behind its debut with the SEC, as well as in other venues. "The whole idea is to take the business reporting supply chain from the current paper-centric model and move it to the Internet," he said.

Furthermore, all this reported data will be machine readable, which means that once all the proper tags are in place (no small task), as well as the correct "decoding" software, one would be able to tell the machine — a computer equipped with individual analytical tools and spreadsheets for analysis — via the software, "Give me everything you have about Company X's stock options for 2004, and, while you're at it, compare it to Company Y's options for the same year." In theory, because the correct taxonomies were used, the numbers that the machine pulls up will be accurate and ready to be compared and analyzed.

[74] Excerpted from "XBRL: Deep Drilling for Financials" by A. Malnig available from http://www.rightbrainpublishing.com/samples/XBRL.pdf

6 XBRL Taxonomy Engineering

Taxonomy writing urgently needs project management and strong direction. The development of these taxonomies, just as in any other large scale software development process, requires careful planning, constant discipline, and sound management to ensure a quality product.
[US SEC Chairman Christopher Cox, San Jose, 2006]

US GAAP Taxonomy Development

As noted in the XBRL US mission, the goal is "to support the implementation of XBRL in the United States through the development of taxonomies relevant for use by US public and private sectors". The US GAAP taxonomy is just one of many XBRL taxonomies being developed worldwide. In January 2007, the Investment Company Institute released for public comment the draft taxonomy for tagging information in the risk/return summary of the mutual fund prospectus. And in February 2007, the US SEC announced a proposal to allow mutual fund companies to submit supplemental tagged information in the risk/return summary section of the prospectus. The role of the XBRL US is to foster taxonomy development – that can take the form of encouraging and supporting outside organizations as they develop a taxonomy themselves, or it can involve actually taking on a contract, like the one with the SEC, to create a taxonomy for another organization. To do this successfully requires a sustainable taxonomy framework. With the US GAAP project, XBRL US builds that infrastructure and establishes the process for developing, bringing to market and ultimately promoting the adoption of all kinds of taxonomies, not just US GAAP. A taxonomy can never be complete. As accounting rules change, as industries and companies change, the taxonomy definitions and items must evolve with them. The US GAAP taxonomies must be maintained and developed. And as marketplaces evolve, there will always be a need for new taxonomies that help define a business information process.[75]

In this chapter, we focus on aspects of the development of XBRL taxonomies. In XBRL projects, taxonomy development is often a central and crucial activity. The shape of taxonomies has a major impact on the quality of later reporting. We will discuss approaches from software, knowledge and ontology development and merge them to achieve a generic XBRL taxonomy engineering approach. We will formally define taxonomy engineering and explain its importance in the following

[75] Excerpted from XBRL US website "Building the US GAAP Taxonomies" available at http://xbrl.us/101/Pages/Build.aspx.

section. Finally, we will explain in detail six phases of a generic taxonomy development process model.

Over the last several years, we have seen the development of several significant taxonomies with associated reporting methods. Analysis of the development processes of these taxonomies as well as project-based experience gives rise to three clear conclusions. First, taxonomy development requires a great deal of time and resources. Second, there is often significant delay in the release of taxonomies according to their pre-defined deadlines. Third, published taxonomies often contain a number of errors, both obvious and subtle.

Challenges in IFRS Taxonomy Development and Maintenance

For example, an incremental upgrade to the International Financial Reporting Standards for General Purpose (IFRS-GP) taxonomy of the International Accounting Standards Committee Foundation (IASCF) to account for new disclosure requirements the reporting year starting on 01 January 2006 was released on 15 August 2006. Moreover the IASCF implemented special bugs reporting system for the IFRS taxonomy where a number of entries have been made. Furthermore the observation of XBRL mailing lists and taxonomy publication websites proves the statement that taxonomies are released with a number of errors.[76]

How, then, can taxonomy development be enhanced and improved? One consideration, which is the focus of this chapter, is to support taxonomy development process and project management, by the use of a taxonomy development process model. XBRL International does not provide such an approach. They understandably leave this aspect of the creation of taxonomies to taxonomy authors and developers. The existing best practices released by XBRL International included the Financial Reporting Taxonomies Architecture (FRTA) merely indicate modeling rules to be followed.

There are several well-established engineering approaches from related domains. Adaptation of readily available development models from other domains would help build generic XBRL taxonomy engineering approach but also make it easier to integrate XBRL projects with software development or ontology building projects. The most significant areas that may have application to business reporting standardization domain are approaches from software engineering, ontology engineering and knowledge engineering. Table 6.1 presents the definitions of these three approaches.

---

[76] See for example XBRL-COREP@yahoogroups.com and http://www.corep.info/corepTaxonomy/taxonomy.html for COREP taxonomy bugs or http://xbrl.iasb.org/int/fr/ifrs/gp/2006-08-15/changelog.html for IFRS-GP taxonomy bugs.

Tab. 6.1: Software, knowledge and ontology engineering definitions

Software engineering	Knowledge engineering	Ontology engineering
"… is the application of a systematic, disciplined, quantifiable approach to the development, operation, and mainte nance of software."	"… refers to the building, maintaining and development of knowledge-based systems. Knowledge engineering understands knowledge that is produced by socio-cognitive aggregates (mainly humans) and is structured according to our understanding of how human reasoning and logic works."	"… is a research methodology which gives us design rationale of a knowledge base, kernel conceptualization of the world of interest, strict definition of basic meanings of basic concepts together with sophisticated theories and technologies enabling accumulation of knowledge which is dispensable for modeling the real world."

Research on methods for constructing ontologies bases on has splitting domain knowledge into different logical components. In software engineering, there has been considerable work on formal methods for software specification, based on the construction and composition of theories, and using category theory. This can be viewed as motivating, simplifying and applying similar ideas to the task of taxonomy engineering. Knowledge engineering, as a software engineering influenced approach, identifies and provides semantic patterns, to describe knowledge in an implementation-neutral way. It operates above the level of any particular representation language, with the objective of reusing the collected semantics. The ontological point view changes the semantic patterns to knowledge patterns. The knowledge patterns are significant as they provide structure to the knowledge, explicitly modularize and separate the patterns from the phenomena in the world. This is, what ontology engineering attempts to achieve. The ontology objects are intended for use within a particular representational scheme in an automated way, with the primary goals of uncovering and making explicit the abstract theories used in an ontology, and capturing the modeling decisions made about these theories apply to the domain of interest. We combine experiences from these three domains to derive formal XBRL taxonomy engineering approach.

6.1 What is XBRL taxonomy engineering?

The approach suggested in this chapter should be helpful for organizing the taxonomy development projects. The phases defined in the taxonomy life cycle as well as the proposed ordering and feedback loops allows a manageable and controllable taxonomy development leading to more quantifiable XBRL projects. The model can be the base for defining the term taxonomy engineering. The definition can be derived and based upon the definition of software engineering suggested by IEEE standard 610.12. Accordingly:

"Taxonomy engineering is the application of systematic, formal, quantifiable approach to the design, building, usage and maintenance of XBRL taxonomies, that is application of software engineering to taxonomies."

Figure 6.1 addresses the intersections among software, knowledge and ontology engineering domains, discussed in the introduction of this paper, as well as allocates taxonomy engineering addressed in the section three among the three domains.

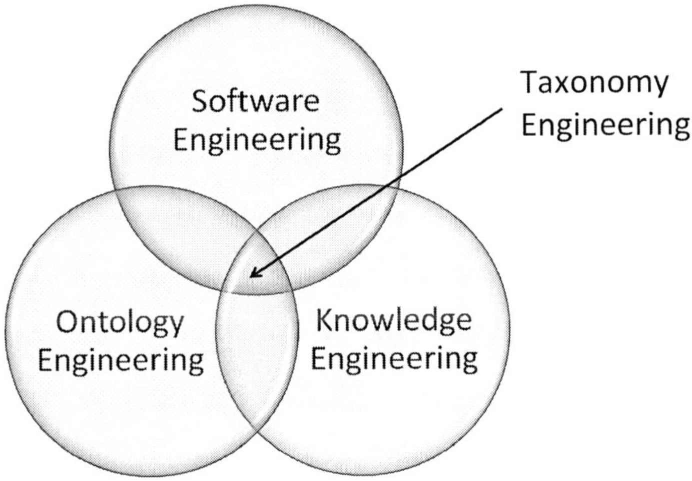

Fig. 6.1: Intersections of software, knowledge and ontology engineering and allocation of taxonomy engineering

This chapter introduces aspects of taxonomy engineering. We define clear phases of taxonomy development. Of course, specific taxonomy development projects can have individual phases we do not include in our model - our method is not monolithic. Further, we draw on measured stages of software development. The impact of agile software development in the software engineering domain must be analyzed in the context of XBRL taxonomy development. Agile software development models are a reaction against the classical phase-oriented heavy software engineering models. These agile programming methods attempt to minimize risk by developing software in short timeboxes, called iterations, which typically last one to four weeks. Each iteration is like a miniature software project of its own and includes all of the necessary tasks to release the mini-increment of new functionality: planning, requirements analysis, design, coding, testing, and documentation. Especially some of eXtreme Programming (XP) practices such as test driven development or collective ownership can be seen in the XBRL taxonomy development projects. Only to some extend our approach considers the impact of these agile approaches on taxonomy engineering.

6.2 Phases of XBRL taxonomy development

XBRL taxonomy development can be regarded as a transfer of the domain knowledge from a domain expert into an implemented knowledge base that is encoded within an XBRL taxonomy. There is a clear application of ontology development models to XBRL taxonomy development, given the importance of knowledge structures in XBRL taxonomy development. As we are interested in software-neutral approaches to taxonomy development, we can reuse some components from ontology engineering.

The analysis of the existing XBRL taxonomy development projects indicates a clear taxonomy life cycle as well as the possibility to recognize clearly defined phases during the process. We observe these process phases in most XBRL projects. This makes a clear case for formalization of the process model. Our approach analyses the taxonomy life cycle in order to recognize and classify the different phases of the taxonomy development. We order and integrate these phases in a process model. We base the process model on the incremental software development model coupled with prototyping. However, the internal activities within each phase come from experiences derived from ontology engineering approaches.

As quoted from Chairman Cox in the introduction to this chapter:

> *"the development of these taxonomies, just as in any other large scale software development process, requires careful planning, constant discipline, and sound management to ensure a quality product".*

Hence we used the development cycle from software engineering to categorize the phases of XBRL taxonomy development. We set out the phases planning and analysis, design, building, testing, publication and recognition and maintenance in the following sections.

6.2.1 Planning and analysis

The XBRL taxonomy development starts with the planning and analysis phase where the taxonomy development project requirements are defined and considered. The first aspect of the analysis is to state which kind of taxonomy is developed. We refer to this as the *taxonomy scope*. XBRL taxonomies can represent core accounting standards such as national GAAP or International Financial Reporting Standards. It can be a national or industry extension to these standards as well as company specific taxonomies.

The core taxonomy compromises knowledge included in a single set of regulations (in case of XBRL FR these regulations often comprise of accounting standards).

The jurisdictional taxonomy extension is a taxonomy using the knowledge base included in the core taxonomy and usually extends it for a certain geographical region. The COREP taxonomy discussed in the previous chapters is subject to extension in a number of European member states. These taxonomy extensions enhance the COREP taxonomy with national or industry specific aspects. In the previous chapters, we discussed FINREP taxonomy as an industry extension to the IFRS taxonomy.

Finally, the reporting entity can build a custom taxonomy extension including individual concepts. The requirement of which taxonomy to build and, in case of an extension taxonomy, which taxonomy to use as a base, should be defined in an early stage of the planning and analysis phase.

The resulting activity is the design of the taxonomy framework. A taxonomy framework can be defined as a way of combining different taxonomies for a jurisdiction or industry. A number of European taxonomies are part of sophisticated frameworks that demonstrates the importance of this activity. Examples for the European taxonomies where the frameworks are available are the Dutch GAAP taxonomy, the COREP taxonomy and the IFRS taxonomy. Such frameworks usually constitute more than one XBRL taxonomy schema file linked to a number of taxonomy linkbases. Moreover, frameworks often enable modularization of XBRL taxonomies. This facilitates users downloading only the taxonomy parts they need. Modularization of XBRL taxonomies means creating a number of schemas and/or linkbases instead of working with monolithic files. The criteria of modularization can be functional (IFRS taxonomy reference linkbase is modularized according to IFRSs) or technical (US GAAP taxonomy provides separate modularized schema file for the technical definitions of the custom data types). We will discuss modularization in detail in the next chapters. How a taxonomy framework is constructed influences the taxonomy architecture that is the mode of modeling and building single taxonomies.

During the later development phases the knowledge from different sources such as regulations, accounting standards or other legal documents, model financial statements, real financial statements have to be gathered. These sources must be clearly set out in the taxonomy requirements prior to the design phase. A clear reference to the knowledge and ontology engineering approaches can be drawn in this part of the taxonomy development. The requirements documentation as a result of the first phase should be part of the taxonomy documentation clarifying the actions taken which is drawn from software engineering.

6.2.2 Design

In ontology engineering, we can see clear phases in the knowledge transfer process. Usually the knowledge needs to be extracted from different sources by the domain expert and codified as a knowledge base by a technical expert. Similar to the knowledge transfer process known from ontology engineering, the reporting knowledge from domain experts must be drawn into the knowledge base during the taxonomy design phase. At this stage, the crucial role of the division of tasks between domain and technical experts must be clear. Observation of XBRL taxonomy development projects shows that there always exists a mixture of domain and technical experts working together to design the taxonomy.

Structured Systems Analysis and Design Method

There exist similar considerations to the domain and technical experts cooperation since the introduction of the Structured Systems Analysis and Design Method (SSADM). The project phases are derived from the business view on the information system, through the logical design to the physical design. SSAMD requires thus close cooperation of the business and technical experts.

We see that the approaches of each group to taxonomy development are very different. The domain experts prefer expressing their knowledge in a structured way. The technical experts prefer to formalize the structured knowledge directly in XBRL code while modeling the taxonomy. The danger of this approach is the transfer process itself, where the structured knowledge may not be appropriate for the restrictions inherent in the XBRL standard.

Codification and Structuring of the Knowledge Base

The IFRSs do not provide any predefined structure of the financial statements. Financial statements should present the *true and fair view* of the reporting entity which makes the IFRS taxonomy highly extensible. But for IFRS taxonomy developers such approach requires an intermediate modeling level while designing a taxonomy.

Other researchers indicate another problem within the modeling process that concerns the subjectivity of the domain experts while modeling the reality. Both issues can disrupt the modeling process. In the absence of formal XBRL modeling notation for taxonomy development, the most common development approach is to use spreadsheets to represent the knowledge base. A so-called information model is created with possible structures that need to be encoded in a subsequent

XBRL taxonomy. The information model can vary from just representation tasks of the reports in the form of tables (e.g. FINREP taxonomy) to a very detailed description of each attribute that should be included in the taxonomy (e.g. German GAAP). Figure 6.2 presents an excerpt from a high-level information model of the Polish COREP taxonomy representing the form for filing financial information.

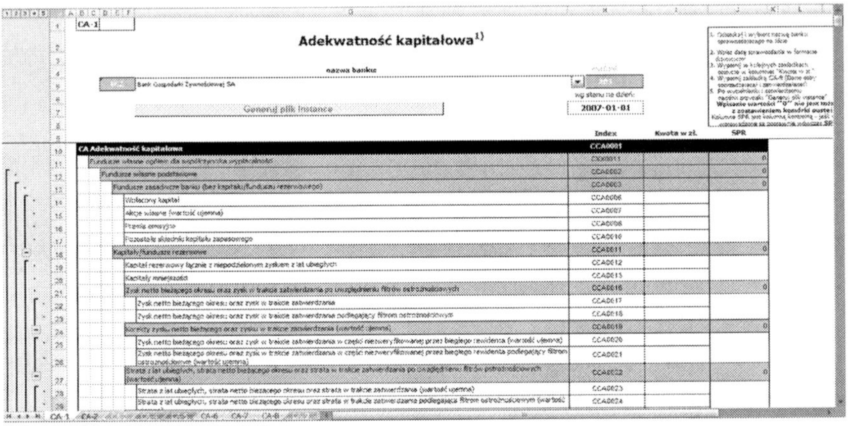

Fig. 6.2: Information model for Polish FINREP taxonomy

The lack of a common modeling approach in XBRL and a formal notation is a major drawback of the standard. With the introduction of multidimensional XBRL taxonomies the modeling aspects are becoming more advanced and the modeling aspects consequentially significantly more important. We will discuss the aspects of the engineering of multidimensional taxonomies in following chapters.

The result of the design phase is the information model and additional documentation that explain the modeling choices. Another aspect of the design phase that we observe in the development of recent XBRL taxonomies is documentation of the technical decisions concerning taxonomy design in a single document often called taxonomy architecture. Thus, the second deliverable from the design phase should be technical taxonomy architecture documentation.

6.2.3 Building

The taxonomy building phase begins after the development of the information model by domain experts is finished. The technical knowledge is necessary to build an XBRL taxonomy and therefore the building phase requires XBRL technical experts. The information model is an output from the design phase and parallel input to the building phase. The main goal of the building phase is to convert the information model in a valid XBRL taxonomy (physical set of XBRL files). This is often performed in an iterative process until the project team achieves the required taxonomy quality.

There are several XBRL taxonomy editing tools available that ease the technical aspects of the production process. Nonetheless, taxonomy building is still a sophisticated task. Similar to the previous phase the potential risk is the transfer of the knowledge base from the information model into the coded structures of the XBRL taxonomy. This transfer process can result in changes or even losses in semantic of the constructed taxonomy. XBRL International has released a document called FRTA with established rules and conventions that assist in a comprehensive manner the usage and performance among different financial reporting taxonomies. Also Hoffman describes 25 so-called taxonomy patterns that define the possible structures appearing in financial reports and their representation in taxonomy code. But taxonomy developers are free to encode the information model according to individual rules as there is no formal notation to support these patterns.

Usually there are a number of so-called taxonomy working drafts to support the visibility of the taxonomy building phase. After each working draft, the feedback is being included in the information model. Another option is that the next working draft fulfils the requirements. Initial taxonomy working drafts usually do not use the full functionality of XBRL, but represent certain aspects of the information model. The usage of available taxonomy editors supports the testing of the taxonomy working drafts at the end of each development cycle. Although extensive tests are rarely conducted in the building phase, the tools ensure XML and XBRL specifications compatibility. The main output of the building phase is the set of taxonomy files itself.

6.2.4 Testing

The penultimate phase of taxonomy construction involves extensive tests and quality assurance. There are various test levels. The most basic prerequisite is compliance of the taxonomy with XML, XML schema, XLink specifications and XBRL specifications. These prerequisites are ensured by using a proper XBRL taxonomy editing tools. When constructing financial reporting taxonomies, compliance with the FRTA rules is recommended.

A second key step is the non-technical domain experts review of the final working draft of the constructed taxonomy. The domain experts ensure that the transformation of the information model into XBRL taxonomy code. In order to provide non-technical experts the possibility of high quality review different visualizations are utilized in the testing phase. Figure 6.3 presents a visualization of the US GAAP taxonomy.

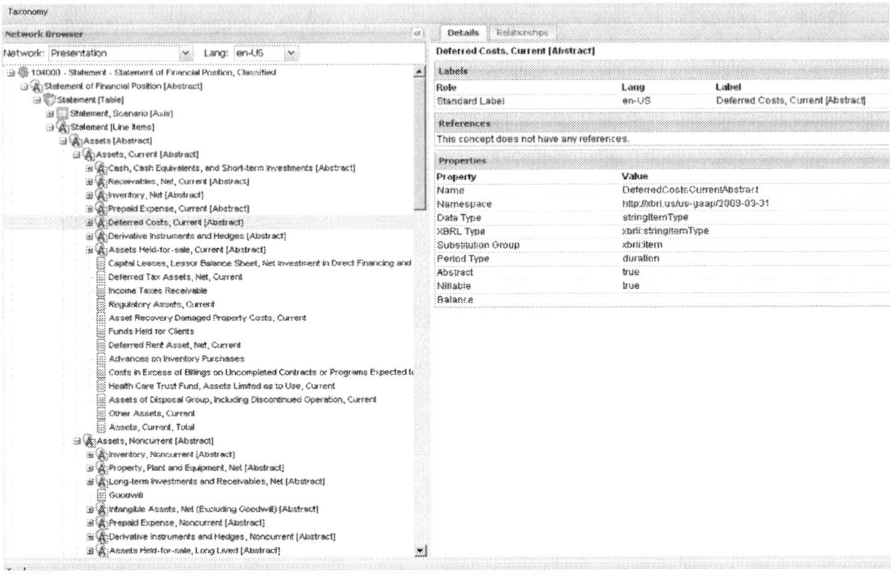

Fig. 6.3: US GAAP taxonomy visualization

The reviewed taxonomy is usually released as an exposure draft to gain user feedback. The feedback is discussed during the building phase with the following revised working draft, tests and exposure draft. Crucial for the test are sample and real instance documents. Sample instance documents are usually replete with artificial numbers. Real instance documents represent sample business reports such as financial statements. Both types of instance documents should be available in order to validate the proper taxonomy design. Potential taxonomy users take often part during the testing phase. Their special task is often the preparing of real instance documents based on the taxonomy exposure draft.

6.2.5 Publication and recognition

The following phase is taxonomy publication and recognition. Typically, the corresponding organization publishes the final XBRL taxonomies on their websites.[77] In addition, the website of XBRL International announces the taxonomies. There is a recognition process at the XBRL International level. This may assign the status acknowledged or approved to a taxonomy. The taxonomy recognition process is mainly applicable to XBRL taxonomies in the public domain. It is rarely applicable to taxonomies created for a special project needs. An acknowledged taxonomy is recognized as in compliance with the XBRL

[77] Often to enable non-technical users viewing of the published taxonomy browser based XBRL viewing tools are implemented.

Specification. An approved taxonomy is recognized as complying with the official XBRL guidelines for that taxonomy type as well as with the XBRL Specification. XBRL International can approve, ask for changes or reject the taxonomy during the recognition process. The result of the publication and recognition phase is the final taxonomy version.

6.2.6 Usage and maintenance

The taxonomy usage and maintenance starts directly after the publication. The taxonomy users are reporting entities and software vendors that build the XBRL reporting capabilities into their software products. The experience derived from developed projects indicates that taxonomy maintenance requires taxonomy developers to monitor the taxonomy usage and track the issues and bugs that users experience with the taxonomy. Feedback from the taxonomy usage and maintenance phase is used in the next version of the information model and improves consequently following taxonomy release. Concern with taxonomy versioning is also a part of the maintenance phase. Approaches from software versioning as well as ontology versioning systems provide a starting point for taxonomy versioning. XBRL International is currently working on a standardized solution to XBRL taxonomy versioning that should enhance the maintenance of the taxonomies from the users' perspective. We discuss versioning of XBRL taxonomies in the final chapter.

Further, there are a number of challenges during the taxonomy maintenance phase. The changes to the underlying regulations can affect the design of the taxonomy and thus the whole development process. Subsequent releases of the taxonomy must also have appropriate documentation especially describing chages compared to the previous release.

6.3 Taxonomy development process model

XBRL taxonomy development strongly relates to ontology engineering because of the knowledge specification in case of both. However, usually approaches to the ontology development are very project and software specific. Therefore, it is not possible to apply them as a generic XBRL taxonomy development process model. The term generic means applicable to all kinds of reporting taxonomies worldwide and not being subject to specific regulations, software used or conducted project. The approach presented in this section is organizing the taxonomy life cycle phases in a process model. In many respects, it resembles more the rigorous and formal software development process than knowledge or ontology development process. The main reason for this is the existence of generic approaches to the software engineering and established process models which can be easily adapted in the XBRL taxonomy development environment.

We see correspondence between software development processes and taxonomy development mainly in the phase structure as well as output-oriented approach. The output oriented approach results in a physical output of each development phase enhancing project management.

Neither the literature nor the documentation of existing XBRL taxonomies provides explicit phases for the taxonomy development[78]. However, observation at XBRL taxonomy developments all over the world, we can see clear phases as we discuss in the previous sections. Taxonomy development starts with planning and analyzing, followed by design. Later, the taxonomy building stage finishes the development with testing, publication and recognition. The final phase is taxonomy usage and maintenance.

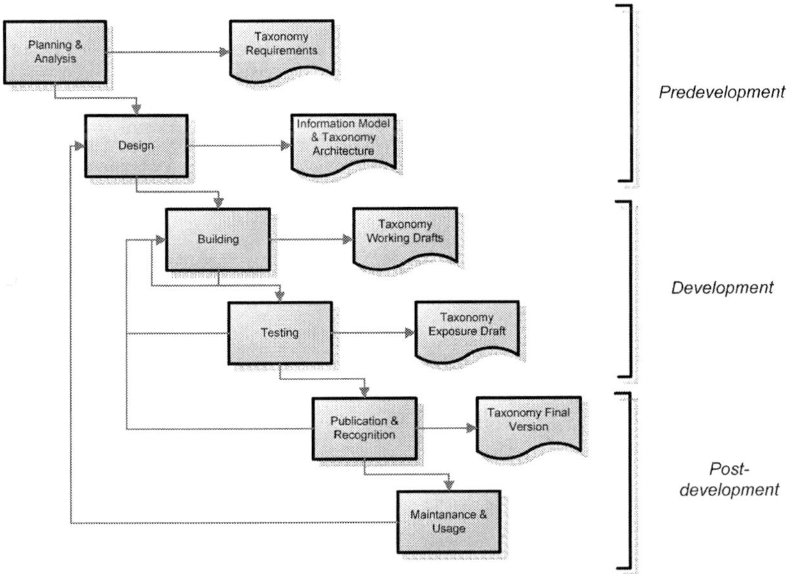

Fig. 6.4: Taxonomy development process model

The phases, together with our observation and cooperation in a number of XBRL taxonomy development projects, allow us to construct an appropriate process model for the taxonomy development. The process model presented in Figure 6.4 reflects in its principal construction the phase model with potential feedback between phases. Similar to software and ontology engineering approaches, there are clear predevelopment, development and post-development components. The

[78] Although the XBRL International released a document called *Taxonomy Life Cycle* the issue that this document concerns is merely the XBRL taxonomy versioning and taxonomy development process as such is not discussed.

phases are requirements, design, building, testing, publication and recognition as well as maintenance and usage. At the end of each phase, there is a formal document or set of files produced. The main feedback cycles are within the building phase while creating a number of taxonomy working drafts, between the testing and building phase as well as between recognition and building phase. Further, at the conclusion of the maintenance and usage phase, the feedback provided leads the changes in the taxonomy information model and implies development of a new taxonomy version.

6.4 Summary

The discussion during several recent XBRL International conferences raised a need for formalizing the taxonomy development approach in a form of a formal and generic process model.[79] Although many such approaches exist in the area of software and ontology engineering they cannot be directly applied in the XBRL domain. Therefore based on the models known from discussed engineering approaches as well as on empirical experience of the authors, especially during the development of the IFRS, Polish GAAP, COREP and FINREP as well as German GAAP taxonomies, an XBRL taxonomy development model is addressed.

The approach presented in this chapter contributes to XBRL in two important ways. First, it provides a general understanding of the relationship among software engineering, knowledge engineering and ontology engineering and places XBRL taxonomy engineering among them. The advantage of this approach is reusing well-established models and approaches. Second, it moves the literature on XBRL taxonomies forward by addressing the phases of taxonomy development together with their content and establishing a formal and generic approach to the XBRL taxonomy development. This contribution should be also regarded in the context of XBRL taxonomy quality management as well as XBRL project management.

6.5 Key terms you should know

- Taxonomy Engineering
- Phases of Taxonomy Development
- Knowledge Engineering
- Software Engineering
- Ontology Engineering

---

[79] See for example FSA Japan's XBRL Project presented by Kobayashi, T. at the 14th XBRL International Conference in Philadelphia in December 2006.

6.6 Case analysis[80]

The Committee of European Banking Supervisors (CEBS) has finalized its common reporting framework COREP (COmmon REPorting) for the new solvency ratio for credit institutions and investment firms under the European Union (EU) capital requirements regime and has also published guidelines establishing a standardized financial reporting framework (FINREP) for financial institutions operating in the EU. The COREP work is primarily focused on regulatory of own funds and the Basel II Pillar I capital requirements pertaining to credit risk, operational risk and market risk. The aim is to reduce the reporting burden on reporting entities and encourage a level playing field across Europe. The COREP project team has completed a harmonized business model for the European solvency reporting requirements, which is published in 18 templates. The FINREP framework, based on 40 templates, will enable credit institutions to use the same standardized data formats and data definitions for prudential reporting in all countries where the framework will be adopted. CEBS believes that this will reduce the reporting burden for credit institutions that operate cross-border, and lower barriers to the development of an efficient internal market in financial services.

CEBS agreed that the Capital Reporting Directive (CRD) for COREP and FINREP implementations should adhere to the following requirements:

- *P1 Flexibility/Extensibility:*
  - P1.a: Each supervisor is allowed to choose the scope, as well as
  - P1.b: The level of aggregation of information required;
  - P1.c: The framework will also allow for flexibility to accommodate differences in the exercise of the national options provided for in the CRD, for instance with reference to the treatment of small institutions.
- *P2 Consistency:* Linking each element to its definition or the description of its use in the applicable European Directive
- *P3 Standardization:* Achieving uniformity through a common approach to calculating and reporting key data elements.

CEBS members developed *data models* and an Information System solution which were designed to support the reporting frameworks and at the same time be compatible with existing reporting systems. CEBS refers to these data models as the *COREP and FINREP Data Models*, and we refer to them as being an additional principle (P4) for this project.

CEBS also provides XBRL taxonomies for the national supervisory solvency reporting and financial reporting. The COREP and FINREP taxonomies are an

[80] Excerpted from "COREP - FINREP Taxonomies: Technical Documentation" available at http://www.corep.info/corepTaxonomy/descriptions/COREP%20-%20FINREP%20Documentation-2007-04-20.pdf

XBRL representation of the harmonized business models and are therefore based on the 18 COREP and 40 FINREP templates, respectively.

The COREP and FINREP taxonomies are designed to be very adaptable by national supervisors. This means that the taxonomies can be either extended or restricted, within certain limits. The work is supported by leading European XBRL experts from various XBRL jurisdictions. The availability of these taxonomies is not intended to influence any national decisions about the methods that will be used for collecting data from the reporting entities. National supervisors, in consultation with their industry, will be free to choose whichever transmission process or processes to be used.

7 Multidimensionality in XBRL

There has been, and still is, a lot of misunderstanding about what is trying to be achieved with XBRL Dimensions. The key here is to minimize the burden on business users for reporting using XBRL.
[Charles Hoffman (the father of XBRL) in his blog]

Multidimensionality in the COREP Taxonomy[81]

The New Basel Capital Agreement, known as Basel II, requires some notable changes in the systems of measurement and control of risks of credit entities and investment firms. It introduces new concepts and requirements. The systems of risk management to which the Agreement makes reference can be implemented in various degrees of sophistication. By measuring the different exposures to risk with greater accuracy, a more advanced system offers such firms and entities the prospect of needing less own funds and using increased financial leverage over secure bases. The national supervisors, in the various central banks, must approve the systems and instruments established. The new reporting tool that is destined to fulfill this function, for the moment in the context of the European Union only, is the COREP XBRL taxonomy. This is based on the mark-up language of the business world, the eXtensible Business Reporting Language, and makes use of the concept of multidimensionality. This concept is being incorporated into the XBRL specification currently in force, since it is necessary for the structure of the new reporting model that is required.

Multidimensionality in XBRL is a relatively new solution for taxonomy modeling in environments when disclosure of information is in *cubes*. These cubes have two or more vectors to analyze and break down the information into subsets of interest to the end-user. Multidimensionality is a term in common use in relation to database modeling and design. We find it in use especially in sales and production environments. It supports end-user querying and displaying information according to defined breakdowns. This may be for some combination by regions, by products, by clients, etc.

This chapter begins with a description of the background business and technical requirements that caused incorporation of dimensions into XBRL specifications. These requirements heavily influenced the approach and solutions applied in *XBRL Dimensions Specification 1.0*. This document defines syntax and logic of the underlying technology to support dimensions. In the process of familiarizing the reader with XBRL dimensions, we present terminology based on the model

---

[81] Excerpted from Ignacio Boixo, "New Technical and Normative Challenges for XBRL: Multidimensionality in the COREP Taxonomy", The International Journal of Digital Accounting Research, Vol. 5, N. 9, 2005, pp. 79-104, available at http://www.data.corep.info/documents/Multidimensionality.pdf.

architecture diagram containing all the components defined in the specification. We also discuss the non-normative section of the standard on modularization of dimensional taxonomies. We illustrate application of dimensions in this chapter with examples of different types of dimensions. We also look at some complex constructs including dimension defaults and *empty hypercubes* and *dimensions*. We draw extensively on practical use of the technology in the COREP and FINREP taxonomies promulgated by the Committee of European Banking Supervisors (CEBS).

We assume familiarity of a reader with XBRL, acquired from the previous chapters of this book when presenting the theory and examples in this chapter.

7.1 Background requirements for dimensions

With the practical application of XBRL to business reporting projects around the world, it quickly became apparent that the existing conceptual aspects of *XBRL 2.1* specification did not completely support the need for exchanging multidimensional information. The market communicated this requirement to the XBRL International. As a result, the community commenced consideration of implementing dimensions into the syntax of taxonomies and instance documents.

To some extent, XBRL 2.1 specification provides some limited means to define several dimensional characteristics of concepts in instance documents. These are identification of a reporting entity, reporting date or period and units of measure which we discussed in previous chapters. Additionally and importantly, the *context* element in instance documents offers two unstructured containers intended to contain supplementary information about reported facts. These are the *segment* and *scenario* elements that may contain any XML (but not XBRL) tags. An example is presented on Code example 7.1.

```
<xbrli:context
id="Year2007_SouthAmerica_UnauditedForecasted">
    <xbrli:entity>
        <xbrli:identifier
scheme="http://www.stockexchange/ticker">ACME</xbrli:identi
fier>
        &lt;xbrli:segment&gt;
            <s:Region>South America</s:Region>
        &lt;/xbrli:segment&gt;
    </xbrli:entity>
    <xbrli:scenario>
        <s:InformationOnData>
            <s:AuditStatus>Unaudited</s:AuditStatus>
            <s:TypeOfData>Forecasted</s:TypeOfData>
            <s:Comments/>
        </s:InformationOnData>
    </xbrli:scenario>
    <xbrli:period>
        <xbrli:startDate>2007-01-01</xbrli:startDate>
        <xbrli:endDate>2007-12-31</xbrli:endDate>
    </xbrli:period>
</xbrli:context>
```

Code example 7.1: Example of context definition with *segment* and *scenario* elements

Initially, *xbrli:segment*[82], as a sub-element of the entity identification, was designed to contain additional information about a reporting party in case the entity identifier was insufficient. This information could include for instance identification of a subsidiary or by products/regions breakdown of operations. In the example presented on Code example 7.1 *xbrli:segment* indicates that facts referred to this context are reported for business activities that identified by its ticker (according to the value of 'scheme' attribute) on *xbrli:identifier* element *ACME* company conducts in *South America.*

The *xbrli:scenario* element, on the other hand, was aimed at capturing additional information about a reported fact. This might include, for example, identification of *actual/forecasted/audited/unaudited* data or applied currency exchange rates. In Code example 7.1, the content of *xbrli:scenario* indicates that values of facts referring to this context are unaudited and forecasted.

Dimensional metadata used in the *xbrli:segment* and *xbrli:scenario* elements was defined as simple or complex XML elements (i.e. *xsd:simpleType* containing

[82] In order to differentiate between XBRL 2.1 specification components and XBRL Dimensions 1.0 specification components we will use namespace prefixes in this and following chapter (respectively *xbrli* as opposite to *xbrldi* and *xbrldt*).

only a value or *xsd:complexType* that can contain other elements). Examples of definitions of such constructs used in Code example 7.1 are presented in Code example 7.2.

```
<xsd:element name="Region" id="s_Region">
    <xsd:simpleType>
        <xsd:restriction base="xsd:token">
            <xsd:enumeration value="Europe"/>
            <xsd:enumeration value="Poland"/>
            <xsd:enumeration value="South America"/>
        </xsd:restriction>
    </xsd:simpleType>
</xsd:element>

<xsd:element name="AuditStatus" id="s_AuditStatus">
    <xsd:simpleType>
        <xsd:restriction base="xsd:token">
            <xsd:enumeration value="Audited"/>
            <xsd:enumeration value="Unaudited"/>
        </xsd:restriction>
    </xsd:simpleType>
</xsd:element>

<xsd:element name="TypeOfData" id="s_TypeOfData">
    <xsd:simpleType>
        <xsd:restriction base="xsd:token">
            <xsd:enumeration value="Actual"/>
            <xsd:enumeration value="Budgeted"/>
            <xsd:enumeration value="Forecasted"/>
        </xsd:restriction>
    </xsd:simpleType>
</xsd:element>

<xsd:element name="Comments" id="s_Comments"
type="xsd:string"/>
<xsd:element name="InformationOnData"
id="s_InformationOnData">
    <xsd:complexType>
        <xsd:sequence>
            <xsd:element ref="s:AuditStatus"/>
            <xsd:element ref="s:TypeOfData"/>
            <xsd:element ref="s:Comments"/>
        </xsd:sequence>
    </xsd:complexType>
</xsd:element>
```

Code example 7.2: Example of XML elements definitions used on *xbrli:segment* and *xbrli:scenario*

The main problem with the approach adopted by XBRL 2.1 specification was the difficulty of indicating in taxonomies the relations between defined items and assumed dimensional breakdowns as there are no common mechanisms serving this purpose[83] and, because of that, it is impossible to validate correctness of reported information with regard to these relations.

There is no mechanism defined in the XBRL 2.1 specification to link the XML constructs that appear in *xbrli:segment/xbrli:scenario* in instance documents and the XBRL concepts in the taxonomy that require this type of contextual information.

The other issue raised by business users with regard to the approach adopted in XBRL 2.1 specification was the lack of a method to define dimensional breakdowns using the functionality that XBRL provides. This includes the possibility to construct relations between concepts, provide labels or references to authoritative literature. Taxonomy developers perceived this as a highly desired feature. This use case formed the basis of the requirements document that underpinned the dimensions specification.

We illustrate this problem in the fragment schema file in Code example 7.2. Here the geographical breakdown of operations is defined as the *s:Region* concept. The data type of this concept reflects the structure of the breakdown. It is *xsd:token* and has an enumeration of acceptable values. In this example, the enumerations are *Europe*, *Poland* and *South America*. This construction disallows the construction of hierarchical relations (e.g. it is impossible to indicate *Poland* as subcomponent of *Europe*), labels (displayed and input values are as the defined enumerations i.e. in English) or the modification of its content by an extension taxonomy.

Domain or business users' need for highly functional dimensional constructs in XBRL appeared to be even more urgent for closed reporting projects[84] in financial institutions sector, where data models are clearly defined and there is no place for misinterpretations. Therefore, the largest project of this kind at that time, the European COREP initiative, eventually became the driving factor and test field for development of support for multidimensionality in XBRL.

---

[83] This information can be stored in taxonomies for example in a form of a custom label but XBRL processors must be additionally programmed to be able to validate it. There is no syntax defined in the XBRL 2.1 specification that allows to indicate the relationship between an XBRL element (i.e. element in *xbrli:item* or *xbrli:tuple* substitution group) and XML construct that is required to appear in context that this XBRL element refers to in instance document.

[84] Meaning that the underlying data model defines all necessary information and extending taxonomy is prohibited.

7.2 Dimensions specification and technical files

XBRL International promulgated the XBRL Dimensions 1.0 Specification as a recommendation on September 18, 2006. Its content begins with a non-normative introduction to the concept of multidimensionality, explaining the business and technical requirements for incorporating dimensions into XBRL and providing hints on modularization of dimensional taxonomies. The normative (i.e. setting rules not providing suggestions or explanations as non-normative) sections two and three define application of XBRL dimensions on taxonomy and instance document levels respectively. To be more precise, section two introduces the technical constructs such as substitutions groups, arcroles, attributes on arcs and concept definitions while section three expresses the validation rules for the content of contexts in instance documents. In appendices, the specification document refers to the error messages and assesses fulfillment of background business and technical requirements.

The two main business and technical needs that the authors of XBRL Dimensions specification faced were alignment with XBRL 2.1 specification and maximal use of XBRL functionality, as we indicated in the previous section.

The first condition concerns compatibility of dimensional taxonomies and reports with XBRL applications developed according to the XBRL 2.1 specification. In other words, it was necessary to load into an XBRL 2.1 compatible processor a taxonomy that contained dimensions. Equally, it was important to validate an instance document with dimensions against a non-dimensional taxonomy. To exemplify this second case, an instance document created based on dimensional extension of the IFRS 2006 version taxonomy where the only modification was incorporation of geographical breakdown dimension for income statement should be valid also against the IFRS 2006 taxonomy itself. Since this requirement was met, the dimensions specification is being referred to as a modular extension to the 2.1 specification.

The later business and technical need relates mainly to the use of XLink technology, in the form of XBRL linkbases, to allow for definition of hierarchical structures of dimensional breakdowns as well as providing mechanisms for labeling and referencing dimensional information to external resources.

The ending of the specification document constitutes a normative code of two XML schema files: *xbrldt-2005.xsd* and *xbrldi-2006.xsd* that contain definitions of concepts, attributes and arcroles used when creating dimensional taxonomies and instance documents respectively. When referring to the contents of these files in this chapter following prefixes are used: *xbrldi:* for *xbrldi-2006.xsd* and *xbrldt:* for *xbrldt-2005.xsd*[85].

---

[85] Other prefixes used in this chapter (*xbrli:*, *xlink:*, *link*, *xsd*: etc) relate to XBRL 2.1 or XML specifications technical files.

7.3 Architecture and terminology

Together with increased functionality, dimensions introduced to the XBRL a new terminology and a handful of new technical constructs. We present the comprehensive overview of the dimensions architecture on taxonomy and instance document level in Figure 7.1. We will explain and refer to this figure many times throughout this chapter.

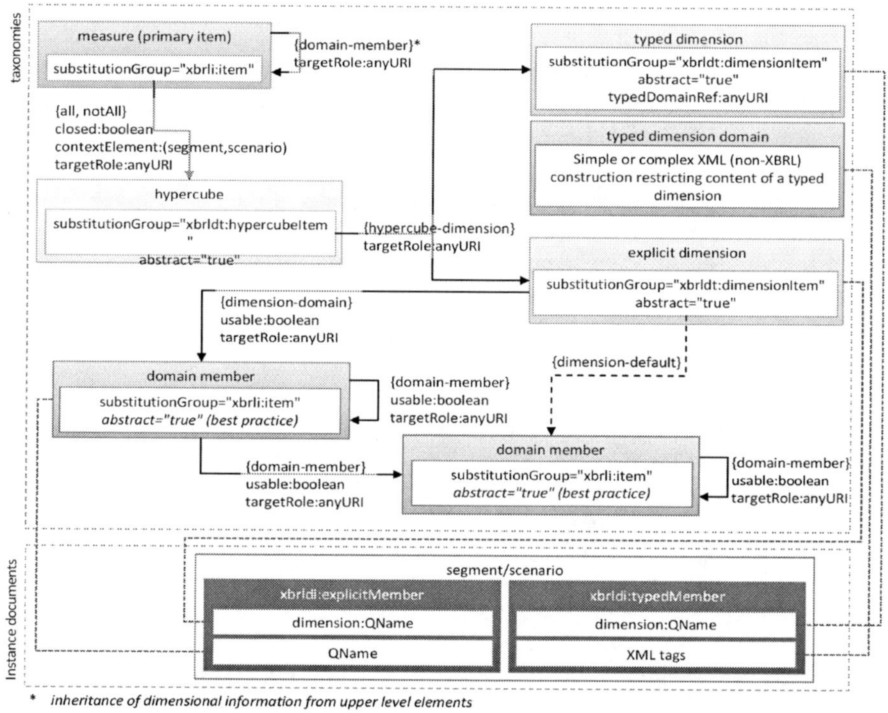

Fig. 7.1: Architecture and terminology of XBRL dimensions

7.3.1 Dimensions application in taxonomies

In general, XBRL Dimensions 1.0 Specification defines new *types* of concepts or assigns existing concepts under the XBRL 2.1 specification a slightly modified role or content. We represent these concepts and their characteristics by rectangles in Figure 8.1. Arrows symbolize arcs with arcroles[86] defined in curly brackets { }. We show attributes that may appear on arcs below each of the arcroles together with their names and content.

Primary item / Measure

The first term introduced by the specification is a *primary item*. We also refer to this as a *measure*. In dimensional logic, measures are basic concepts. For example, in an accounting context these measures include *Revenues* and *Assets*. *Measures* are usually all concepts that appear on the face of the financial statement (i.e. in *Balance sheet*, *Profit or loss* or *Cash flows statements*) and are further itemized and analyzed in details in notes and disclosures.

In taxonomies, we can indicate the dimensional information associated with these primary items. For example, we can state that all concepts from *Income statement* must have a geographical breakdown. The information producer must then assign these breakdowns later in contexts in the instance documents.

In XBRL technical language, primary items are concepts of the *xbrli:item* substitution group[87], so typical reportable concepts defined according to the base XBRL 2.1 specification.

The key difference between non-dimensional and dimensional taxonomies is the characterization of the hierarchical trees of relations between primary items. In non-dimensional taxonomies we only apply *parent-child* relations in the presentation linkbase. Conversely, in the dimensional taxonomies, we can construct the relations between measures in the definition linkbase using arcs with the *domain-member* arcrole.

An important aspect of the *domain-member* relations is inheritance of multidimensional information. If an upper-level concept is assigned dimensional information, all the lower-level concepts in the hierarchical tree structure inherit this characteristic.

Indication of the multidimensional information that is applicable to a measure is performed by attaching to it a hypercube.

---

[86] Arcroles defined by XBRL Dimensions 1.0 specification are referred to in this chapter with their ids not URIs because they are shorter (keep in mind that arcs declarations refer to URIs). The same logic applies in this chapter when referencing roles used on extended links.

[87] Elements defined in *xbrli:tuple* substitution group are not allowed to be used with dimensional constructions defined by XBRL Dimensions 1.0 specification. Tuples and dimensions in some cases may be treated as substitutes.

Hypercube item

A *hypercube* is an artificial construct used to bind dimensions together in order to produce a *Cartesian product* of their breakdowns. Figure 7.2 presents a model of a hypercube, that combines *Clients*, *Products* and *Regions* dimensions that results (as a *Cartesian product*) in a set of all ordered pairs whose components are enumerations of each of the dimensions, for example (< *4 years old; Cars; Africa*), (< *4 years old; Cars; Asia*), (< *4 years old; Cars; Europe*), (< *4 years old; Dolls; Africa),* etc.

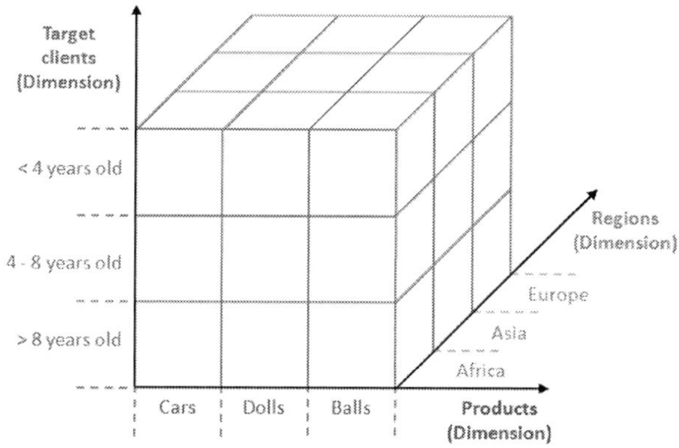

Fig. 7.2: Model of a hypercube

From the XBRL technical perspective, a hypercube is an abstract concept defined in *xbrldt:hypercubeItem* substitution group. As a derivation from the *xbrli:item* substitution group, a hypercube can participate in networks of relations and be assigned labels and references.

Apart from the *all* arcrole we use to indicate existence of certain dimensional information for a particular measure and its subconcepts, taxonomy developers are also able to create exclusions with *notAll* arcroles. The *all* arcrole connects a measure to a hypercube implying the use of all combinations resulting from a Cartesian product of all dimensional breakdowns. Conversely, the *notAll* arcrole allows for prohibition of undesired combinations. For example attaching a hypercube presented on Fig. 7.2 to a measure using *all* arcrole would imply, that a measure can be reported with dimensional information referring to any pair resulting from the Cartesian product of the three dimensions. To exclude combinations of pairs (for example < *4 years old; Dolls; Africa*) or entire blocks (> *8 years* and *Dolls* regardless of region) a separate hypercube must be created and linked to a measure using *notAll* arcrole. We describe the mechanisms for defining multidimensional breakdowns and exclusions later in this chapter.

To identify particular dimensions bound together by a hypercube, taxonomy developers use *hypercube-dimension* arcs that connect hypercube with the concepts representing dimensional breakdowns.

Dimension item and its domain

In general, dimensions in XBRL are each of the various types of breakdowns of contextual information by which we can report a given measure. As presented in Figure 7.2, these could be *Target clients*, *Products* and *Regions*.

Technically, these breakdowns are represented by abstract concepts defined in the *xbrldt:dimensionItem* substitution group. They have their breakdowns described in the definition linkbase or by using regular XML structures. In a similar fashion to hypercubes, dimension items can participate in relations and be labeled and referenced to external resources.

We refer to breakdowns of dimensions in the XBRL dimensions terminology as *domains*, for which their content can be implicitly or explicitly identified in taxonomies.

We perform implicit identification with the use of *typed dimensions*. This occurs when a breakdown structure, or domain, of a dimension is unknown or so impractically large for explicit enumeration. As an alternative to listing all possible values, taxonomy developers can therefore impose restrictions on the content of a domain of a typed dimension. The resulting *typed domain* is an XML, and not XBRL,[88] element. It cannot, therefore, participate in networks of relations. Instead, it is referenced from the typed dimension definition by *xbrldt:typedDomainRef* attribute which points to its location (similarly to the *xlink:href* attribute). A typed domain can be a simple or a complex XML construction depending on business requirements. For example, in reporting on a capital adequacy ratio, the so-called *obligor grade* is defined as a non negative integer with an unknown range instead of naming each possibility by creating an XBRL concept to represent it and linking all enumerations in hierarchical structures. This approach was introduced here because banks and other credit institutions are allowed to use different scales to classify obligors. These typed domains constitute the same content of *xbrli:segment* or *xbrli:scenario* elements as anticipated in the XBRL 2.1 specification (and presented in Code example 7.1), but allows for performing validations in relation to reported measures. We present an example of application of typed dimension and typed domain later in this chapter.

An *explicit dimension* in XBRL is a dimension for which a structure of a breakdown is identified in the taxonomy in the form of concepts defined in *xbrli:item* substitution group related to the dimension and to one another in the definition linkbase via arcs with specific arcroles. In the XBRL dimensions terminology, these breakdowns are domains consisting of members.[89] The top-level members link to the dimension via an arc with a *dimension-domain* arcrole.

---

88 XBRL concepts are not allowed on *xbrli:segment* and *xbrli:scenario* containers.

89 There is no clear distinction between a domain and a member (especially that every domain could be a member of a wider domain and every member could be a domain of its further breakdown) therefore in this book domain is referred to as a complete (full) breakdown of a dimension while a member is each single enumeration from this set.

The rest of the relations within the breakdown (i.e. relations between members) are constructed using arcs with a *domain-member* arcrole.

Application of the same arcrole for definition of hierarchical structures for primary items and domain members allows for measures to be used as dimensional breakdowns. The reverse relationship also holds.[90] However, there is a prohibition on the creation of circles. These are situations when a measure has itself as dimensional information. Domain members for which there is no intention of reuse as measures are defined as abstract items. This prevents them from being reported in instance documents as regular financial concepts.

In order to increase comparability and tackle validation issues that appear when applying dimensions in a taxonomy, developers are allowed to define a default member for each explicit dimension using an arc with a *dimension-default* arcrole. The default member is usually the top-level member that aggregates the rest of the breakdown or, in other words, the total of a domain. We explain the implications of use of a default member for a dimension later in the chapter.

Explicit or typed dimension

It is up to the business requirements and taxonomy developers to decide whether to use explicit or typed dimension to reflect particular breakdowns. For example, geographical division can be explicitly defined as concepts reflecting names of all continents, countries, etc. or deliberately left open as a string value of a typed dimension domain.

In practice, explicit dimensions allow for higher comparability of data and wider use of XBRL functionality. Breakdowns of explicit dimensions are organized in hierarchical structures. Modification of these structures comes by extending taxonomies with the addition of concepts and inserting, prohibiting or overriding relations. Domain members can have different kinds of labels and references to external sources. Typed dimensions are inherently more flexible. However, their application may result in inconsistencies between reports and difficulties in their further processing. Therefore, wherever feasible and reasonable, we recommend use of explicit dimensions.

Characteristics of arcroles

As indicated above, the XBRL Dimensions 1.0 specification defines new arcroles together with their characteristics in the form of attributes that may be applied on relationships' definitions in order to provide additional information about a dimensional construct and increase functionality of the solution as a whole. Table 7.1 summarizes information about arcroles defined in the specification and lists attributes that must or can be put to use on each of the arcs[91].

---

[90] This solution may be applied for example for notes and disclosures to a financial statement when a primary financial statement information is reused as classes. Correctness of such approach may raise doubts from the database modeling point of view.

[91] Order of arcroles appearing in dimensional taxonomies one after another is strictly defined in the specification and referred to as *consecutive relationships*.

Tab. 7.1: Dimensional arcroles and their attributes

Arcrole id	Explanation	Attributes
'all'	connects a measure to a hypercube implying use of dimensions attached to this hypercube and their specified breakdowns	closed:boolean contextElement:(segment/ scenario) targetRole:anyURI
'notAll'	connects a measure to a hypercube prohibiting use of dimensions attached to this hypercube and their specified breakdowns	closed:boolean contextElement:(segment/ scenario) targetRole:anyURI
'hypercube-dimension'	connects a hypercube and a dimension item	targetRole:anyURI
'dimension-domain'	connects a dimension item to its top level members in every variation of a breakdown	usable:boolean targetRole:anyURI
'domain-member'	defines hierarchical relations for measures and domain members; in case of measures implies inheritance of dimensional characteristics from upper-level concepts	usable:boolean targetRole:anyURI
'dimension-default'	links dimension item to its default member (usually total of the full breakdown)	

As we show in Table 7.1, when creating arcs with arcroles *all* and *notAll*, the taxonomy developer must use the *xbrldt:contextElement* attribute to indicate which of the two containers *xbrli:segment* or *xbrli:scenario* is chosen to store dimensional information defined in the particular hypercube. The taxonomy developer should apply this decision consistently to each dimension. If necessary, the taxonomy developer can use both containers to express different types of breakdowns.

Another dimensional characteristic contained by arcs with *all* and *notAll* arcroles is *xbrldt:closed* attribute expressing whether a context in instance document is allowed to contain more information than defined by the specific hypercube. For example, suppose that *Revenues* (primary item) in one note to the financial statement requires a hypercube containing *Geographical* and *By products* breakdowns. In other note, however, we require only the *Geographical breakdown*. If the taxonomy developer leaves the later hypercube open (i.e. value of *xbrldt:closed* attribute is *false*) it would imply the use of the same context for *both* cases. As a result, the instance document would report the same values for *Revenues* for enumerations of *Geographical breakdown* irrespective of the *By products* breakdown. We therefore recommend closing of hypercubes (attached to measures using arc with *all* arcrole) so that XBRL dimensions compatible processors treat the hypercubes separately. Importantly, the default value of *xbrldt:closed* attribute is *false*. We present an explanation on how XBRL processors validate hypercubes later in this chapter.

When defining dimensional breakdowns using arcs with *dimension-domain* and *domain-member* arcroles it is possible to exclude undesired members from being used (reported) in contexts in instance documents but keeping them included in breakdowns' structures. This helps us to organize the hierarchical relations. This approach is similar to the way taxonomy developers use abstract items to organize the hierarchical structure of measures in the presentation linkbase. To indicate that a particular domain member is not meant to be used as contextual information, the *xbrldt:useable* attribute (on arc pointing to it) is assigned value *false*.[92] The default value of this attribute is *true*.

In order to make it possible to reuse already defined structures and allow for prohibition of undesired dimensions' enumerations or combinations of these, the dimensions specification introduced the *xbrldt:targetRole* attribute. This can be in use on every dimensional arc, apart from the *dimension-default* arc. Introduction of this attribute was necessary in order to meet business requirements but raised many controversies on the technical side. Generally, in the XBRL 2.1 specification the definition of each set of relations was in a separate extended link role. When applying dimensions it is possible to cross the borders of a single extended link role and refer to structures defined in other extended link roles via the *xbrldt:targetRole* attribute. The value of this attribute is an URI representing *roleURI* of the other extended link. We present an example and discuss the implications of use of the *xbrldt:targetRole* attribute later in this chapter.

[92] This value is also applied when some parts of breakdown of a dimension are meant to be reused, therefore separate trees in hierarchical structures of domains are created.

Summary and examples of introduced terminology

Table 7.2 provides a summary of the main dimensional terms together with examples.

Tab. 7.2: Summary explanation and examples of dimensional terms

Term	Explanation	Examples
primary item (measure)	basic financial/accounting terms that can be reported with dimensional context	Revenues Assets Liabilities
dimension item	each of different types of breakdowns that can be reflected in dimensional context for a measure	By regions breakdown By clients breakdown
domain	complete breakdown of a dimension	list of countries groups of customers
domain member	each enumeration of a domain	Europe, Asia, … men, women, children, …
hypercube	ordered list of dimensions which Cartesian product of members constitutes (or is prohibited for) dimensional context	By regions and clients breakdown Exclusion of children in Europe
dimension default	default member of a dimension, usually aggregator (total) of the entire domain	Counties, Total Clients, All

Presented above terminology and constructs are used in the processes of designing and building of dimensional taxonomies. Referring to the examples we provide in Table 7.2, a taxonomy developer could attach to a primary item (for example *Revenues*) the *By regions and clients breakdown* hypercube using arc with *all* arcrole. The hypercube would in turn refer to *By regions breakdown* and *By clients breakdown* dimension items via arc with *hypercube-dimension* arcrole. Further hierarchical structure of geographical breakdown would consist of *Countries, Total* concept that would be linked to *By regions breakdown* with an arc of *dimension-domain* arcrole. It would simultaneously be a source of arcs with *domain-member* arcrole pointing to the *Europe* and *Asia* members. A similar construction would appear for the clients division with *Clients, All* concept as a target of *dimension-domain* and source of *domain-member* arcs. As a result, a measure linked using arc with *all* arcrole to the *By regions and clients breakdown* hypercube could be reported in an instance document in different variations created as a result of the Cartesian product of dimensional breakdowns' enumerations. In this example, *Revenues* could be assigned values in contexts in instance documents for pairs: (*Countries, Total* and *Clients, All*), (*Countries, Total* and *men*), (*Countries, Total* and *women*), (*Countries, Total* and *children*), (*Europe* and *Clients, All*), (*Europe* and *men*), etc.

7.3.2 The application of dimensions in instance documents

The example we describe above indicates that dimensional information constitutes a part of the way in the definition of contexts in instance documents. Taxonomies can regulate the content of these contexts by indicating the applicable combinations of dimensions where we must see joint reporting. Taxonomies also explicitly enumerate all possible members of dimensions or imply restrictions on the content of domains of typed dimensions.

At a technical level, dimensional information in instance documents is stored in *xbrli:segment* and/or *xbrli:scenario* concepts that are deliberately left open and unstructured by the XBRL 2.1 specification to allow incorporation of any XML constructs[93]. In order to create a standardized manner for the embedding of dimensional information into contexts, the XBRL Dimensions 1.0 specification equips instance creators with two new concepts and a new attribute. The formal definition of these new constructs is in the *xbrldi-2006.xsd* XML schema file, which code is embedded in the XBRL Dimensions 1.0 specification document.

An example of dimensional information defined on the *xbrli:segment* element is presented in Figure 7.3.

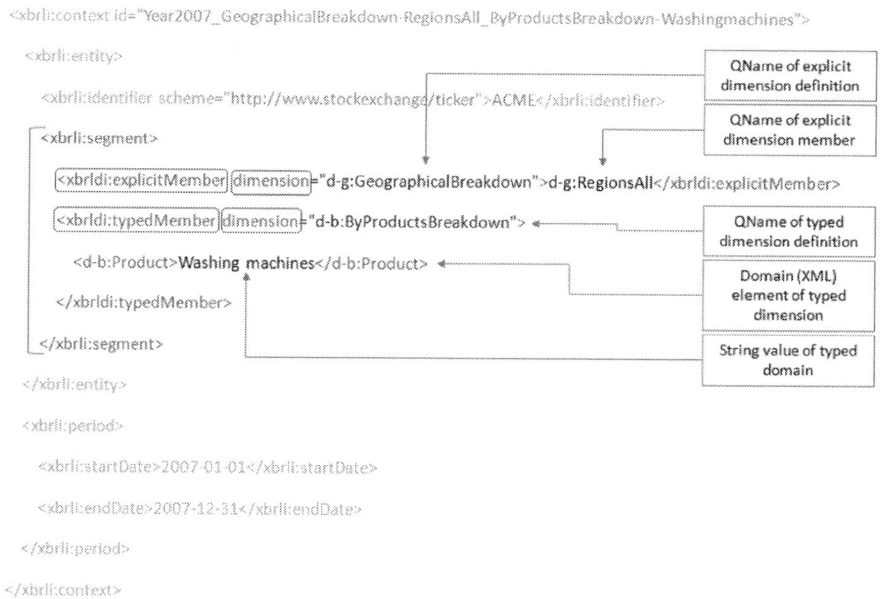

Fig. 7.3: Example of dimensional information in context in instance document

[93] Explanation of the intended content and a difference between *xbrli:segment* and *xbrli:scenario* elements is presented in the background section at the beginning of this chapter.

As we show in Figure 7.3, explicit dimensions are coded in contexts using the *xbrldi:explicitMember* element. Conversely, we define typed dimensions using the *xbrldi:typedMember* element. The *dimension* attribute must appear on each of these elements. Its value refers to the qualified name of a dimension item. The content of the *xbrldi:explicitMember* element itself is a qualified name of a valid member of the dimension item indicated by 'dimension' attribute. For typed dimensions, value of *xbrldi:typedMember* element is an XML simple or complex element defined as a typed domain of the dimension item referenced by *dimension* attribute.

Facts reported in instance documents refer to contexts that provide dimensional information according to the rules defined by appropriate hypercubes in taxonomies. The correctness of these references as well as the validity of *xbrli:segment* or *xbrli:scenario* content is checked by XBRL dimensions compliant processors, as each measure can appear in different sets of dimensional breakdowns. Earlier in the chapter, we reviewed the complexity of this situation in the example explaining use of the *xbrldt:closed* attribute. Here, as we present in Figure 7.4, the instance document must report *Revenues* (primary item) for *all* regions where the company operates as well by major product and by regions where it is sold.

Geographical breakdown of revenues

	Europe	Asia	Australia
Revenues			

Revenues from major product

	Dolls	
	Europe	Asia
Revenues		

Fig. 7.4: Example of data model where a measure is reported in two different sets of dimensional breakdowns

As we shown in Figure 7.4, *Revenues* in one note to the financial statement (Revenues from major product) is assigned a hypercube containing *Products* dimension which indicates that the main product is *Dolls* and *Regions* dimension showing that *Europe* and *Asia* is where the company sells the *Dolls* product. The other note (Geographical breakdown of revenues) reflects the requirement to report *Revenues* in the entire *Regions* dimension. In this latter case, there must be a value for all regions.

In order to make it possible to report a primary item with different sets of dimensional information, there must be a definition for each set in a different extended link role as we display in Figure 7.5:

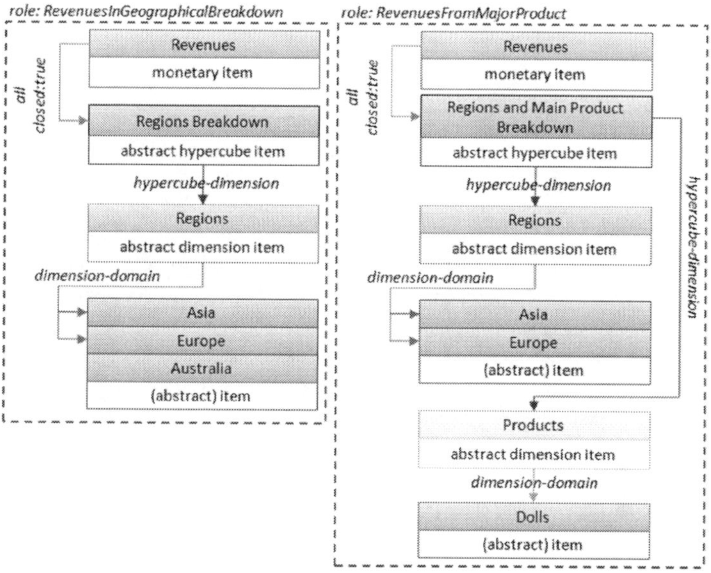

Fig. 7.5: Example of taxonomy architecture where a measure is reported in two different sets of dimensional breakdowns

An XBRL processor that validates an instance document against a taxonomy modeled as we present in Figure 7.5, would allow *Revenues* to be reported in five different contexts, viz[94]: *Asia*, *Europe*, *Australia*, *Asia and Dolls*, *Europe and Dolls*. Hypercubes referring to different sets of dimensions are defined in different extended link roles that are not related to each other (for example via *xbrldt:targetRole* attribute). Similarly, the definition of more than one hypercube in a single extended link role results in the combination of all dimensional information together when performing validations. In this example, in the *RevenuesFromMajorProduct* extended link role there could be two hypercubes linked to the *Revenues* primary item. One would refer to the *Regions* dimension and the other to the *Products* dimension.

This merger of dimensional information can also be performed with regard to inheriting dimensional characteristics even from the different extended link roles that are connected and discovered via *xbrldt:targetRole* attribute as we show in Figure 7.6.

---

94 It is important that the arc with *all* arcrole in *RevenuesInGeographicalBreakdown* extended link role has the value of *xbrldt:closed* attribute equal to *true*. Otherwise, *Revenues* referring to *Dolls* in *Asia* and to *Asia* only can be interpreted by a processor as the same fact although it is not necessarily the case, especially when a company sells also other products in this region. Similar logic applies to *Dolls* in *Europe* and *Europe* only.

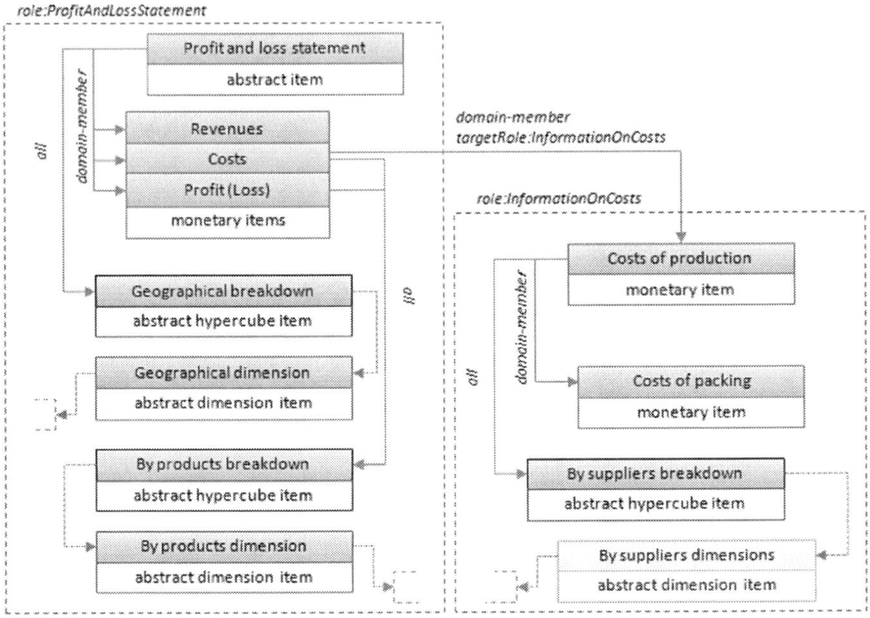

Fig. 7.6: Inheritance of dimensional information

According to Figure 7.6 (and if we assume that the values of all *xbrldt:closed* attributes are *true*) we can report:

- *Revenues* for information defined by the *Geographical breakdown* hypercube,
- *Profit (Loss)*, *Costs*, *Cost of production* and *Costs of packing* for information defined by *Geographical breakdown* and *By products breakdown* hypercubes simultaneously (i.e. Cartesian product as pairs of domain members from *Geographical dimension* and *By products dimension*),
- *Costs of production* and *Costs of packing* for information defined by *By suppliers breakdown.*

7.4 *Summary*

- The XBRL Dimensions specification 1.0 defines syntax and logic of the underlying technology to support dimensions.
- XBRL 2.1 specification provides some limited means to define several dimensional characteristics of concepts in instance documents. These are identification of a reporting entity, reporting date or period and units of measure.
- In dimensional logic, measures are basic concepts. For example, in an accounting context these measures include *Revenues* and *Assets*.
- A hypercube is an artificial construct used to bind dimensions together in order to produce a Cartesian product of their breakdowns.
- In general, dimensions in XBRL are each of the various types of breakdowns of contextual information by which we can report a given measure.
- An explicit dimension is a dimension for which a structure of a breakdown is identified in the taxonomy in the form of XBRL concepts.
- A typed dimension occurs when a breakdown structure of a dimension is unknown or so impractically large for explicit enumeration.
- Domain members are enumerated concepts defined for a given domain.

7.5 *Key terms you should know*

- Hypercube
- Dimension
- Typed dimension
- Explicit dimension
- Primary item
- Measure
- Domain
- Domain member

7.6 *Case analysis*[95]

The Association of Government Accountants (AGA) has long supported the use of XBRL to potentially improve the transparency and analysis in government financial reporting. Accordingly, AGA decided to implement a research project to study the benefits of developing and using an XBRL-taxonomy to tag data in a state's Comprehensive Annual Financial Report, or CAFR.

The biggest curve ball came when it was discovered that in order to produce a taxonomy that could render the Oregon Comprehensive Annual Financial Report (CAFR), an XBRL specification with dimensions would have to be used. This issue stems from the columnar presentation of the Oregon CAFR, which has data elements defined on the stubs (x) and columns (y), along with date specificity, hence the dimension. For example, under Current Assets on the Statement of Net Assets and Activities, Cash and Cash Equivalents are shown in the dimension of Primary Government, Government Activities.

[95] Excerpted from AGA, "XBRL and Public Sector Financial Reporting: Standardized Business Reporting: the Oregon CAFR Project", available at http://www.agacgfm.org/research/downloads/CPAGNo16.pdf

8 XBRL Dimensional Engineering

XBRL is like a shotgun, you can bring a nice piece of meat home or you can shoot yourself in the foot
[Father of XBRL Charles Hoffman, 16th XBRL International Conference, Vancouver, 2007]

Opening Vignette: IFRS Taxonomy Modules Manager[96]

The International Accounting Standards Committee (IASC) Foundation today announced the release of the new IFRS Taxonomy Modules Manager (ITMM 2.0). Based on the IFRS Taxonomy 2008, which consists of over 400 files (representing components of financial statements) in more than 40 folders, the license-free ITMM 2.0 offers taxonomy users many new features:

- The files can be combined with one another in any combination
- The preparer has an entry point that combines for example:
  - Consolidated statement of financial position, by order of liquidity
  - Consolidated income statement, by function of expense
  - Consolidated statement of cash flows, using the direct method
- An interactive graphical interface that guides the user through the selection of the necessary IFRS modules
- An entry point (in the form of a schema or empty instance document) that is the starting point for entity-specific extension or direct filing
- Users can navigate across the IFRSs as well as the structure of financial statements
- A normal mode for first-time users, and advanced settings (together with expert mode) for experienced users.

In this chapter, we extend our discussion on dimensions in the previous chapter. The XBRL Dimensions 1.0 specification created a full range of new modeling possibilities in the engineering of XBRL taxonomies. These additional semantics not only extend the understanding of metadata that is going to be reported but also introduces new validation possibilities thus enhancing the data quality. We will use a number of examples in this chapter to introduce advanced aspects of engineering XBRL dimensional solutions.

---

96 Excerpted from the IASC Foundation XBRL news website, available at http://www.iasb.org/News/XBRL/The+IASC+Foundation+publishes+new+IFRS+Taxonomy+Module+Manager.htm.

8.1 Modularization of dimensional taxonomies

The extent of modularization of XBRL taxonomies has been an issue for taxonomy developers. Observing the development of the IFRS taxonomy, we can see growing sophistication of modularization. First, the introduction of dimensions explicitly addressed the modularization issues in the specification. The non-normative introduction to the XBRL Dimensions 1.0 specification contains a section that explains how dimensional taxonomies can be modularized in terms of the files' content and organization. This modularization allows upgrade of non-dimensional taxonomies with dimensional constructs. Modularization supports highly reusable taxonomy frameworks. We present a graphical structure of this model approach in Figure 8.1.

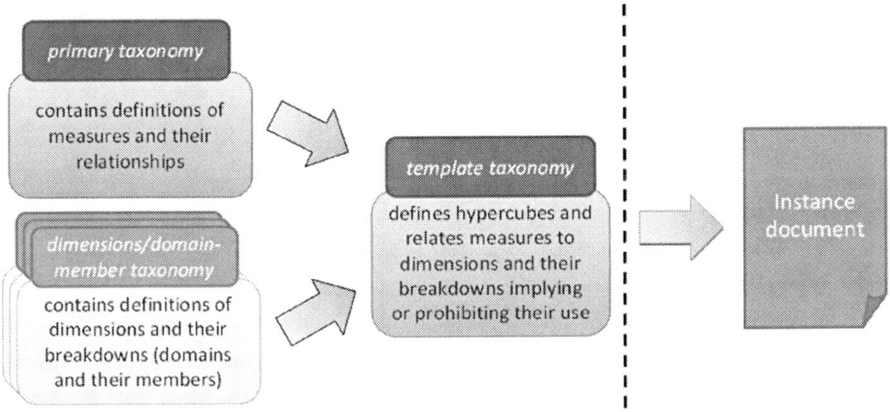

Fig. 8.1: Model approach to modularization of dimensional taxonomies

Taxonomies developed under the XBRL 2.1 specification consist only of measures and make use of no dimensional concepts or relations. As the specification suggests, and as we show in Figure 8.1, the modularization structure assumes that these constitute separate sets of files referred to as the *primary taxonomies*.

Dimensions/domain-member taxonomies define dimension items and their domains (members and their hierarchical structures). They may also indicate default members for each of the dimensions. Best practice suggests that the definition of each dimension is in a separate taxonomy (XBRL Schema file with corresponding linkbases). This separate taxonomy can be applied for measures where and when required.

The taxonomy architect indicates the use of selected dimensions for particular sets of measures in the *template taxonomy*. This taxonomy imports applicable primary and dimensions/domain-member taxonomies, defines hypercubes and uses dimensional arcroles to indicate existence of appropriate relations.

We present an example of such modularization in Figure 8.2.

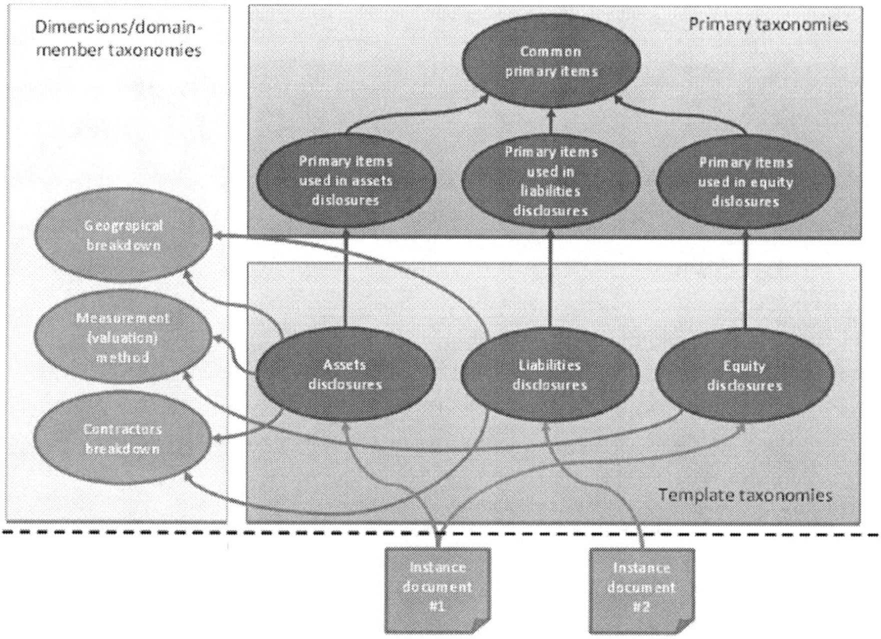

Fig. 8.2: Example of modularization of dimensional taxonomies

Figure 8.2 is an example of modularization of disclosures in financial statements. Judging from the architecture of the taxonomy, the underlying data model defines separate sets of information for assets, liabilities and equity disclosures. Each of these sets is represented by a primary taxonomy importing a *Common primary items* taxonomy defining measures reusable across disclosures. These taxonomies could contain presentation relations between the measures stressing their use in non-dimensional contexts[97].

The definitions of dimensions and their breakdowns are in separate dimensions/domain-member taxonomies. These dimensional taxonomies can be imported every time a particular breakdown is necessary. The example presented in Fig. 8.2 indicates three different breakdowns: geographical, contractors and measurement (valuation) method.

Each of the primary taxonomies is referenced by its template counterpart that imports applicable for the sets of measures dimensional breakdowns, defines hypercubes and all the other required relations. In the example illustrated in Figure 8.2, only *Assets disclosures* uses all three of the dimensional breakdowns. The other templates refer only to the applicable breakdowns.

[97] Example of simultaneous use of measures in dimensional and non-dimensional context is described later in this chapter when presenting concept of dimension default member and empty hypercubes.

Another important conclusion that stems from the example is that breakdowns can be defined just once and then are available for use in different templates. In other words, if geographical breakdown is in use in the disclosures about assets and liabilities, the definition is made just once with many subsequent uses in a variety of use cases.

8.2 Examples of use of dimensions

This part of the chapter consists of four examples that should assist the reader to understand XBRL dimensions. It describes in detail the application of terms and architecture introduced in the theoretical section and presents practical dimensional taxonomy modeling and instance document creation rules.

8.2.1 Explicit dimensions example

The first example relates to the use and application of explicit dimensions and presents one of the possible taxonomy modeling approaches.

The business requirement background for the taxonomy design is to define a short *Profit and loss statement* consisting of *Revenues*, *Costs of production* and *Profit (Loss)*. Additionally, reporting is necessary for *Geographical breakdown* of *All regions*, *Poland*, *Germany* and *Austria* and simultaneously in *By products breakdown* enumerated as *All products*, *Cars*, *Boats* and *Ships*. We illustrate the data model that accords to these assumptions in Figure 8.3.

		Profit and loss statement		
		Revenues	Costs of production	Profit (Loss)
All products	All regions			
	Poland			
	Germany			
	Austria			
Cars	All regions			
	Poland			
	Germany			
	Austria			
Boats	All regions			
	Poland			
	Germany			
	Austria			
Ships	All regions			
	Poland			
	Germany			
	Austria			

Fig. 8.3: Data model of explicit dimensions example

In general, the header of the columns of the table in Figure 8.3 represents primary items. The headers of rows correspond to two different dimensional breakdowns: by products on the left in green and by regions on the right in red. The two gray cells reflect additional assumption towards this example stating that *Revenues* from sales of *Boats* and *Ships* don't occur in Austria as this country has no access to open water reservoirs. *Costs of production* are generated in this region by seats factory located in Vienna therefore *Profit (Loss)* can also be estimated (although it will always be a loss).

From the instance document perspective, the white cells in Figure 8.3 are facts that can be reported where headers of columns define concepts and headers of rows stand for different dimensional contextual information.

We show the example of explicit dimensional taxonomy architecture and content that result from the business requirements and the data model in Figure 8.4.

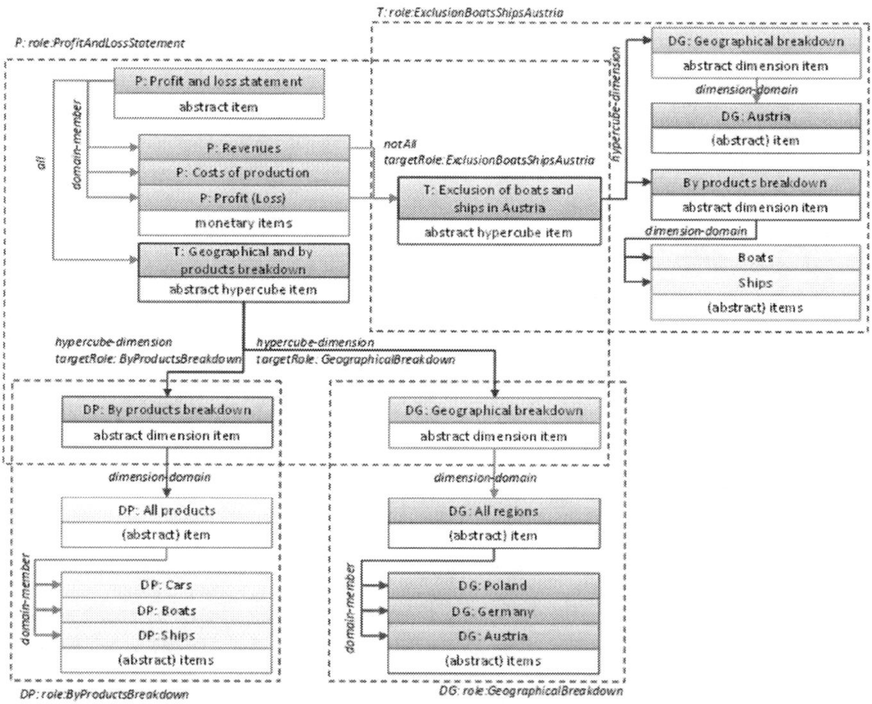

Fig. 8.4: Graphical diagram of explicit dimension example taxonomy architecture and content

The modeling of the taxonomy commences with the decision on the extent of modularization. For this example, as we present in Figure 8.5, there are four separate sets of files with following distinguishing prefixes:

- P: for primary taxonomy,
- DP: for *By products breakdown* dimensions taxonomy,
- DG: for *Geographical breakdown* dimensions taxonomy,
- T: for template taxonomy.

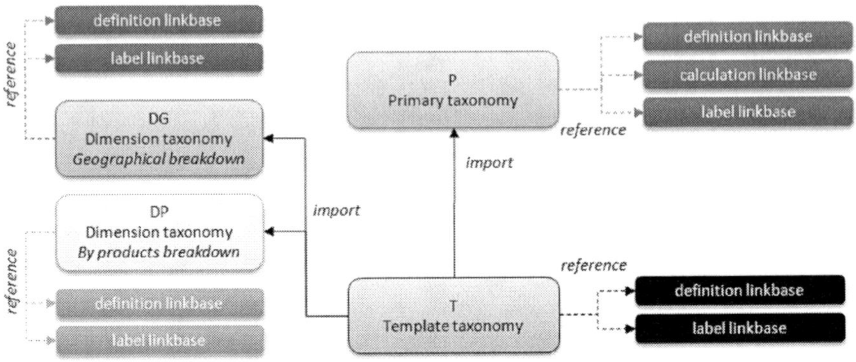

Fig. 8.5: Modularization architecture of the explicit dimension example

We present our modularization architecture in Figure 8.5. This architecture allows reuse of dimensions as well as application of only one of the breakdowns if the other is irrelevant for a particular report or a report fragment. It also increases flexibility and further extensibility of the entire framework of taxonomies by allowing us to incorporate the change once, (for example extend the breakdown of a dimension in a dimensional taxonomy) and automatically apply it in many places. The breakdown is referenced using the *xbrldt:targetRole* attribute.

The taxonomy development procedure starts with the definition of a primary taxonomy or breakdowns. In real XBRL adoption projects, taxonomies are created basing on data models that define sets of all reports together with commonly and locally applied dimensions. It is irrelevant whether the development starts with primary or dimensional taxonomies, as they do not directly link to each other. Instead, they connect via a template.

Primary taxonomy

The primary taxonomy in this example defines an abstract *Profit and loss statement* concept and three monetary measures *Revenues*, *CostOfProduction* and *ProfitLoss* together with their labels. Additionally, primary taxonomy defines a role with id *ProfitAndLossStatement* that we use in extended links in the definition and calculation linkbases[98].

We construct the calculation linkbase for the primary taxonomy with two arcs that have *summation-item* arcroles from *Profit (Loss)* to *Revenues* and from *Profit (Loss)* to *Costs of production*. They have a weight attribute of *1* and *-1*, respectively[99].

---

[98] In this example it is assumed that *Profit and loss statement* is reported only with dimensional information. Implications of this assumption are discussed later in this chapter in section devoted to dimension default member and empty hypercubes and dimensions.

[99] *Revenues* and *Profits (Loss)* have *credit* nature of *xbrli:balance* attribute while *Costs of production* are *debit*.

In order to allow use of dimensional arcroles, appropriate *link:arcroleRef* elements must be used in the definition linkbase. We present the full set of dimensional arcroles references in Code example 8.1.

```
<link:linkbase (…) >
    <link:arcroleRef
arcroleURI="http://xbrl.org/int/dim/arcrole/all"
xlink:type="simple"
xlink:href="http://www.xbrl.org/2005/xbrldt-2005.xsd#all"/>

    <link:arcroleRef
arcroleURI="http://xbrl.org/int/dim/arcrole/dimension-
default" xlink:type="simple"
xlink:href="http://www.xbrl.org/2005/xbrldt-
2005.xsd#dimension-default"/>

    <link:arcroleRef
arcroleURI="http://xbrl.org/int/dim/arcrole/dimension-
domain" xlink:type="simple"
xlink:href="http://www.xbrl.org/2005/xbrldt-
2005.xsd#dimension-domain"/>

    <link:arcroleRef
arcroleURI="http://xbrl.org/int/dim/arcrole/domain-member"
xlink:type="simple"
xlink:href="http://www.xbrl.org/2005/xbrldt-
2005.xsd#domain-member"/>

    <link:arcroleRef
arcroleURI="http://xbrl.org/int/dim/arcrole/hypercube-
dimension" xlink:type="simple"
xlink:href="http://www.xbrl.org/2005/xbrldt-
2005.xsd#hypercube-dimension"/>
    <link:definitionLink (…) >
        (…)
    </link:definitionLink>
</link:linkbase>
```

Code example 8.1: References to dimensional arcroles from the definition linkbase

In this example, it is enough for the taxonomy builder to reference in the definition linkbase of the primary taxonomy only the arcrole with *domain-member* id. We then apply it on arcs inside the *ProfitAndLossStatement* extended link role that point from the abstract *Profit and loss statement* concept to three non-abstract monetary items. We illustrated this in Figure 8.4.

Dimensions taxonomies

The next step in development of the example taxonomy is to define dimensions and their breakdowns. Because of the assumed modularization architecture we present in Figure 8.5, each of the dimensions taxonomies consists of an XBRL schema file that refers to the definition and label linkbases and imports *xbrldt-2005.xsd* in order to enable defining dimension items.

The *Geographical breakdown* dimensional taxonomy defines a *Geographic breakdown* abstract dimension item and its domain that consists of the *All regions*, *Poland*, *Germany* and *Austria* members.

The *By products breakdown* is an abstract dimension item for the other dimension and its domain members are *All products*, *Cars*, *Boats* and *Ships*.

In both cases, the domain members of dimensions are unlikely to be reused as primary items. They do not represent basic financial terms. Rather they are characteristics of financial terms (therefore facts reported in an instance document stating that *Boats* equals 100EUR or *Poland* being reported as a *This is a country* string are senseless) so their XBRL representation are abstract items.

The structure of hierarchical dependencies of domain members and dimension items is in the definition linkbase. The linkbase uses dimensional arcroles as we present in Figure 8.4. These structures are likely to reflect the complete set of each breakdown, which can be later imported where needed and restricted only to the applicable measures.

Template taxonomy

In this example, the template taxonomy imports the primary taxonomy and both dimensional taxonomies.

Inclusion of full breakdowns

In order to apply the full breakdowns of dimensions, the taxonomy developer needs to define a hypercube (an abstract item in *xbrldt:hypercubeItem* substitution group). The instance documents reference neither *name* nor *id* of a hypercube. Nevertheless, we recommend that taxonomy developers construct and apply a naming convention to name and label hypercubes logically and consistently across the taxonomy. In this example, the hypercube combines the geographical and by product breakdowns. We therefore label it *Geographical and by products breakdown* and we introduce the names accordingly (i.e. camel case with no spaces between words).

In order to apply simultaneously both dimensional characteristics to all primary items, the hypercube is linked via arc with the *all* arcrole to the top-level concept. In our case this is the *Profit and loss statement* abstract item in the *ProfitAndLossStatement* extended link role. In the same extended link both dimension items connect to the hypercube. This implementation is via an arc with a 'hypercube-dimension' arcrole. We illustrate this situation in Figure 8.4. We present a fragment of code in Code example 8.2.

```
<link:definitionLink xlink:type="extended"
xlink:role="http://explicit.example/p/role/ProfitAndLossSta
tement">

<link:loc xlink:type="locator"
xlink:href="p.xsd#p_ProfitAndLossStatement"
xlink:label="ProfitAndLossStatement"/>

<link:loc xlink:type="locator"
xlink:href="t.xsd#t_GeographicalAndByProductsBreakdown"
xlink:label="GeographicalAndByProductsBreakdown"/>

<link:definitionArc xlink:type="arc"
xlink:arcrole="http://xbrl.org/int/dim/arcrole/all"
xlink:from="ProfitAndLossStatement"
xlink:to="GeographicalAndByProductsBreakdown" order="4.0"
xbrldt:contextElement="segment" xbrldt:closed="true"/>

<link:loc xlink:type="locator"
xlink:href="dg.xsd#dg_GeographicalBreakdown"
xlink:label="GeographicalBreakdown"/>

<link:definitionArc xlink:type="arc"
xlink:arcrole="http://xbrl.org/int/dim/arcrole/hypercube-
dimension" xlink:from="GeographicalAndByProductsBreakdown"
xlink:to="GeographicalBreakdown" order="1.0"
xbrldt:targetRole="http://explicit.example/dg/role/Geograph
icalBreakdown"/>

<link:loc xlink:type="locator"
xlink:href="dp.xsd#dp_ByProductsBreakdown"
xlink:label="ByProductsBreakdown"/>

<link:definitionArc xlink:type="arc"
xlink:arcrole="http://xbrl.org/int/dim/arcrole/hypercube-
dimension" xlink:from="GeographicalAndByProductsBreakdown"
xlink:to="ByProductsBreakdown" order="2.0"
xbrldt:targetRole="http://explicit.example/dp/role/ByProduc
tsBreakdown"/>
    (...)
</link:definitonLink>
```

Code example 8.2: Code expressing linking hypercubes and dimension items

The fragment of code we show in Code example 8.2 contains locators that refer to the top-level primary item, hypercube and both dimension items as well as arcs reflecting links between these concepts. The values of *xlink:href* attributes on locators point to different XBRL schema files according to the assumed modularization architecture that we presented in Figure 8.5.

On the arc with *all* arcrole linking top level primary item and the hypercube there are two attributes specified: *xbrldt:contextElement* and *xbrldt:closed*. The first, as we explained earlier in this chapter, indicates that the dimensional information in instance documents must be reported on *xbrli:segment* element. The latter limits the content of *xbrli:segment* only to the defined dimensional information.

Additionally, there are *xbrldt:targetRole* attributes on arcs with *hypercube-dimension* arcrole which allow for reuse of full breakdowns that we predefine in dimensions taxonomies. This construction indicates that the *Geographical breakdown* should be available in the extended link with roleURI *http://explicit.example/dg/role/GeographicalBreakdown* an we define details of *By products breakdown* in the *http://explicit.example/dp/role/ByProductsBreakdown* extended link. Both roles in use as values of *xbrldt:targetRole* attribute must be referred to in the definition linkbase of the template taxonomy as we present in Code example 8.3.

```
<link:roleRef
roleURI="http://explicit.example/dg/role/GeographicalBreakd
own"
xlink:type="simple"
xlink:href="dg.xsd#GeographicalBreakdown"/>

<link:roleRef
roleURI="http://explicit.example/dp/role/ByProductsBreakdow
n"
xlink:type="simple"
xlink:href="dp.xsd#ByProductsBreakdown"/>
```

Code example 8.3: References of extended link roles (defined in dimensions taxonomies) in the definition linkbase of the template taxonomy

The procedure we set out above leads to the creation of the dimensional information for the entire *Profit and loss statement*.

Excluded combinations

Following the business requirements for this taxonomy, the next step is to create exclusions for combinations of:

- *Austria* from *Geographical Breakdown* and
- *Boats* or *Ships* from *By products breakdown* for Revenues.

The procedure begins with the definition of a new extended link role *ExclusionBoatsShipsAustria* in the template taxonomy. We create this in order to contain relations that reflect the exclusion. We need an additional extended link role, as both *Geographical breakdown* and *By products breakdown* dimension items already participate in relations in *ProfitAndLossStatement* extended link role. It is impossible to have two different groups of subconcepts in a single set of relationships (one extended link role).

Similarly, it is impossible to reuse the hypercube, and in this case it is also enough to define a new one. Therefore additional abstract hypercube item is created and labeled *Exclusion of boats and ships in Austria.*

When constructing relationships, this hypercube becomes the first node in the *ExclusionBoatsShipsAustria* extended link role. Both dimension items connect to it via arcs with the *hypercube-dimension* arcrole. Further breakdown of dimensions is limited only to the excluded members linked to the dimension items using arcs with *dimension-domain* arcrole as we present schematically in Figure 8.4.

To apply these exclusions to *Revenues* measure, *Exclusion of boats and ships in Austria* hypercube links to this primary item via arc with the *notAll* arcrole in the *ProfitAndLossStatement* extended link role. Additionally, this arc carries the *xbrldt:targetRole* attribute refers to the *http://explicit.example/t/role/ExclusionBoatsShipsAustria* roleURI where the information on exclusion is available. We present the definition of this arc in relation to *Revenues* in the code in Code example 8.4.

```
<link:definitionLink xlink:type="extended"
xlink:role="http://explicit.example/p/role/ProfitAndLossSta
tement">

<link:loc xlink:type="locator"
xlink:href="p.xsd#p_CostsOfProduction"
xlink:label="CostsOfProduction"/>

<link:loc xlink:type="locator"
xlink:href="t.xsd#t_ExclusionBoatsShipsAustria"
xlink:label="ExclusionBoatsShipsAustria"/>

<link:definitionArc xlink:type="arc"
xlink:arcrole="http://xbrl.org/int/dim/arcrole/notAll"
xlink:from="CostsOfProduction"
xlink:to="ExclusionBoatsShipsAustria" order="1.0"
xbrldt:targetRole="http://explicit.example/t/role/Exclusion
BoatsShipsAustria" xbrldt:contextElement="segment"
xbrldt:closed="false"/>
(...)
</link:definitionLink>
```

Code example 8.4: Fragment of code expressing reference to the excluding hypercube

As we indicate in Code example 8.4, in order for the exclusion to be valid, the *xbrldt:contextElement* attribute value on *notAll* arcrole must be identical to the previously defined arc with the *all* arcrole.

Extending the example

The procedure we describe above results in the exclusion of undesired combinations to specific measures from the whole set of possibilities defined by a Cartesian product of both full sets of breakdowns.

Accordingly, one could easily modify the content of breakdowns in dimensions taxonomies that would be applied *automatically* in every referring template. For example, extension of the geographical breakdown by *Spain* in the *DG* dimensional taxonomy would result in changes in every one of the template taxonomies that refer to the full breakdown of this dimension.

If necessary, we can create additional exclusions to prohibit other combinations to particular measures, for example *Cars* in *Poland* or *Boats* in *Germany*.

Alternative modeling approach

It is important to stress that the same data model can result in different design of taxonomies depending on the modeling approach. An alternative to the definition of a breakdown and exclusion of unwanted combination, as in this example, is to identify a Cartesian product applicable for each of the measures or for sets of measures separately. Referring to this example, the taxonomy developer would achieve the same result by splitting the table into three extended link roles as in Figure 8.6.

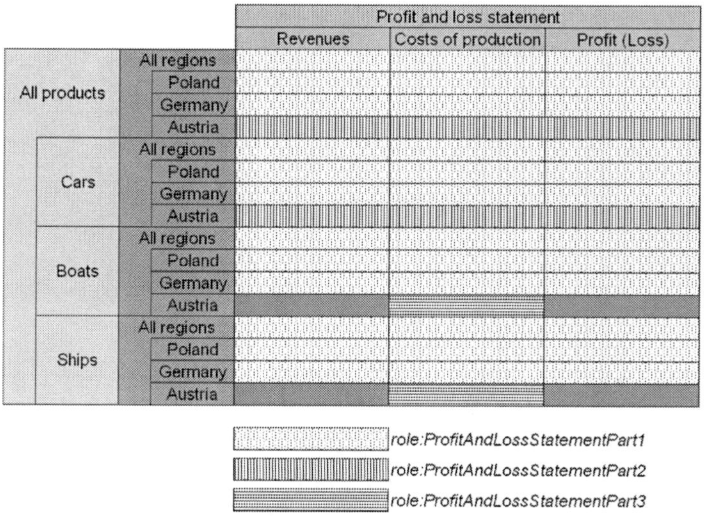

Fig. 8.6: Alternative modeling approach to explicit dimensions example

As Figure 8.6 shows, in order to reach the same effect with regard to allowed and disallowed combinations of dimensions (Cartesian product) for particular measures the taxonomy developer could construct three extended link roles:

1. The extended link with role id *ProfitAndLossStatementPart1* that we show in Figure 8.7. The top-level abstract that gathers all the measures we assign to a hypercube that reuses the *By products breakdown* structure that we define in the extended link with the role id *ByProductsBreakdown*. For the *Geographical breakdown* we attach only the *All regions*, *Poland* and *Germany* domain members to the dimension item in the *ProfitAndLossStatementPart1* extended link role.
2. The extended link with the role id *ProfitAndLossStatementPart2* presented in Figure 8.8. Here the measures are assigned to a hypercube that refers to *All products* and *Cars* from *By products breakdown* and *Austria* from *Geographical breakdown.*
3. We show the extended link with the role id *ProfitAndLossStatementPart3* in Figure 8.9. In this extended link, the not reportable measure is *Revenues*. The other measures are meant to be provided with dimensional contextual information for *Austria* of *Geographical breakdown* and *Boats* and *Ships* domain members of *By products breakdown.*

Note that we reused the same hypercube to combine dimensions in all the three extended links. Although it is not required, we recommend reuse of hypercubes where possible, in order to decrease redundancy.

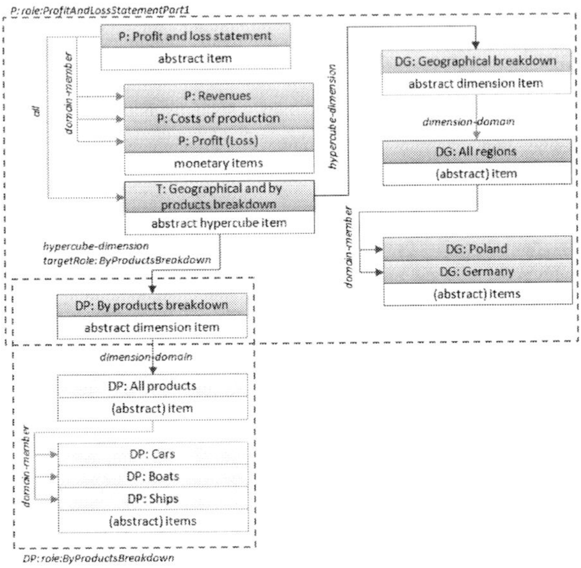

Fig. 8.7: *ProfitAndLossStatementPart1* extended link structure

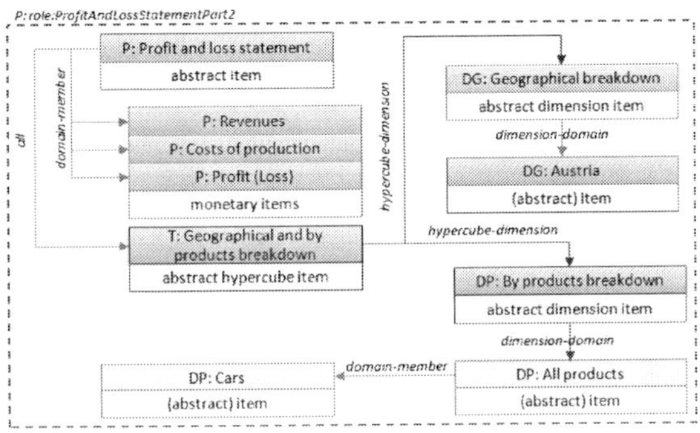

Fig. 8.8: *ProfitAndLossStatementPart2* extended link structure

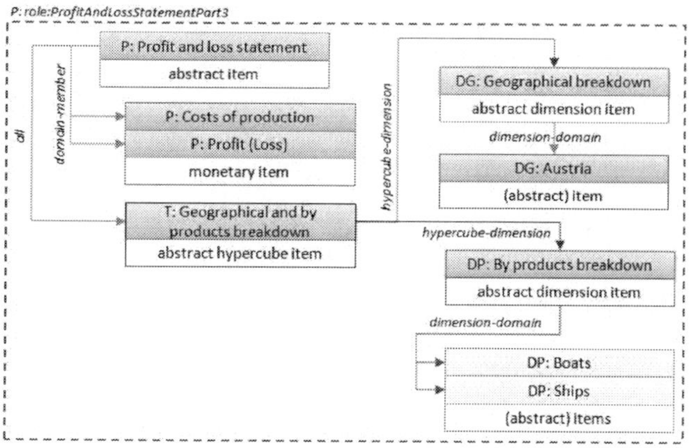

Fig. 8.9: *ProfitAndLossStatementPart3* extended link structure

Although the modeling approach is indifferent from the perspective of the content of instance documents, it may result in other issues relating to correct understanding of the taxonomy.

Figure 8.10 presents the rendering[100] of the reverse-engineered (from the taxonomy) data model of the alternative modeling approach to the explicit dimensions example.

role:ProfitAndLossStatementPart1

		Profit and loss statement		
		Revenues	Costs of production	Profit (Loss)
All products	All regions			
	Poland			
	Germany			
Cars	All regions			
	Poland			
	Germany			
Boats	All regions			
	Poland			
	Germany			
Ships	All regions			
	Poland			
	Germany			

role:ProfitAndLossStatementPart2

		Profit and loss statement		
		Revenues	Costs of production	Profit (Loss)
Austria	All products			
	Cars			

role:ProfitAndLossStatementPart3

		Profit and loss statement	
		Costs of production	Profit (Loss)
Austria	Boats		
	Ships		

Fig. 8.10: Reverse-engineered data model of the alternative modeling approach to explicit dimensions example

[100] Although XBRL dimensions were not designed in principle for rendering purposes, due to the lack of any other solution (at the moment of writing of this book XBRL Rendering specification is an Internal Working Draft) they are used by some applications for reproduction of the underlying data model in a tabular format.

What may be confusing about the data model presented in Figure 8.10 is that *All regions* from the *ProfitAndLossStatementPart1* extended link role consist only of *Poland* and *Germany* while the value of measures reported for this dimensional information should include *Austria* and possibly other regions not explicitly named by this breakdown.

Other issues related to the presented alternative modeling approach consist of lower reuse of predefined full breakdowns of dimensions and discrepancy between the reverse-engineered data model (illustrated in Figure 8.10) and the base data model (presented in Figure 8.6).

Of course, one could think of more ways of transforming the business requirements of this example into a taxonomy using other modeling techniques. Nevertheless, the modeling approach should be consistent across the entire taxonomy and optimal in terms of logic and code consumption. It is important to distinguish between the changes in modeling approaches that do not affect the data model represented by the taxonomy and the actual changes to the data model.

Instance document

The instance document that accords to the example taxonomy refers to the template taxonomy schema file via *link:schemaRef* element. If all the values of the data model we illustrate in Fig. 8.3 are to be reported, the instance document must define a total of sixteen contexts. Each contains in the *xbrli:segment* element a pair consisting of one member from each dimension. We illustrate an example of one of the contexts definitions in Code example 8.5.

```
<xbrli:context id="Year2007_GeographicalBreakdown-
Germany_ByProductsBreakdown-Ships">
 <xbrli:entity>
  <xbrli:identifier
scheme="http://www.stockexchange.com/ticker">ACME</xbrli:id
entifier>
   &lt;xbrli:segment&gt;
    <xbrldi:explicitMember
dimension="dg:GeographicalBreakdown">dg:Germany</xbrldi:exp
licitMember>
    <xbrldi:explicitMember
dimension="dp:ByProductsBreakdown">dp:Ships</xbrldi:explici
tMember>
   &lt;/xbrli:segment&gt;
  </xbrli:entity>
  <xbrli:period>
   <xbrli:startDate>2007-01-01</xbrli:startDate>
   <xbrli:endDate>2007-12-31</xbrli:endDate>
  </xbrli:period>
</xbrli:context>
```

Code example 8.5: Example of a context definition in instance document for explicit dimensions example

Validation

XBRL processors that are "dimensions aware" must not report insufficient or additional dimensional information if the value of *xbrldt:closed* attribute on every arc with *all* arcrole is set to *true*. The processor must also indicate an error if a measure refers to the contexts defining prohibited in the taxonomy combinations for this particular measure. Examples are the gray cells in Figure 8.3).

As we indicate in previous chapters, the XBRL 2.1 specification does not allow for cross-context validation of calculation rules. Therefore, the processor can only check the correctness of calculations in the example only for each row of the table presented in Figure 8.3. This is shown in the calculation linkbase of the primary taxonomy (i.e. *Profit (Loss) = Revenues – Cost of production*). In other words, creation of calculations between domain members that would be validated by processors in instance documents (e.g. *Revenues* from *All regions = Revenues* from *Austria + Revenues* from *Poland + Revenues* from *Germany*) is out of scope of the XBRL Dimensions 1.0 specification and was left to be implemented as part of the functionality of upcoming XBRL Formula 1.0 specification.

Typed dimension example

As we discuss earlier in this chapter, XBRL allows us to define explicit dimensions (enumerated breakdowns consisting of XBRL concepts) or typed dimensions that refer to typed domains which are XML constructs. The instantiation of these constructs appears in contexts in instance documents.

Typed dimensions are generally in use when it is impractical or impossible to enumerate explicitly a breakdown of a dimension. In that case, it is more reasonable to define a constraint on the data type (e.g. string, integer, etc.) of a typed domain and allow creators of instance documents to input appropriate values.

The following example presents the development process of a taxonomy with a typed dimension and the resulting construction of instance documents.

As we indicate in Figure 8.11, this example shows how to model trade receivables and liabilities in a breakdown of contractors[101]. Contractors are referred to by internal codes used by a reporting entity.

[101] This data model could be easily reflected in a taxonomy using tuples. Indeed, dimensions are currently often used as a replacement of tuples. Although typed dimensions are more natural substitutes of tuples, some taxonomies, such as US GAAP, use explicit dimensions for this purpose. This approach is possible when taxonomies are allowed to be extended by reporting entities.

Code of Contractor	Trade receivables and liabilities	
	Trade receivables	Trade liabilities
...	...	...

Fig. 8.11: Data model of typed dimension example

We show the assumed modularization of the resulting taxonomy into three logical sets of files in Figure 8.12.

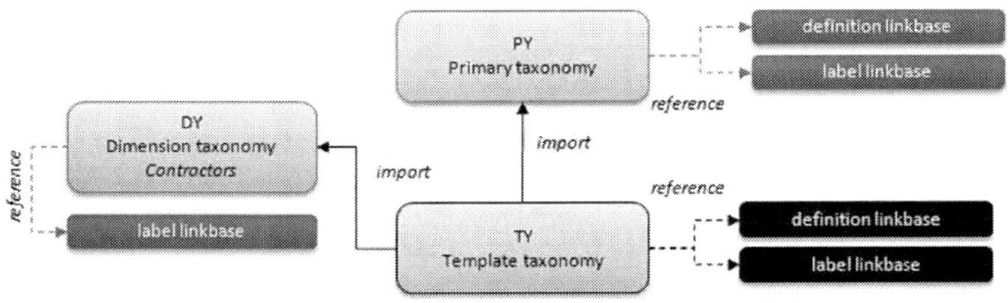

Fig. 8.12: Modularization of typed dimensions taxonomy example

Primary taxonomy (prefixed in this example *PY*) defines and labels three items: an abstract *Trade receivables and liabilities* and two monetary items *Trade receivables* and *Trade liabilities*. It also defines an extended link role *TradeReceivablesAndLiabilities* and constructs *domain-member* relations in the definition linkbase as we show in Figure 8.13.

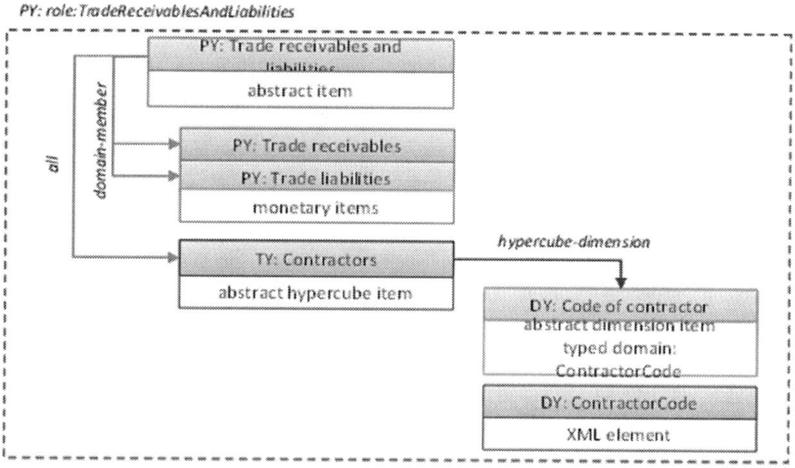

Fig. 8.13: Diagram of the typed dimension example taxonomy architecture

The dimensional taxonomy (prefixed in this example *DY*) imports *xbrldt-2005.xsd* schema file and defines the dimension item *Code of contractor* and its typed domain *ContractorCode*. We present the code that reflects this situation in Code example 8.6.

```
<xsd:element name="CodeOfContractor"
id="dy_CodeOfContractor" type="xbrli:stringItemType"
abstract="true" nillable="true" xbrli:periodType="instant"
substitutionGroup="xbrldt:dimensionItem"
xbrldt:typedDomainRef="#dy_ContractorCode"/>

<xsd:element name="ContractorCode" id="dy_ContractorCode">
   <xsd:simpleType>
      <xsd:restriction base="xsd:string">
        <xsd:pattern value="[A-Z]{3}[0-9]{4}"/>
      </xsd:restriction>
   </xsd:simpleType>
</xsd:element>
```

Code example 8.6: Code presenting definition of typed dimension and its domain

As indicated by the upper orange rectangle on Code example 8.6, *Code of contractor* dimension item contains on its declaration additional attribute *xbrldt:typedDomainRef*. This indicates typed domain by pointing to a file and concept id in the same manner as *xlink:href* attribute[102].

As we indicate earlier in this chapter, the typed domain is an XML (not XBRL) construct. As such, it cannot appear in linkbases. It can be instantiated in the contexts in instance documents. Therefore, the dimensional taxonomy in this example does not define any relations in the definition linkbase.

In the example, the possible content of the typed domain is limited to combination of three capital letters and four digits that represents the assumed pattern for codes of contractors used by a reporting entity.

The template taxonomy (prefixed *TY*) imports the primary and dimensional taxonomies (as presented in Figure 8.12). It defines the *Contractors* hypercube item. In the definition linkbase, the hypercube links from the abstract *Trade receivables and liabilities* item via an *all* arcrole and to the dimension item using an arc with the *hypercube-dimension* arcrole. We present this in Code example 8.7. The arc with the *all* arcrole contains *xbrldt:contextElement* attribute indicating *xbrli:segment* element as a container of dimensional information in an instance document.

Instance document

Instead of choosing from predefined list of domain members of a dimension, as is the case with explicit dimensions, enumerations' values of breakdowns of typed dimensions are defined by the instance document creator. The creator may be an individual or a computer application. These values must be created according to the structure of a typed domain, which may be complex (e.g. contain other elements and restrictions on their content) or simple as in this example.

Code example 8.7 presents an example of a context definition with typed dimension and a fact referring to it. The *xbrldi:typedMember* element appears on *xbrli:segment* container of a context, points by *dimension* attribute to the *Code of contractor* typed dimension via its *QName* and contains the typed domain instantiation as a value. Content of the typed domain is validated according to the restrictions defined in the appropriate schema file (*DY*).

[102] Because in this example typed domain is defined in the same file as typed dimension, file name is not included in the reference. If it was defined in a different file (e.g. *typedDomains.xsd*) value of the *xbrldt:typedDomainRef* would be *typedDomains.xsd#td_ContractorCode* (where *td_ContractorCode* is a value of *id* attribute of a typed domain definition element).

```
<xbrli:context id="End2007_ABC1234">
    <xbrli:entity>
        <xbrli:identifier
scheme="http://www.stockexchange.com/ticker">ACME</xbrli:id
entifier>
        &lt;xbrli:segment&gt;
            <xbrldi:typedMember
dimension="dy:CodeOfContractor">

<dy:ContractorCode>ABC1234</dy:ContractorCode>
            </xbrldi:typedMember>
        &lt;/xbrli:segment&gt;
    </xbrli:entity>
    <xbrli:period>
        <xbrli:instant>2007-12-31</xbrli:instant>
    </xbrli:period>
</xbrli:context>

<py:TradeReceivables decimals="0"
contextRef="End2007_ABC1234"
unitRef="USD">100</py:TradeReceivables>
```

Code example 8.7: Example of context definition with typed dimension and a fact referring to it

8.2.2 Dimension default example

Dimensions can be assigned default values from the set of their domain members. Usually, the dimension default is used when a breakdown has a logical top-level concept being simultaneously an aggregator of all enumerations of a breakdown (a total of all domain members). According to section 2.7 of the XBRL Dimensions 1.0 specification, each dimension can have only *one* default member which is set globally. For some dimensions a concept of a default value is not applicable. It happens in particular when a dimension breakdown consists of alternatives such as *solo/consolidated, audited/unaudited.* In some cases, however, it is logical to embed in the taxonomy information that, for example, audited consolidated data is default if not explicitly restated in an instance document.

Taxonomy

The following description of application of dimension default domain member is based on the slightly modified example we used to explain explicit dimensions. We present the appropriate data model in Figure 8.14.

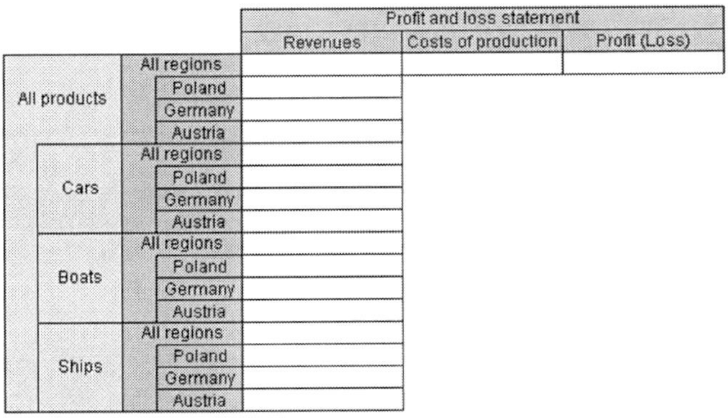

Fig. 8.14: Data model for the dimension default example

As we indicate in Figure 8.14, only *Revenues* are meant to be reported with dimensional context for the entire *Geographical and by products* breakdown, while information on *Costs of production* and *Profit (Loss)* is necessary only for *All products* and *All regions*.

In this case, the taxonomy developer could either create an additional hypercube excluding combinations of each country and each product for both measures *Costs of production* and *Profit (Loss)* or define default values for dimensions in form of their top level domain members.

Figure 8.15 presents a diagram of the example taxonomy. It is similar to the explicit dimensions example in terms of modularization and content. The main difference is that *Geographical and by products breakdown* hypercube is attached to *Revenues* primary item (and not to *Profit and loss statement* abstract) and there are no exclusions defined as they do not appear in the data model presented in Figure 8.14.

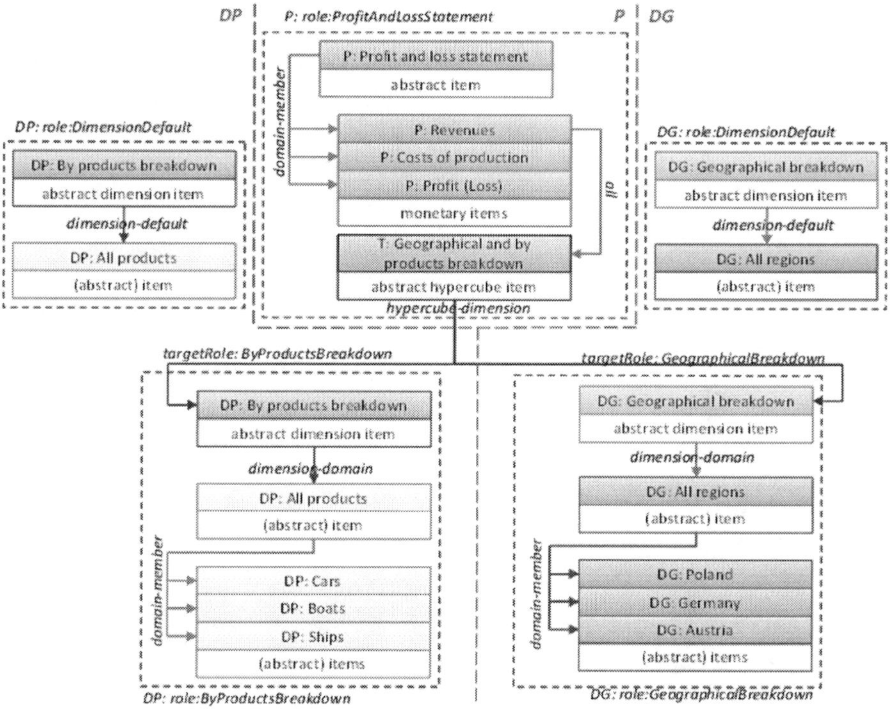

Fig. 8.15: Graphical diagram of dimension default example

In comparison to the explicit dimensions example we add two relations in each of the dimensions taxonomies. As we indicate in Figure 8.15, the default domain members link to the dimension items via arc with a *dimension-default* arcrole. We present the code for this situation in Code example 8.8.

```
Fragment of the definition linkbase of the geographical
breakdown dimensional taxonomy:

<link:roleRef
roleURI="http://dimensiondefault.example/r/role/DimensionDe
fault" xlink:type="simple"
xlink:href="r.xsd#DimensionDefault"/>

<link:definitionLink xlink:type="extended"
xlink:role="http://dimensiondefault.example/r/role/Dimensio
nDefault">

<link:loc xlink:type="locator"
xlink:href="dg.xsd#dg_GeographicalBreakdown"
xlink:label="GeographicalBreakdown"/>

<link:loc xlink:type="locator"
xlink:href="dg.xsd#dg_AllRegions"
xlink:label="AllRegions"/>

<link:definitionArc xlink:type="arc"
xlink:arcrole="http://xbrl.org/int/dim/arcrole/dimension-
default" xlink:from="GeographicalBreakdown"
xlink:to="AllRegions" order="1.0"/>

</link:definitionLink>

Fragment of the definition linkbase of the by products
breakdown dimensional taxonomy:

<link:roleRef
roleURI="http://dimensiondefault.example/r/role/DimensionDe
fault" xlink:type="simple"
xlink:href="r.xsd#DimensionDefault"/>

<link:definitionLink xlink:type="extended"
xlink:role="http://dimensiondefault.example/r/role/Dimensio
nDefault">

<link:loc xlink:type="locator"
xlink:href="dp.xsd#dp_ByProductsBreakdown"
xlink:label="ByProductsBreakdown"/>

<link:loc xlink:type="locator"
```

```
xlink:href="dp.xsd#dp_AllProducts"
xlink:label="AllProducts"/>

<link:definitionArc xlink:type="arc"
xlink:arcrole="http://xbrl.org/int/dim/arcrole/dimension-
default" xlink:from="ByProductsBreakdown"
xlink:to="AllProducts" order="1.0"/>

</link:definitionLink>
```

Code example 8.8: Fragments of code from definition linkbases of dimensions taxonomies illustrating indication of default domain members for dimensions

As we discussed, the definition linkbases of both dimensional taxonomies employ the same custom extended link role that we define in a separate schema file. This allows us to reuse information about dimension defaults[103].

Instance document

The major consequence of a dimension having a default member is that this information must not appear in contexts in instance documents. In other words, the XBRL processor assumes that every context without any information on the particular dimension contains a default value of that dimension[104]. Referring to the example, the *clean* context (i.e. without *xbrli:segment* and *xbrli:scenario* subconcepts) is automatically interpreted as a context representing *All products* value of the *By products breakdown* and *All regions* enumeration of *Geographical breakdown*. Furthermore, information about these members of dimensions does not appear in contexts even in combination with other dimensions.

In other words, in this example the lines of code:

- *<xbrldi:explicitMember dimension="dg:GeographicalBreakdown"> dg:AllRegions</xbrldi:explicitMember>*
- *<xbrldi:explicitMember dimension="dp:ByProductsBreakdown"> dp:AllProducts</xbrldi:explicitMember>*

are not allowed with regard to the appropriate (indicated by *xbrldt:contextElement* attribute) context container.

[103] Other solution could be to define these relations in the standard extended link role, custom roles created for this purpose in each of the dimensional taxonomies or the same roles that are used to store information about the entire breakdowns of dimensions.

[104] At the moment of writing this book there is a strong discussion on the mailing list of the base specifications maintenance working groups whether the globally defined dimension default value applies to all measures or only these to which the dimension (that has a default member) is assigned by any hypercube or for these hypercubes that do not implicitly or explicitly exclude this dimension. In our example the first interpretation applies.
This issue is crucial especially as the information on a dimension default member must not appear in instance documents.

Figure 8.16 summarizes the allowed content of a context's dimensional containers for instance documents based on a taxonomy with and without a definition of a default dimension member.

		Without default dimensions		With default dimensions	
		By products breakdown:	*Geographical breakdown:*	*By products breakdown:*	*Geographical breakdown:*
All products	All regions	*All products*	*All regions*		
	Poland	*All products*	*Poland*		*Poland*
	Germany	*All products*	*Germany*		*Germany*
	Austria	*All products*	*Austria*		*Austria*
Cars	All regions	*Cars*	*All regions*	*Cars*	
	Poland	*Cars*	*Poland*	*Cars*	*Poland*
	Germany	*Cars*	*Germany*	*Cars*	*Germany*
	Austria	*Cars*	*Austria*	*Cars*	*Austria*
Boats	All regions	*Boats*	*All regions*	*Boats*	
	Poland	*Boats*	*Poland*	*Boats*	*Poland*
	Germany	*Boats*	*Germany*	*Boats*	*Germany*
	Austria	*Boats*	*Austria*	*Boats*	*Austria*
Ships	All regions	*Ships*	*All regions*	*Ships*	
	Poland	*Ships*	*Poland*	*Ships*	*Poland*
	Germany	*Ships*	*Germany*	*Ships*	*Germany*
	Austria	*Ships*	*Austria*	*Ships*	*Austria*

Fig. 8.16: Content of context's dimensional container in instance document based on a taxonomy without and with default dimension members definitions

Definition of a default dimension member is a sensible solution in taxonomy design. In our example, it is clear that the amounts of *Revenues*, *Assets* etc. reported in the context with no dimensional information is applicable to all of the *All regions*, *All products*, *All clients,* etc. breakdowns.

Because of the treatment of *clean* contexts as dimensional, the definition of default dimension members increases the feasibility of implementing calculation linkbase based rules. In this example, we can define mathematical expressions between *Revenues*, *Costs of production* and *Profit (Loss)* measures and other measures defined in the base, non-dimensional context.

8.2.3 Empty hypercubes and empty dimensions

This section of the chapter addresses the presentation and explanation of use of two constructs that improve XBRL validation of instance documents against dimensional taxonomies: empty hypercubes and empty dimensions. These constructs apply especially in closed reporting by disallowing redundant data. We typically see closed reporting in a variety of regulatory environments, where the regulator wishes to receive data with a high degree of reliability and may not need a great deal of extensibility from the organizations submitting fillings. Use cases covered by empty dimensions and empty hypercubes include:

- signaling of reportable and non-reportable items or;
- indicating items that are meant to be reported only/also in base (non-dimensional) context.

Before presenting an example, we provide a short introduction and explanation of key issues.

Background

Under the XBRL 2.1 specification, an instance document can include facts reported for every non-abstract concept defined in any of the schema files that participate in the DTS. Moreover, as we discuss in the introduction to the chapter, an fact can reference many contexts which *xbrli:segment* or *xbrli:scenario* containers cannot be restricted with regard to their content. This may result in instance documents reporting redundant (facts that are not meant to be reported at all) or inappropriate (facts referring to unrequested context) data.

According to best practices for the creation of XBRL taxonomies, all facts that may appear in instance documents should participate in networks of relations that taxonomies define. Before the introduction of dimensions within the XBRL family of standards, it was appropriate that a presentation linkbase includes the representation for all these reportable items. For example, the *Assets* item typically appeared in a *BalanceSheet* extended link. When an entity reports a balance sheet, they draw on this link. The development of dimensions in taxonomies changes this best practice. The treatment of reportable items splits between the presentation and definition linkbases[105] and not only presentation linkbase Also a number of taxonomies decide to use definition linkbase only without considering presentation linkbase at all. There are two situations when a discoverable concept (i.e. a concept defined in one of schema files that constitutes the DTS) participates in neither presentation nor definition linkbase relationships.

First, it can arise because of extension of an *external taxonomy* and the use of only a part of concepts that it defines. For example, the FINREP taxonomy supports regulatory reporting for financial institutions. The FINREP taxonomy is an extension of the IFRS taxonomy (version 2006). However, this particular regulatory reporting requires only a subset of the base IFRS taxonomy. There are over 4,000 concepts in the base taxonomy, which represent the complete *Bound Volume* version of the IFRS standards. FINREP has only some 400 of these concepts in scope. As a result, all the other concepts (approximately 3,600) can be assigned values in instance documents prepared by reporting entities according to the FINREP taxonomy notwithstanding that they are not required and do not take part in relations reflecting FINREP data model.

A similar situation appears when a taxonomy is *modularized* with separate schema files defining common concepts. These sets of shared definitions are usually broad and fit many areas. Therefore, each taxonomy that imports common items schema files uses only some of their content depending on necessity. For example, COREP modularization structure consists of three common primary

[105] Generic link specifications allows for further custom extension of forms in which reportable elements are indicated in taxonomies.

taxonomies that define items shared by some eighteen templates that reflect different logical parts of underlying data model.

Both situations that we describe above that use external taxonomies and modularized taxonomies may result in items being in schema files but not in use in either the presentation or definition linkbases that mirror the data model. According to the XBRL specification, and as enforced in XBRL validators[106], these concepts may be in instance documents.

The second use case relates to reporting items in inappropriate or not required contexts. The solution to these issues is in the XBRL Dimensions 1.0 specification. The specification allows the taxonomy architect to define restrictions on the content of *xbrli:segment* and *xbrli:scenario* containers. In order to provide full information on demand of a taxonomy developer regarding context content that each item can refer to, every concept in an instance document must relate to a hypercube. This applies even though, as we describe in the following example, some hypercubes are, by design, left empty.

Example

This example explains when and how to use empty hypercubes and empty dimensions. The data model for the example taxonomy is presented on Fig. 8.17:.

Base taxonomy:

Balance Sheet

Balance Sheet	
Assets	
Non Current Assets	
Current Assets	
Equity	
Liabilities	

Extension taxonomy:

Balance Sheet

Balance Sheet	
Assets	
Non Current Assets	
Current Assets	
Equity and Liabilities	

Information on Assets in Largest Subsidiaries

	Largest subsidiary	Second largest subsidiary
Assets		
Non Current Assets		
Current Assets		

Fig. 8.17: Data model for empty hypercube and empty dimension example

[106] It is possible to include additional rules in a validator that would reject an instance document containing too much data but this is performed either using formula linkbase or supplementary (not a base) XBRL validation.

8.2.4 Base taxonomy

We assume in this example the use of an external taxonomy. This base taxonomy (prefixed in this example as *EPB*) reflects a simple Balance Sheet that consists of *Assets*, *Non Current Assets*, *Current Assets*, *Equity* and *Liabilities*. The relations between these items come in the extended link role with id *BalanceSheet* in the presentation linkbase. As with most of the taxonomies that are meant to be extensible and reusable as a whole or in parts (such as IFRS or US GAAP), this taxonomy defines no restrictions on both reportable and non-reportable items or on the content of additional contextual data containers.

Extension taxonomy

Extension primary taxonomy (prefixed in this example *EPE*) imports the base taxonomy. According to the data model presented on Fig. 8.17, the concepts of the Balance Sheet inherited from the base taxonomy need to be modified so that *Equity* and *Liabilities* are replaced with one *Equity and Liabilities* item. In order to implement the required changes, arcs pointing from the *Balance Sheet* abstract item to the *Equity* and *Liabilities* are prohibited. At the same time, we define another monetary item, a new *Equity and Liabilities* concept. We link this in an extended link with the role id *BalanceSheet* in the presentation linkbase to the *Balance Sheet* abstract item. We present the presentation linkbases of the base and the extension primary taxonomies in Figure 8.18.

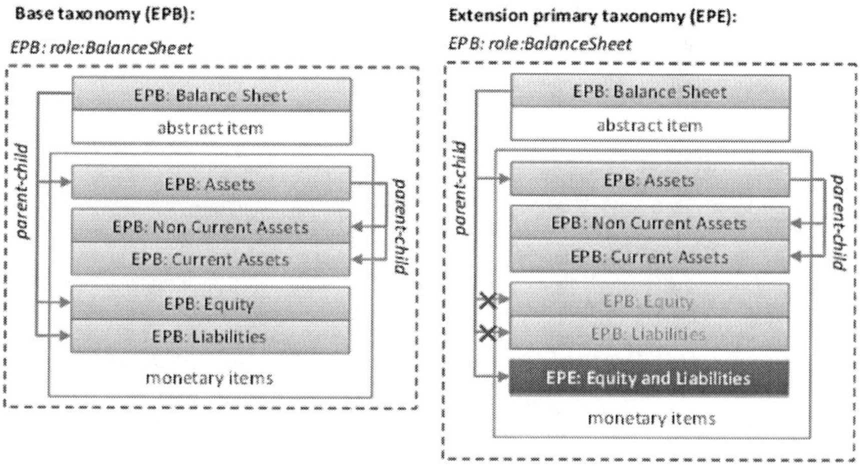

Fig. 8.18: Presentation linkbases of base and extension primary taxonomies

Additionally, the extension taxonomy data model requires creation of a dimensional table to disclose information on *Assets*, *Non Current Assets* and *Current Assets* in two largest subsidiaries. For this purpose, the extension primary taxonomy defines the extended link role with id *InformationOnAssetsInSubsidiares*. We use this extended link role in the definition linkbase to link *Assets* to *Non Current Assets* and to *Current Assets* using arcs with *domain-member* arcrole.

The next step involves creation of a separate dimensional taxonomy (prefixed in this example *EPES*) that defines the *Subsidiaries Breakdown* dimension item and its two domain members *Largest Subsidiary* and *Second Largest Subsidiary*. We construct the *dimension-domain* relations between the dimension item and its domain members in the definition linkbase inside the extended link role of *SubsidiariesBreakdown* id.

Finally, a template taxonomy (prefixed in this example *ETE*) imports extension primary taxonomy and dimensional taxonomy, defines a hypercube *Subsidiaries Information*. We link it in the *InformationOnAssetsInSubsidiares* extended link role from *Assets* measure using arc with *all* arcrole containing the *xbrldt:contextElement* attribute indicating *xbrli:segment* as a dimensional information container. Later, the hypercube is connected to the *Subsidiaries Breakdown* dimension item via arc with *hypercube-dimension* arcrole. The *xbrldt:targetRole* attribute on this arc refers to the extended link roleURI of *SubsidiariesBreakdown* id defined in the dimensional taxonomy.

We present the structure and content of the definition linkbases' results from the steps described above in Figure 8.19.

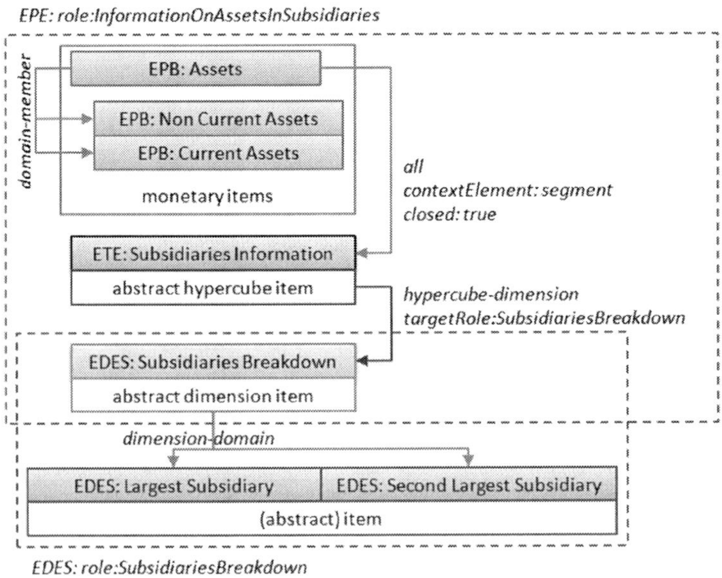

Fig. 8.19: Structure of the definition linkbases content reflecting dimensional table from data model for empty hypercubes and empty dimensions example

Non-reportable concepts – empty dimensions

As we discuss in the introduction to this section of the chapter, one of the problems that taxonomy developers must deal with when constructing extension or modularized taxonomies are concepts that are in the schema files of DTSs but that do not participate in relationship linkbases. In some reporting environments, this may allow reported facts in instance documents that the developer does not desire to see reported.

In this example, the base taxonomy contains definitions of *Equity* and *Liabilities* monetary items. Because of modification of the taxonomy to match the extension taxonomy data model a single *Equity and Liabilities* item replaces the two items. In order to prevent unwanted items from being reported, taxonomy developer can use the empty dimension construction.

To explain the idea of empty hypercubes and empty dimensions in this example, we create an additional dimensional taxonomy. This approach is in line with assumed modularization of dimensional taxonomies. This modularization increases reusability and decreases redundancy[107]. Therefore, an additional dimensional taxonomy (prefixed in this example *EDEH*) defines a common structure reused for indication of non-reportable items. It consists of an extended link role with id *NonReportable*, an abstract concept *Non reportable*, a hypercube *Empty Dimension Hypercube* and a dimension item *Empty Dimension.* In the definition linkbase, inside extended link role with id *NonReportable*, *Empty Dimension Hypercube* connects via an arc with *all* arcrole to the abstract *Non Reportable* item and refers to *Empty Dimension* using arc with *hypercube-dimension* arcrole.

In order to indicate items that the taxonomy creator does not wish to report, *Equity* and *Liabilities* link via arc with a *domain-member* arcrole to the *Non Reportable* abstract in the *NonReportable* extended link role in the definition linkbase of the template taxonomy. We present this in Figure 8.20.

[107] In some cases it is more reasonable to indicate non-reportable and reportable with base context items in custom extended link roles for each of the templates.

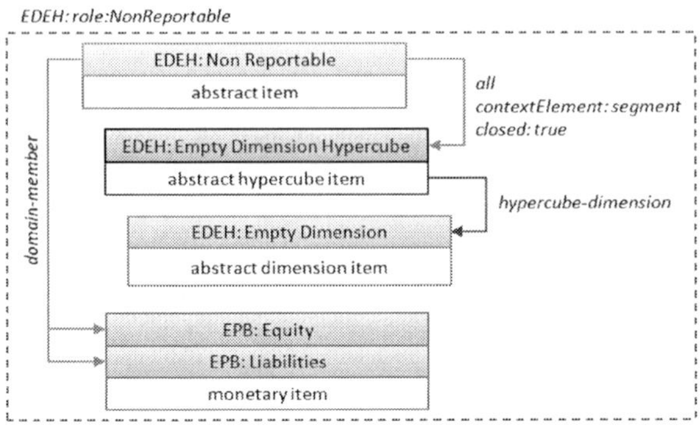

Fig. 8.20: Indication of non-reportable items

Because of the procedure described above, there will be no occurrence of the *Equity* and *Liabilities* item in instance documents, as it is impossible to create a valid context to which they can refer.

According to the XBRL Dimensions 1.0 specification, the *xbrldi:explicitMember* element is an XML element whose content must be a *QName* (qualified name) of a domain member of a dimension item indicated by *dimension* attribute. Because the example taxonomy does not provide any breakdown for *Empty Dimension*, there is no content for *xbrldi:explicitMember* element. We present this situation in Code example 8.9 as a validation error.

```
<xbrli:context id="End2007_EmptyDimension">
 <xbrli:entity>
   <xbrli:identifier
scheme="http://www.stockexchange.com/ticker">ACME</xbrli:id
entifier>
   &lt;xbrli:segment&gt;
   <xbrldi:explicitMember
dimension="edeh:EmptyDimension"></xbrldi:explicitMember>
   &lt;/xbrli:segment&gt;
 </xbrli:entity>
 <xbrli:period>
  <xbrli:instant>2007-12-31</xbrli:instant>
 </xbrli:period>
</xbrli:context>

<epb:Equity decimals="0"
contextRef="End2007_EmptyDimension"
unitRef="USD">10000</epb:Equity>

<epb:Liabilities decimals="0"
contextRef="End2007_EmptyDimension"
unitRef="USD">20000</epb:Liabilities>
```
Code example 8.9: Disallowed empty content of *xbrldi:explicitMember* element

In this example, validation of context reference from *Equity* and *Liabilities* items in instance document is performed only with regard to the *Empty Dimension Hypercube* as it is the only hypercube and dimensional information defined for these two concepts. Values of *xbrldt:contextElement* and *xbrldt:closed* attributes on the arc with *all* arcrole are meaningless as the concept of empty dimension is enough to effectively prevent items from being reported.

Items reportable in base context – Empty hypercube

When developing taxonomies where some items come with dimensional information and some not, there is a strong need to indicate those concepts that should build from a base context. This is for at least three reasons.

Firstly, navigation in dimensional taxonomies and discovery of reportable tables is complicated. The data model is reflected partly in presentation and partly in definition linkbases. Internationally accepted best practices for dimensional taxonomies do not yet exist. This results in taxonomies being incompatible with each other, hard to understand in relation to data model and containing redundant information. Despite of that, it is generally possible to locate and explore reportable structures by looking for non-abstract items in presentation linkbase and extended link roles which contain at least one *all* arcrole in the definition linkbase. In general, presentation linkbase becomes obsolete as *parent-child* relations can be easily replaced with *domain-member* hierarchical structures in the definition linkbase[108]. In that case, it is useful to indicate which items from the definition linkbase are meant to be reported only in the base (non-dimensional) context.

Secondly, providing all items in a taxonomy with dimensional information (even if it is only to say that there is no dimensional information for a particular item) results in an increase of validation level and higher quality of instance documents in terms of their content matching exact requirements of taxonomy developers. The indication that some items are not meant to be reported with additional contextual information prevents reporting entities from doing so.

The third reason is a consequence of XBRL dimensions logic. This applies to concepts that can be in a report with base and dimensional context at the same time. In this example, at least two of these reasons justify application of empty hypercubes.

As we present in the data model in Figure 8.25, *Assets*, *Non Current Assets* and *Current Assets* measures are meant to be reported in base context according to the content of extended link role with id *BalanceSheet* in presentation linkbase and in dimensional context for *Subsidiaries Breakdown* defined in *InformationOnAssetsInSubsidiaries* extended link role in definition linkbase.

[108] One important characteristic that is missing in definition linkbase is *preferredLabel* attribute which according to XBRL 2.1 specification can be used on arcs with *parent-child* arcrole in presentation linkbase increasing its functionality for example by allowing to build tables of movements and display different period start (beginning balance) and period end (ending balance) labels.

Leaving the taxonomy content limited only to structures presented in Figure 8.18 and Figure 8.19, would not allow the instance document to report *Assets*, *Non Current Assets* and *Current Assets* in the base context, as these measures are assigned dimensional information which must be used in the *xbrli:segment* element[109].

A different situation relates to the *Equity and Liabilities* primary item, which is in use only in the *BalanceSheet* extended link role in the presentation linkbase. This item can be reported in the base context, as there is no dimensional information defined for it in the definition linkbase. Because of this, it can also be reported in any context including *Subsidiaries Breakdown* and whichever XML structure a reporting entity decides to use either on *xbrli:segment* or *xbrli:scenario* containers.

In order to resolve the two issues we describe above, we create an additional dimensional taxonomy for this example (*EDEH*) that contains a definition of an abstract item labeled *Adimensional* and two hypercube items *Empty Hypercube (Segment)* and *Empty Hypercube (Scenario)*. In the extended link role with id *Adimensional*, the hypercubes link to the abstract primary item using arcs with *all* arcrole but different values of the *xbrldt:contextElement* attribute: *segment* for *Empty Hypercube (Segment)* and *scenario* for *Empty Hypercube (Scenario)*. It is important that the value of *xbrldt:closed* attribute is in both cases set to *true* as otherwise empty hypercubes make it possible to report items in base context but do not prevent from reporting too much contextual data.

The next step is to link *Assets*, *Non Current Assets*, *Current Assets* and *Equity and Liabilities* using arcs with *domain-member* arcrole to the *Adimensional* abstract item, which takes place in the definition linkbase of the template taxonomy. We graphically present the procedure we describe above in Figure 8.21.

[109] Other solution to enable reporting items with dimensional information in base context is assigning every dimension with a default domain member, but as presented in this example, it is not always reasonable as some dimension have breakdowns without a logical aggregator, common top level element or assumed standard value.

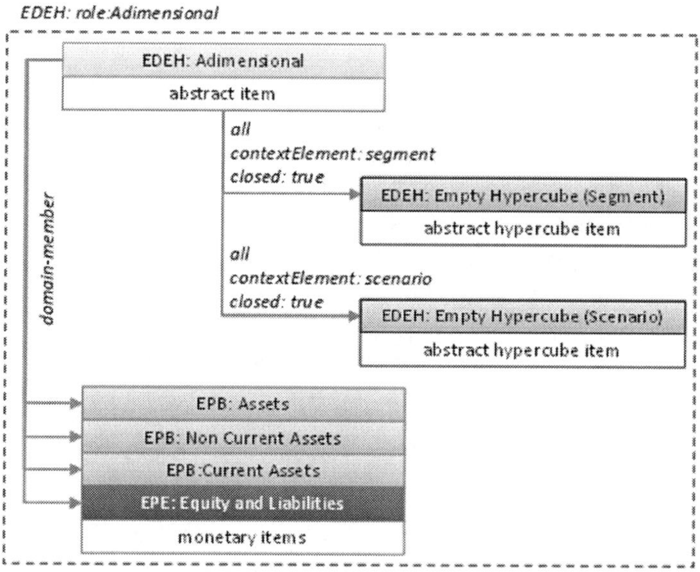

Fig. 8.21: Indication of items reportable in base context

Empty hypercube suggests XBRL validators, that one of the dimensional information containers indicated on *xbrldt:contextElement* attribute must have empty content and therefore must not appear[110]. Because there are two additional contextual information containers: *xbrli:segment* and *xbrli:scenario* it is crucial to prohibit *both*.

To sum up, the empty dimension prevents unwanted items from reporting while the empty hypercube indicates which items are meant to be reported only/also with the base (non-dimensional) context. This simplifies our understanding of a taxonomy in relation to its data model and improves alignment of the reports with requirements of taxonomy developers.

[110] According to XBRL 2.1 specification elements *xbrli:scenario* and *xbrli:segment* if appearing in instance document must not be empty.

8.3 Summary

- Primary taxonomy contains definitions of measures and their relationships.
- Dimensions/domain-member taxonomies define dimension items and their domains (members and their hierarchical structures).
- Template taxonomy which imports applicable primary and dimensions/domain-member taxonomies, defines hypercubes and uses dimensional arcroles to indicate existence of appropriate relations.
- *xbrldt:targetRole* attributes on arcs allow for reuse of predefined structures and breakdowns
- Dimensions can be assigned default values from the set of their domain members.
- Empty hypercubes and empty dimensions are mechanisms for improving XBRL validation of instance documents for closed reporting cycles.

8.4 Key terms you should know

- Modularization
- Primary taxonomy
- Domain member taxonomy
- Template taxonomy
- targetRole attribute
- Exclusions
- Closed hypercubes
- Dimension default
- Empty hypercubes
- Empty dimensions

8.5 Case analysis

As we indicate at the beginning of this chapter, European taxonomies for solvency and financial reporting of credit institutions were the test field for development and implementation of dimensions. By now, the COREP taxonomy is seen as one of the most complex applications of this relatively new technology.[111]

In general, COREP and FINREP taxonomies (referred to jointly as COFINREP) create a framework for the Committee of European Banking Supervisors (CEBS). These taxonomies concern, respectively, the reporting of the solvency data for credit institutions and investment firms, and establishing standardized financial reporting guidelines for credit institutions in the EU.

The main reason for use of XBRL as a standard to reflect COREP and FINREP data in electronic format stems from business requirements of the Capital Reporting Directive (CDR) of the CEBS. These guidelines provide flexibility to extend the scope of required data by national supervisors while at the same time preserving consistency and facilitating data exchange at the European level. This standardization should improve once the XBRL Formulas and Functions specifications become recommendations. Such recommendations should allow advanced business rules in taxonomies.

Although we treat these two taxonomies as one framework and given that they use the same dialect of XML, COREP and FINREP taxonomies are technically different in many ways. These differences result from regulations that are basis for each part of the framework – the use case. The COREP taxonomy reflects the international standard for monitoring of financial institutions. The Basel II Pillar I regulations relate to the capital requirements and encompass credit, operational and market risk. As there may be assessment of credit risk that uses standardized and internal ratings-based approaches, all the aspects of monitoring are included in XBRL taxonomies. The reporting requirements are set out in the 2006/48/EU and 2006/49/EU Directives.

[111] More information on COREP and FINREP can be obtained from www.corep.info or www.finrep.info websites.

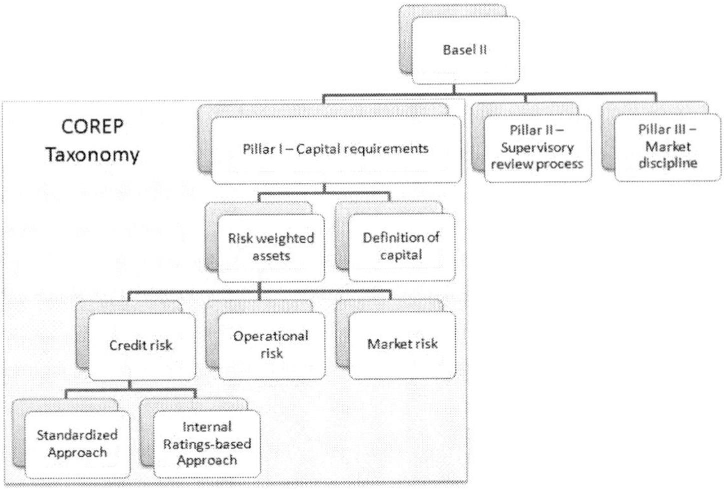

Fig. 8.22: COREP taxonomy framework in relation to Basel II requirements

In opposite to the regulations that drive the design of the COREP taxonomy, the business case behind FINREP builds on financial reporting by financial institutions within the ambit of the International Financial Reporting Standards. The International Accounting Standards Committee Foundation has a pre-existing taxonomy for IFRS. A decision was to use and then extend the IFRS taxonomy to meet the reporting requirements of financial institutions. There were clear apparent advantages arising from employment of an established foundation. Unfortunately for the FINREP taxonomy developers the IFRS taxonomy, at least in the relevant 2006 version, is not dimensional.

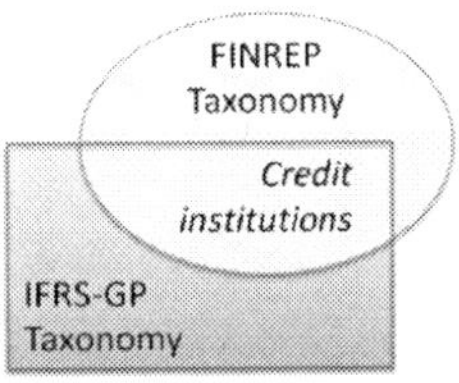

Fig. 8.23: FINREP taxonomy in relation to IFRS

Maximizing the use of the IFRS made it impossible to create similar data models for COREP and FINREP. The first taxonomy is highly dimensional. Measures and dimensions are clearly set out in the data model. The final version of the taxonomy reflects this data model. We present this in Figure 8.24.

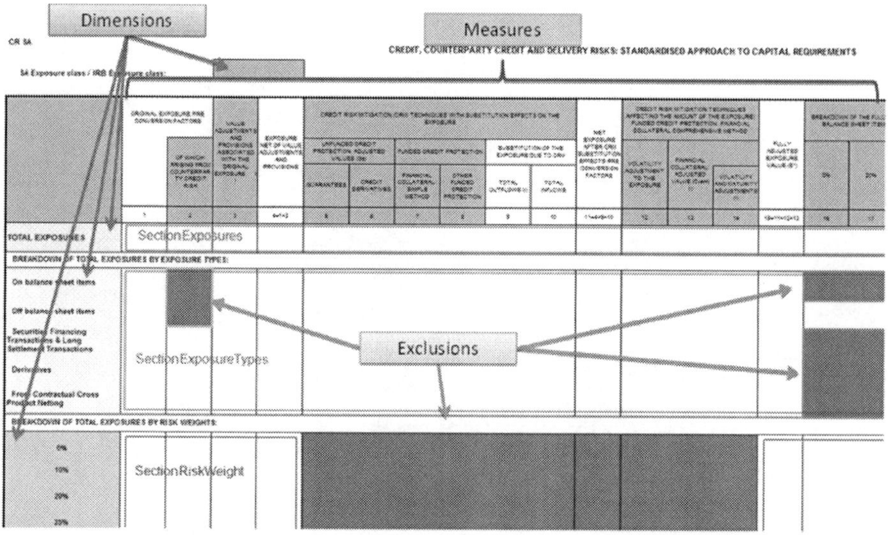

Fig. 8.24: Example of the data model of the COREP taxonomy

The COREP taxonomy is also highly modularized. Each of eighteen templates has its own primary taxonomy. Additionally three common primary taxonomies are ready for reuse depending on the type of risk assessed.

Due to its dependence on IFRS, FINREP does not employ dimensions as widely. We present an example of the FINREP data model in Figure 8.24. It also has a lower level of modularization. There are only two *sacks* of concepts definitions: one (schema file) imported from IFRS and the other concepts to reflect specific needs of credit institutions' reports.

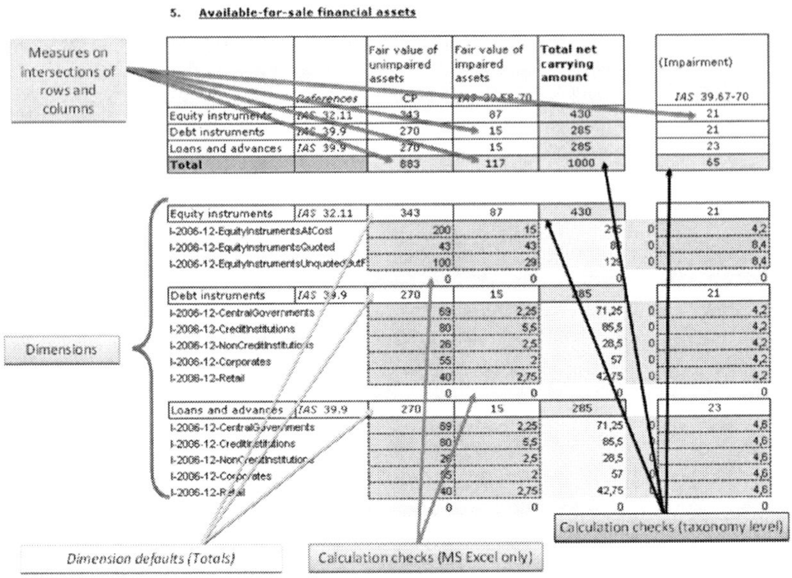

Fig. 8.25: Example of data model of FINREP taxonomy

The first versions of the FINREP taxonomy were monolithic. Subsequently there was a decision to modularize it at the relationships level. A separate taxonomy represents each set of tables distinguished in the data model. This results in some 40 templates.

As we present in the XBRL Dimensions architecture and terminology section of this chapter, multidimensionality of COREP and FINREP taxonomies relates to treating business concepts such as *Assets*, *Profit*, *Loans*, etc. as measures and the breakdowns in which they may be reported as dimensions. The COREP taxonomies employs twelve explicit and nine typed dimensions, of which two are complex FINREP uses ten explicit and two typed dimensions. The maximum number of dimensions attached to one hypercube amounts to four in COREP and three in FINREP. The COREP Taxonomy (version 1.2.4) defines some 386 concepts (310 excluding abstracts). A full report in an instance document is estimated to consist of 12,000 records for the Standardized Approach and 15,000 for internal ratings based approach. These correspond respectively to 1,200 and 1,500 different combinations of dimensions. The FINREP taxonomy (version 1.3) defines 1,727 concepts and employs 381 IFRS concepts. There are 1,911 non-abstract measures in the presentation and definition linkbases Some 364 of these come from IFRS. Although much more extensive than COREP in terms of the number of primary items defined, the estimated maximal number of records in a FINREP instance document is less than 3000. There are approximately 100 combinations of dimensions. Both taxonomies use advanced dimensional constructs (i.e. empty hypercubes and hypercubes with empty dimensions) to improve XBRL validation.

9 Introduction to Latest XBRL Technologies

XBRL is rapidly becoming an integral part of the world's business reporting framework. This development in a very short period of time is a testament to the hard work of all of those involved with XBRL International—in most cases, volunteers who had a vision of the benefits of the convergence of technology and business reporting.
[Chairman of the Trustees of the IASC Foundation, Gerrit Zalm, at 17th XBRL International Conference, Eindhoven]

Opening Vignette: XBRL Technologies[112]

There are some significant conceptual questions about the future roadmap for the XBRL standards themselves, and how they will evolve. In addition to the core XBRL specification, there are a number of supplemental modules on various development tracks; these include specifications for versioning, dimensions, formulas and functions. These developments in turn will impact future taxonomy efforts, and the creation of XBRL enabled software. The market needs clear information about the future development of the XBRL specifications, so that decision makers and developers can make the right investments to support these future capabilities.

The development of a standard is an evolving process. With an increasing number of XBRL implementations worldwide, adopters discover issues, identify new requirements, develop common practices and often devise new solutions to existing problems. All these findings may be subsequently incorporated into the XBRL standard or assist in its broader acceptance.

The first implementers of the XBRL standard pointed to the need to address three areas related to the validation of data and maintenance of XBRL projects:

- Allowing advanced formulas and business rules to be included in the taxonomy and processed by respective software;
- Supporting versioning of XBRL taxonomies;
- Allowing rendering of data encoded with XBRL.

The primary drivers for introduction of the Formula linkbase was the business requirement to disclose calculations and *advanced business rules*. These were either not supported or were directly prohibited by the XBRL 2.1 specification. For example, the XBRL specification allows calculation relationships to be set out in the calculation linkbase. However, the functionality of this linkbase does not allow the representation of calculations between concepts in two different period natures. In other words, the Specification does not allow addition of a concept

[112] Excerpted from R. Corey Booth, "Speech by SEC Staff: Remarks Before the 13th XBRL International Conference" available at http://www.sec.gov/news/speech/2006/spch051606rcb.htm.

reported at a moment in time with a concept reported for a period. This requirement is clear from the logical and mathematical perspective but in practice accountants and auditors often calculate between different period types. Support for business practice impacts the level of adoption of the standard and consequently the consortium considered enabling such calculations as important step forward.

The requirement for addressing *versioning* originated from changes in taxonomies that arise from amendments in underlying regulations or reporting standards. Since participants throughout the entire business reporting value chain use taxonomies, changes in taxonomies affect both their internal IT solutions (e.g. mapping from ERP/data warehouse to XBRL reports) and reporting procedures. The adopters of XBRL indicated that provision of a standardized, technical solution that describe the nature of changes between two versions of taxonomies would significantly foster adoption of the standard.

The primary requirement for addressing advance *rendering* of instance documents arose from limitations of the presentation linkbase. Particularly the inability to present in a standardized manner intersection tables (such as *Movements in Assets* or *Statement of Changes in Equity*) has driven the development of the rendering specification.

In this chapter, we introduce these three technologies. We describe some areas of their application. We only provide a relatively brief discussion of Versioning and Rendering technologies since their specifications are only available in *Working Draft* or *Candidate Recommendation* versions at the time of writing.

9.1 Introduction to XBRL Formulas[113]

Development of the Formulas specification came from the limitations of the original XBRL 2.1 specification. The document constrained the calculation linkbase relationships:

- Prohibited cross-context calculation (e.g. summation between stock and flow);
- Did not support taxonomic construction of advanced logical or mathematical rules.

There were design reasons for these limitations. For example, it is not appropriate to mix numeric values captured for *period* and *as of* dates. These limitations significantly limited implementation of XBRL taxonomies in important

[113] At the moment of writing, a Candidate Recommendation of the Formulas specification was published; therefore authors are aware that certain areas may change in the final public version of the specification. Readers are encouraged to follow the latest news on the www.xbrl.org for new publications.

information transfers. As we analyze the first constraint, we will draw on the following example.

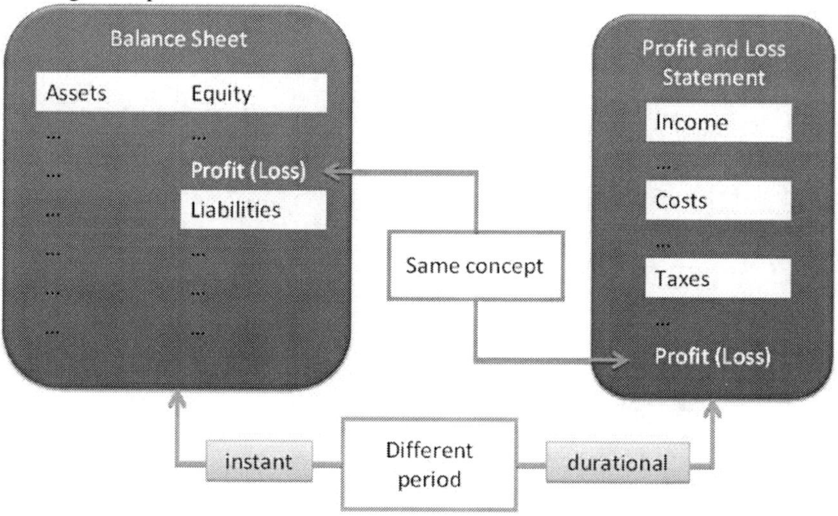

Fig. 9.1: Example of cross-context calculation

Advanced calculation

The IFRS XBRL taxonomy includes representations of the Balance Sheet and the Income Statement that we typically find in a corporation's annual report. These two statements make use of the same concept, viz: *Profit (Loss)*. However, in the *Balance Sheet* most items are of the *instant* reporting period nature (reported as of date). In the Income Statement, however, most items are of the *duration* reporting period nature (reported for a period).

The Income Statement describes *Profit (Loss)* as *duration* item. In the Balance Sheet, in the Equities section Profit (Loss) is calculated with other *Equities* items to derive the total value of *Equities*. These latter items are defined at an instant of time. Fig. 9.1 presents an example of a cross-context calculation, such as between the two statements we discuss in this section.

Before the Formulas specification, one of these calculation relationships (addition of Profit Loss to Equity or calculation of its value in the Income Statement) cannot be defined in an XBRL taxonomy. The current Candidate Recommendation of the Formulas specification allows cross-context calculation in the formulas linkbase.

We can see the second constraint in the following example. Advanced, logical business rules are a common part of contemporary digital reporting. Tax forms, for example, often embed logical expressions in the completion process. A common example here might be the following statement on the tax form presented in Fig. 9.2:

- If the value of the Income Tax is more than X please complete Section A

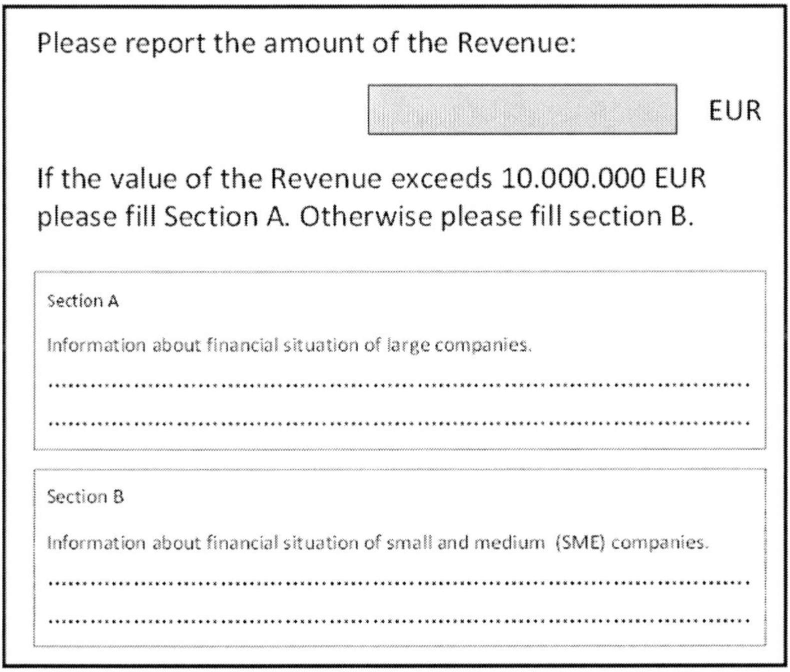

Fig. 9.2: Advanced business rule example

A standard XBRL calculation linkbase could not represent this condition. The prime reason was the restricted functionality of the calculation linkbase, which allowed only weighted calculation of the following nature:

- ParentConcept = +/- WeightA * ChildConceptA
  +/- WeightB * ChildConceptB ...

As a consequence, the calculation linkbase was not able to capture advanced expressions such as logical, conditional statements (if ... then). The current Candidate Recommendation allows defining logical relationships. Having described the background of the Formulas specification we will now focus on the general framework of the XBRL Formulas.

9.1.1 XBRL formulas framework

First, it is important to note that the Formulas linkbase makes use of the following technologies:

- XLink 1.0,
- XPath 2.0.

Development of the Formulas specification considers other XML-based technologies such as XQuery and Schematron.

XPath
A language designed to navigate and select the contents of the XML documents. XPath allows for selection of XML nodes and computation of values. The XBRL Formulas specification uses the XPath to define the formulae (an expression that should be evaluated).

XQuery
A language designed for querying collections of data stored in XML documents (reports). It supports queries on selected portions of data according to given criteria, extract them from the XML document and manipulate the extract to fit particular purposes. The selected extracts of data may comprise of values of XML tags, values of attributes, XML nodes and other information. The design of language is very similar to SQL, which is the most common database query language.

Schematron
A language to define rules that evaluate the existence of patterns in an XML document's tree. Assertions of presence or absence of various patterns of XML code structure allows for strong validation of XML document contents.

The following table presents a simplified glossary that should aid understanding the general framework. We encourage interested readers to analyze the Formulas specification in detail.

Tab. 9.1: Glossary of terms used in XBRL formulas

Term	Explanation
formula	A formula expresses a set of rules applied to variables. These rules result in a new XBRL fact. *Example:* *Assets = Equity + Liabilities (result stored in Balance concept as true or false)*
variable	A variable could be either a fact or a general variable. A fact variable refers to a single fact or a sequence of facts from an XBRL instance document assuming the given filters. *Example:* *$factVariable1 (to which filtering mechanism assigns a value of an XBRL fact from the instance document – e.g. a value of Assets for company ABC reported for the end of 2007)* A general variable can refer to a broader range of values. *Example:* *$generalVariable (to which the filtering mechanism assigns anything, which is not a fact – e.g. a value of a context or a unit)*
source	Source accompanies the formula to give information on the source of aspect rules from the target XBRL document. Source is used for matching aspects of formula outcome with variables aspects. Source attribute is also used on other concepts to identify source of data applied in particular context. *Example:* *A formula can have one of the facts from the instance document assigned as its source. This fact works as a reference for the processor to evaluate any aspect, which is not explicitly stated in the filters (used by implicit filtering mechanism). This allows the preparer of a formulae to avoid time-consuming description of all aspects that should apply*

	while selecting a fact from the instance document. Rather than that, the processors uses source to assign default values of all aspects which "should be" processed automatically.
aspect	Aspects allow to refer to all information surrounding facts in the XBRL instance documents (e.g. entity, period, scenario, segment, units). A concept name is ultimately also one of the formulas aspects. Certain limitations exist concerning tuples. *Example:* *<formula:aspects>* *<formula:entityIdentifier value="'CompanyA'"/>* *</formula:aspects>* *The above declaration means that implicit filters will be assuming default value of entity equal to "CompanyA" while selecting facts from the instance documents to bind to variables.*
filter	Filters allow to select target facts from XBRL instance documents and bind them to fact variables or variable sets. *Example:* *<cf:conceptName* *xlink:type="resource"* *xlink:label="**conceptName**"* *<cf:concept>* *<cf:qname>**test:assets**</cf:qname>* *</cf:concept>* *</cf:conceptName>* *The above filter declaration selects the facts from the instance document which are reported using concept test:assets.*

Figure 9.3 presents a general application of XBRL formulas.

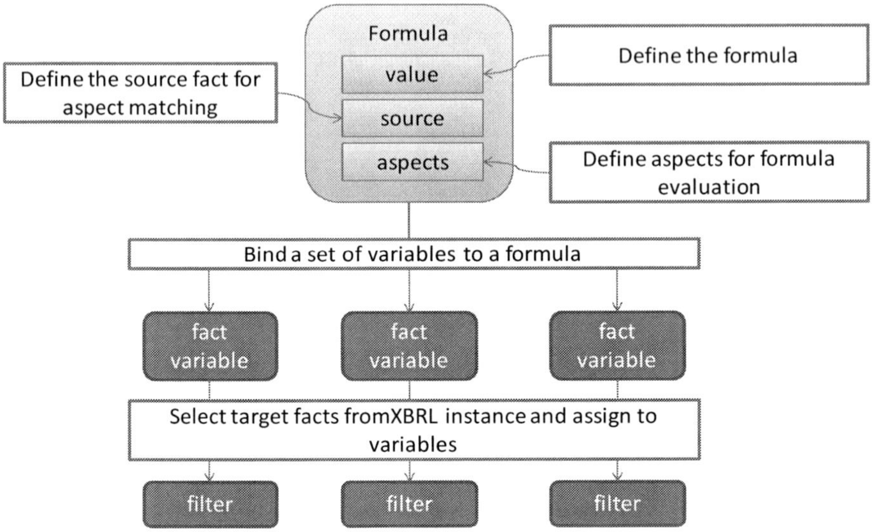

Fig. 9.3: General XBRL formula framework

In general, the formulas work as follows:

1. Filters select the fact (or group of facts) from the XBRL instance document.
    a. During selection of facts, filters evaluate the aspects (both: those defined explicitly and those used by implicit filtering mechanism).
    b. If implicit filters are in use during selection, implicit filters use the source on the formula to match facts for appropriate aspects.
2. Selected facts link to the variable. If during filtering multiple facts are selected, they can be bound as sequence of facts to the variable.
3. The formula is then evaluated. The XBRL Formulas – aware processor uses the XPath expression defined as the value of the formula and tests it by using facts selected for the variables.
4. The result is stored in the concept identified in the aspects section

We will now analyze an example of a simple formula coded according to the Formulas specification.

The exemplary formula shall base on the following concepts:

1. Assets (monetary, debit)
2. Liabilities (monetary, credit)
3. Equity (monetary, credit)
4. Balance (Boolean)

Type attribute indicates the type of values that can be assigned to the particular concept (types can be selected from the built-in XBRL types or defined by user). Examples of types include monetary, Boolean, string, data and other values.

Balance attribute – an attribute in use to indicate the accounting nature of the concept. According to the XBRL specification, balance can take two values: debit or credit. Following the basics of accounting, assets and costs are usually of a debit nature whereas liabilities, equity and income are usually of a credit nature. Some concepts from cash flow statement can have an ambiguous nature. The formula will check if:

$$Assets = Equity + Liabilities$$

The result of the formula check will be stored in the *Balance* concept, indicating true if data in the instance document match the formula or false if not. We present a graphical illustration of the above formula in Fig. 9.4.

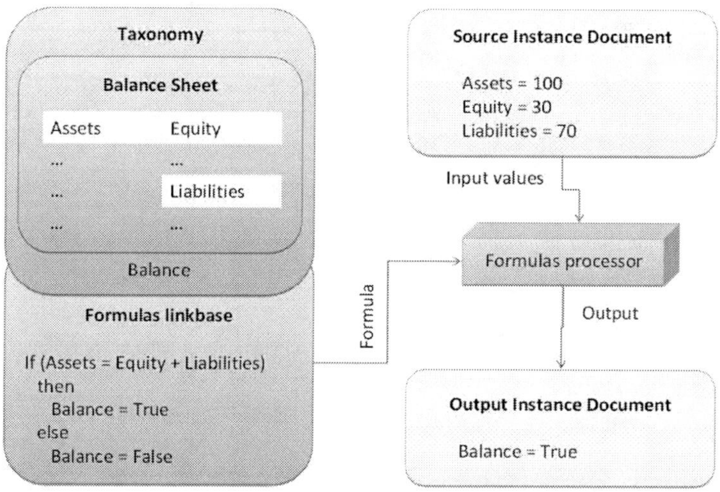

Fig. 9.4: Sample XBRL formula

The code example below presents the XBRL code of the formula presented in Fig. 9.4.

```
[declarations of formula specification prefixes and
namespaces]

xmlns:ca="http://xbrl.org/2008/assertion/consistency"
xmlns:ef="http://xbrl.org/2008/filter/entity"

[linkbase reference]
```

```
<xsd:import namespace="http://xbrl.org/2008/formula"
schemaLocation="http://www.xbrl.org/2008/formula.xsd"/>

[declarations of formula specifications files to be
imported]

<xsd:import
namespace="http://xbrl.org/2008/assertion/value"
schemaLocation="http://www.xbrl.org/2008/value-
assertion.xsd"/>

<xsd:element name="assets" id="sample_assets"
type="xbrli:monetaryItemType"
substitutionGroup="xbrli:item" nillable="true"
xbrli:balance="debit" xbrli:periodType="instant"/>
<xsd:element name="equity" id="sample_equity"
type="xbrli:monetaryItemType"
substitutionGroup="xbrli:item" nillable="true"
xbrli:balance="credit" xbrli:periodType="instant"/>
<xsd:element name="liabilities" id="sample_liabilities"
type="xbrli:monetaryItemType"
substitutionGroup="xbrli:item" nillable="true"
xbrli:balance="credit" xbrli:periodType="instant"/>
<xsd:element name="balance" id="sample_balance"
type="xbrli:booleanItemType" substitutionGroup="xbrli:item"
nillable="true" xbrli:periodType="instant"/>
</xsd:schema>
```

Code example 9.1: Formulas example - sample schema

The above example contains declaration of formulas specification schemas namespaces and import declarations for those schemas. The schema also defines three components and a single resulting concept of the formula.

We will now analyze the formulas linkbase containing definition of our formula. The linkbase is using the Generic linkbase declarations (generic arcs).

```
<link:arcroleRef
arcroleURI="http://xbrl.org/arcrole/2008/variable-filter"
xlink:type="simple"
xlink:href="http://www.xbrl.org/2008/variable.xsd#variable-
filter"/>

<link:arcroleRef
arcroleURI="http://xbrl.org/arcrole/2008/variable-set"
```

```
xlink:type="simple"
xlink:href="http://www.xbrl.org/2008/variable.xsd#variable-
set"/>

<formula:formula xlink:type="resource"
xlink:label="assets_eq_equityPlusLiabilities"
value="$var:assets eq ($var:equity +$var:liabilities)"
source="var:assets" aspectModel="dimensional"
implicitFiltering="true">
 <formula:aspects>
  <formula:concept>
   <formula:qname>sample:balance</formula:qname>
  </formula:concept>
 </formula:aspects>
</formula:formula>

<variable:factVariable xlink:type="resource"
xlink:label="assets_variable" bindAsSequence="false"/>

<variable:variableArc xlink:type="arc"
xlink:arcrole="http://xbrl.org/arcrole/2008/variable-set"
xlink:from="assets_eq_equityPlusLiabilities"
xlink:to="assets_variable" order="1.0" name="var:assets"/>

<cf:conceptName xlink:type="resource"
xlink:label="assets_concept">
 <cf:concept>
  <cf:qname>test:assets</cf:qname>
 </cf:concept>
</cf:conceptName>

<variable:variableFilterArc xlink:type="arc"
xlink:arcrole="http://xbrl.org/arcrole/2008/variable-
filter" xlink:from="assets_variable"
xlink:to="assets_concept" order="1.0" complement="false"
cover="true"/>

<variable:factVariable xlink:type="resource"
xlink:label="equity_variable" bindAsSequence="false"/>

<variable:variableArc xlink:type="arc"
xlink:arcrole="http://xbrl.org/arcrole/2008/variable-set"
xlink:from="assets_eq_equityPlusLiabilities"
xlink:to="equity_variable" order="2.0" name="var:equity"/>
```

```
<cf:conceptName xlink:type="resource"
xlink:label="equity_concept">
 <cf:concept>
  <cf:qname>test:equity</cf:qname>
 </cf:concept>
</cf:conceptName>

<variable:variableFilterArc xlink:type="arc"
xlink:arcrole="http://xbrl.org/arcrole/2008/variable-
filter" xlink:from="equity_variable"
xlink:to="equity_concept" order="1.0" complement="false"
cover="true"/>

<variable:factVariable xlink:type="resource"
xlink:label="liabilities_variable" bindAsSequence="false"/>

<variable:variableArc xlink:type="arc"
xlink:arcrole="http://xbrl.org/arcrole/2008/variable-set"
xlink:from="assets_eq_equityPlusLiabilities"
xlink:to="liabilities_variable" order="3.0"
name="var:liabilities"/>

<cf:conceptName xlink:type="resource"
xlink:label="liabilities_concept">
 <cf:concept>
  <cf:qname>test:liabilities</cf:qname>
 </cf:concept>
</cf:conceptName>

  <variable:variableFilterArc xlink:type="arc"
xlink:arcrole="http://xbrl.org/arcrole/2008/variable-
filter" xlink:from="liabilities_variable"
xlink:to="liabilities_concept" order="1.0"
complement="false" cover="true"/>
```

Code example 9.2: Formulas example - sample linkbase

Analyzing the above linkbase, we now identify the steps to define an XBRL formula:

1. Declare necessary namespaces and arcroles from formulas schemas.

This step allows using concepts defined by the XBRL Formulas specification. The XBRL processors use these declarations to process the formulas.

2. Declare the formula and input XPath expression as its value.

This declaration allows presenting to the processor what is to be evaluated. The value of the formula represents the test that the processor will perform.

3. Declare other formula attributes[114]:
   a. Source,
   b. Aspect model,
   c. Information on use of implicit filtering.

4. Declare formula's output concept.

This declaration tells the processor where the output of the formula should be stored.

5. For each variable used by the formula:
   a. Declare whether it is a fact variable,
   b. Bind the variable with the formula using variable-set arc,
   c. Define the filter to select the fact (concept and contextual information) to bind to the variable,
   d. Bind the fact with the variable by the variable-filter arc.

The Formulas specification allows definition of two types of formulas:

- Formulas – these result in a new item (might be used for new items derivation);
- Assertions – used for checking consistency of source items or computed items and source items or for checking existence of items.

Formula vs. Assertion use cases

Formula
The Central Bank in Germany would like to generate a report back to the filer (which uses the IFRS XBRL taxonomy) and which contains the resulting concept named Balance. The Balance concept should indicate to the filer that the formula: Assets = Equity + Liabilities and reports *True* if the formula is correct or *False* if incorrect. For this purpose, the Central Bank should use the formula construct.

[114] See Table 1: Glossary of terms used in XBRL formulas for details.

Assertion
The Central Bank in Brazil would like to test the values reported by their filers using IFRS XBRL taxonomy for the Bank's internal purposes and further internal processing. The Bank would like to check existence of facts (if the facts were reported since, for instance, a group of facts is required) or would like to assess whether the reported facts' values match those computed based on the formula. The outcome of the assertion is not to be reported back to the filer. Therefore, the Bank will use the assertion construct rather than the formula one.

The Formulas specification also allows the use of two aspect models for aspect matching:

- Dimensional,
- Non-dimensional.

Dimensional aspect model
This model allows verifying aspects, which use the Dimensions specification[115]. These aspects are defined as content of the segment and scenario elements in the context in the XBRL instance document. They use the constructs defined by the Dimensions specification, such as hypercubes and dimensions. The dimensional aspect model indicates to the implicit filtering mechanism that the aspects that address the content of the segment and scenario elements according to the Dimensions specification should be included during aspects evaluation.

Non-dimensional aspect model
The XBRL 2.1 specification indicates that the content of segment and scenario elements in the context in the XBRL instance document may include any XML-valid declaration. This allowed users to specify further the contextual information in the instance document indicating, for instance, that data that use this context has a "revised" or "budgeted" or other nature. The content of segment and scenario was later constraint by the Dimensions specification. To process the aspects which address the content of the segment and scenario elements and which do not use the Dimension specification constructs a user may indicate in the formula that it should follow the non-dimensional aspect model.

A detailed description of the difference between the two models is in the Formulas specification.

---

[115] For details about the Dimensions specification and constructs that this specification defines please the chapters on XBRL Dimensions.

9.1.2 Implicit filtering

Implicit filtering is an important mechanism that allows for automatic matching of aspects that the formula does not explicitly define. Implicit filtering allows selection of the facts to bind correctly with variables and reduces the number of declarations required for facts selection. Further details about implicit filtering are in the Formulas specification.

9.1.3 Summary

The above sections provide an initial description of XBRL Formulas. Readers are encouraged to stay up to date with latest releases of the specification. The Formulas specification creates a powerful environment for processing of XBRL instances, derivation of facts, transformation of values and validation of data. The current XBRL International taxonomies accompanied with formulas linkbases will provide an efficient and flexible platform for business reporting. At the date of writing of this chapter, no software vendor has yet to release a product with full support for formulas linkbase processing. However, there is already some vendor support for the definition of formulas. They use a variety of techniques and standards including XPath. It is possible that the XBRL Formulas specification combined with dimensional taxonomies will change the design and processing of data in business reporting.

9.2 Introduction to XBRL versioning

XBRL taxonomies contain definitions of concepts used for business reporting purposes. These concepts often come after analysis of underlying legal regulations or de facto standards. In the case of the IFRSs, the authoritative literature is in the IFRS Bound Volume from the IASB. The IASB updates the IFRS Bound Volume annually. The update includes the latest changes in the financial reporting domain and IASB discussions. Updates to the IFRS taxonomy come in line with changes of the Bound Volume. Documentation of changes between versions of the taxonomies comes in external files or is not available at all. Examples include the *Change Log* published by the IASC Foundation to indicate changes between the 2005 and 2006 versions of the IFRS taxonomies[116]. However, with numerous projects worldwide facing the same requirement for a standardized methodology for documentation of changes between taxonomies, the XBRL International commenced development of the XBRL Versioning specification. The primary

[116] See:
http://www.iasb.org/xbrl/ifrs_taxonomy/previous_taxonomies/2006-08-15/changelog.html

rationale for this effort is to provide users and adopters with a standardized mechanism to support the transition from older to newer version of a given XBRL taxonomy.

At the date of writing of this chapter, the Public Working Draft of the XBRL Versioning specification (XVS 1.0) was available. Readers are encouraged to stay up to date with the latest releases of this documentation on the www.xbrl.org.

The following diagram provides an overview of how we expect the XBRL Versioning to work. The versioning report document's changes apply to the XBRL semantic level. The mechanisms defined by the Versioning specification rest on the XBRL Infoset documentation.

XBRL Infoset[117]

A document explaining in a standardised manner the content of the Discoverable Taxonomy Set. The XBRL Infoset does not constitute a specification but rather provides a general manner of explaining what the standard DTS contains.

We represent the framework of the Versioning report in Fig. 9.5.

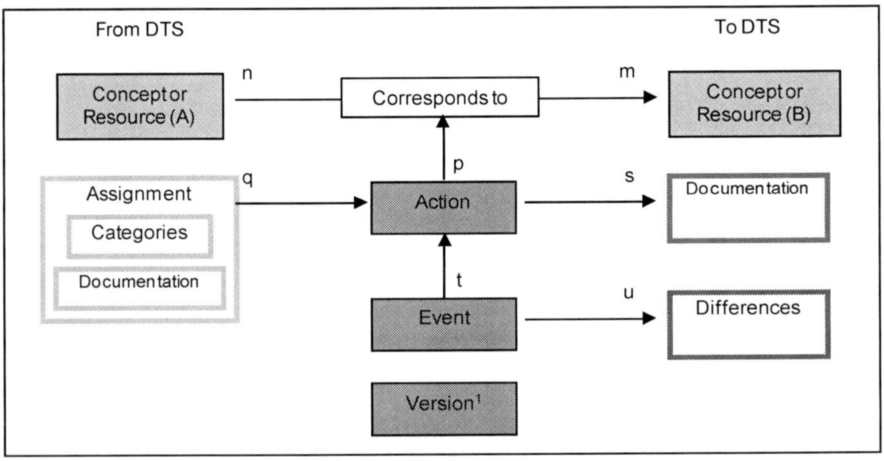

Fig. 9.5: Content of the version information item[118]

The base information about change between two concepts (or resources) is in the Event. Event shows what the change between two DTS contents was.

[117] For details see: http://www.xbrl.org/Specification/Infoset/XIS-PWD-2007-11-28.htm

[118] Source: I Hernandez-Ros, XBRL Versioning Specification, Public Working Draft 1.0, http://www.xbrl.org/Specification/Versioning/XVS-PWD-2007-11-28.htm, accessed 2008-04-20.

DTS (Discoverable Taxonomy Set)

In the physical aspect, the DTS represents the set of files that create the taxonomy and should be available to XBRL processors when processing the taxonomy. For instance, an IFRS taxonomy extension prepared by the CEBS (e.g. FINREP taxonomy) contains extension files defined by this institution but also includes the original IFRS XBRL taxonomy files defined by the IASC Foundation XBRL Team.
The DTS also represents the content of the taxonomy. For instance, an IFRS extension taxonomy includes Balance Sheet and Income Statement modules but also defines new reports (e.g. Environmental Impact Assessment).

Differences present the *diffing* results come together with Events. There can be groupings of those Events that relate to one concept (resource) in *Actions* that indicate set of changes applied. Actions in turn can be associated with additional human readable *Documentation* of the action and *Assignment* presenting the reasons for changes. Those reasons may be predefined (business, technical or errata) or of a user-defined type.

Eventually the versioning report accompanies the *Version* component, which provides general information about the source and target Discoverable Taxonomy Sets versioned. The *Version* component indicates the starting and ending points of the versioning analysis.

This approach assumes that versioning information is stored in the instance document. However, there is another initiative within the XBRL International Working Groups to define versioning information using XLink and store it as one of the additional linkbases.

9.3 Introduction to XBRL rendering

Since the beginning of the development of the XBRL standard, visual presentation of XBRL instance documents has been a key requirement for users. Since taxonomies are in a tree-like fashion (XML), it was difficult to render the instance documents in a report-like form of tables, paragraphs and headers. Even development of the XBRL Patterns document did not solve the issue of XBRL rendering.

Patterns document

This document was developed by Charles Hoffman indicating how certain structures from financial reports should be defined in the XBRL taxonomy presentation linkbase. Since the presentation linkbase uses a traditional XML, tree-like structure, tables like Movements in Equity, which in the financial reports are often presented in a tabular form, required *translation* mechanism. This translation was standardized by the official XBRL Patterns documentation.

Before the XBRL International working groups commenced discussion on the requirements for a Rendering specification, adopters implemented temporary solutions to address this issue. Some adopters utilized XSLT style sheets, whereas other implemented proprietary solutions to present XBRL documents in a standardized and user-friendly format. The prime reason for addressing the Rendering issue originated from the requirement of user-friendly presentation of data to regulatory filers and other participants in various information value chains. However soon the rendering issue included other aspects including assurance of the quality of the data reported. Users indicated the requirement of visual verification of XBRL data in a credible, faithful and valid manner. The recent publication of the *Inline XBRL* (*iXBRL*) specification constitutes the first step to address this issue.

The Inline XBRL specification allows XBRL instance documents tags to be embedded in an HTML page. The design of the XML and XBRL standards were for appropriate structure of metadata. Conversely, the focus of HTML is on presentation of the data in a user-friendly, readable format. The XML community has a specific translation language (XSLT) to provide a flexible mechanism for the transformation of XML data into the HTML format. Since HTML follows the XML design (currently the W3C Consortium recommends use of XHTML, an XML equivalent of HTML) the XBRL Rendering Working Group identified a potential combination of both standards as desired at operational level. In other words, HTML documents became a skeleton for presentation of the XBRL data. Inline XBRL document contains three types of tags:

- HTML Markup tags;
- Inline XBRL tags;
- Other tags as defined by the specification.

We show the concept behind Inline XBRL in the following representation:

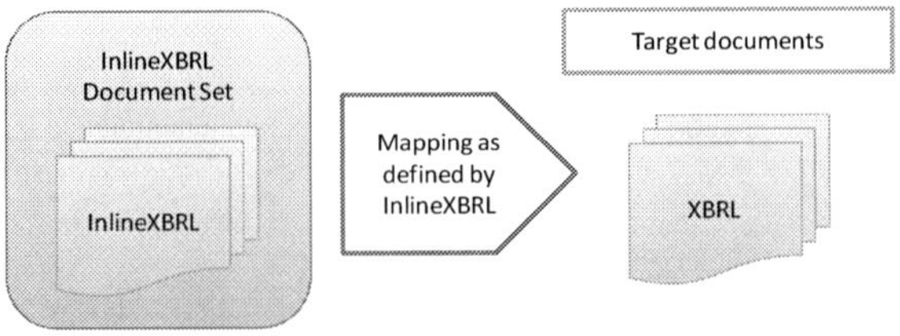

Fig. 9.6: Inline XBRL document set

The result of the mapping should be a valid XBRL instance document. The example below presents sample code of an Inline XBRL document:

```
<td class="rightalign">
  <b>
    <ix:nonFraction
       ix:name="pt:TangibleFixedAssets"
       contextRef="e2003"
       id="s2-1"
       precision="4"
       unitRef="GBP">7464</ix:nonFraction>
  </b>
</td>
<td class="rightalign">
  <ix:nonFraction
       ix:name="pt:IntangibleFixedAssets"
       contextRef="e2003"
       precision="3"
       unitRef="GBP">750</ix:nonFraction>
</td>
```

Code example 9.3: Code example of Inline XBRL document[119]

The above example presents rendering of two monetary items in form of an HTML table.

- Tangible Fixed Assets,
- Intangible Fixed Assets.

InlineXBRL makes use of several elements:

- ix:denominator,
- ix:exclude,
- ix:footnoteLink,
- ix:fraction,
- ix:header,
- ix:hidden,
- ix:nonFraction,
- ix:nonnumeric,
- ix:numerator,
- ix:references,
- ix:resources,
- ix:tuple.

[119] Source: I. Stokes-Rees, P. Allen, Specification for Inline XBRL 0.56, Public Working Draft, http://www.xbrl.org/Specification/inlineXBRL-spec-PWD-2008-03-05.html, accessed 2008-04-21.

The above elements control the content of the XBRL instance document in a manner that allows for their appropriate rendering in the HTML format. The Inline XBRL elements address various rendering approaches that allow:

- Rendering of non-fraction and fraction items;
- Indicating the nominator and denominator of fraction items;
- Rendering of footnotes, headers, references and resources;
- Hiding of certain XBRL items;
- Rendering of complex repetitive structures, notably tuples.

For further reference and detailed description about the nature of the above elements, we encourage readers to read the Inline XBRL specification. The notion of Inline XBRL focuses on embedding Inline XBRL tags in HTML documents. However, there is another activity within the Rendering Working Group that focuses on rendering XBRL instance document with information provided in special rendering linkbases. This approach will give taxonomy developers the ability to define standard ways of rendering of taxonomies. At the data of writing no specification of rendering linkbase was available therefore readers are encouraged to visit www.xbrl.org for the latest releases.

9.4 Summary

New technologies in XBRL arise from user requirements to address certain areas of business reporting standard not described, or causing issues, by the XBRL specification. The Formulas specification, which at the date of writing was in the most stable Candidate Recommendation release presents an important platform supporting the transformation of data. The versioning specification provides support for maintenance of XBRL taxonomies and therefore fosters their adoption. The rendering mechanism allows for standardized presentation of XBRL data to users, which should aid assuring high data quality and help users verify the data provided in instance documents.

Naturally, software vendors will require certain time to be able to implement the new specifications. Several software companies claimed advanced stage of development of respective solutions or even draft public releases. However, the key test of the efficiency of new technologies will come when projects worldwide will make use of their features.

9.5 Key terms you should know

- XBRL formulas
- XBRL versioning
- XBRL rendering
- Inline XBRL
- Variable
- Filter
- Assertion
- Formula
- InfoSet

9.6 *Case analysis*[120]

The exchange and validation of financial data are common practices in many industries, and the banking industry is no exception. In fact, FDIC-insured financial institutions (financial institutions or FIs) in the United States and federal banking regulatory agencies (agencies) have been exchanging and validating financial data since the 1800s.

Historically, the agencies published data series metadata that included forms and instructions; however, formulas applied by the agencies to check for mathematical and logical relationships were not regularly or systematically provided to the FIs. The agencies experimented with providing formula metadata in text files, PDF files, and spreadsheets. However, the agencies' ability to express precise formulas that described critical relationships within a data series was limited with these formats. Within the U.S. commercial banking sector, a Call Report is a well known data series that represents a structured and well defined set of quarterly financial data submitted to federal regulators by the majority of institutions. Timely, accurate, and high quality data are critical to regulators and are used in off-site monitoring systems, examination processes, and policymaking. The publication of these data on the Internet promotes financial transparency and helps the FDIC achieve its mission of "preserving and promoting public confidence in the U.S. financial system."

The agencies' ability to express formulas that ensure mathematical and logical consistency is critical. The creation and use of these formulas have evolved over the years. Even though the agencies shared the same common forms and instructions, no common way to communicate and exchange these complex formulas among the agencies, vendors and FIs existed. Eventually each agency developed its own proprietary set of formulas and processing systems, and over time the agencies developed an elaborate process flow that was opaque, inefficient, and labor intensive. The Federal Financial Institutions Examination Council (FFIEC) took the first step toward achieving federal financial regulatory data transparency through the Call Report Modernization project. This effort developed and implemented the Central Data Repository (CDR) which makes use of an international financial reporting standard to define metadata, publish taxonomies, exchange information, and receive and process data reported by federally regulated financial institutions.

The agencies selected XBRL as the non-proprietary, open standard to define and exchange financial reporting data. The use of XBRL would allow FFIEC analysts to define regulatory reporting metadata, such as the concept name (the data element to be collected), data type, instructions, and calculations. However,

[120] Excerpted from FDIC, "Implementing XBRL Formulas", available at http://www.fdic.gov/bank/ImplementingXBRLFormulas.pdf

the functionality to express complex validation formulas was lacking. Alternative solutions to expressing these formulas (such as SQL, Java, and MathML) were considered, but the ultimate solution was to provide an XML layer that would define and publish a formula, provide transparency, encourage re-use, and remain within the bounds of the XBRL specification. The technology needed to include any language that could express a mathematical equation and allow for the "transformation" into another other language, such as SQL, Java, or C#. XPath was selected as a basis for the new XBRL extension because XPath was an XML specification and would provide a way to define "the pointers" to variables that participate in a given formula.

References and Recommended Readings

Boritz, J. E.; Won, G. N.: Security in XML-based financial reporting services on the Internet, in: Journal of Accounting and Public Policy, No. 24, 2005, pp. 11-35.

Bovee, M., A. Kogan, K. Nelson, R. P. Srivastava and M. A. Vasarhelyi. 2005. Financial Reporting and Auditing Agent (FRAANK) and eXtensible Business Reporting Language (XBRL). Journal of Information Systems 19 (1): 19-41.

Debreceny, R. S. and G. L. Gray. 2001. The production and use of semantically rich accounting reports on the Internet: XML and XBRL. International Journal of Accounting Information Systems 2: 47-74.

Debreceny, R.; Felden, C.; Piechocki, M.: New Dimensions for Business Reporting and XBRL, Deutscher Universität-Verlag, Wiesbaden 2007.

Debreceny, R.: Research into XBRL – Old and New Challenges, in Debreceny, R.; Felden, C.; Piechocki, M.: New Dimensions for Business Reporting and XBRL, Deutscher Universität-Verlag, Wiesbaden 2007.

Debreceny, R. S.; Chandra, A.; Cheh, J. J.; Guithues-Amrhein, D.; Hannon, N. J.; Hutchison, P. D.; Janvrin, D.; Jones, R. A.; Lamberton, B.; Lymer, A.; Mascha, M.; Nehmer, R.; Roohani, S.; Srivastava, R. P.; Trabelsi, S.; Tribunella, T.; Trites, G.; Vasarhelyi, M. A.: Financial Reporting in XBRL on the SEC's EDGAR System: A Critique and Evaluation, Journal of Information Systems, 19, 2, 2005.

DeRose, S.; Maler, E.; Daniel, R. Jr.: XML Pointer Language (XPointer) Version 1.0, W3C, 2001, http://www.w3.org/TR/2001/CR-xptr-20010911/, last call 09.08.2008.

Engel, P.; Hamscher, W.; Shuetrim, G.; Kannon, D. v.; Wallis, H: Extensible Business Reporting Language (XBRL) 2.1, XBRL International, 2003, http://www.xbrl.org/Specification/XBRL-RECOMMENDATION-2003-12-31+Corrected-Errata-2005-11-07.rtf, last call 18.07.2008.

Garbellotto, G.; Cohen, E. E.: XBRL Global Ledger Framework – SRCD Module – Public Working Draft Overview, XBRL International, 2007, http://www.xbrl.org/int/gl/2007-05-23/XBRL-Global-Ledger-Framework-SRCD-PWD-2007-05-23.rtf, last call 18.07.2008.

Garbellotto, G.; Hannon, N.; Why XBRL Is a "Business" Reporting Language, in: Strategic Finance, May 2005, pp. 57-61.

Goto, M.; Hamscher, W.: XBRL Taxonomy Versioning Requirements, XBRL International, 2002, www.xbrl.org/tr/2002/XBRL-Versioning-Req-WD-2002-10-01.doc, last call 07.08.2008.

Greener, A.: Summary of XBRL boundary debate, OASIS, 2004, http://www.oasis-open.org/archives/tax/200403/msg00055.html, last call 07.08.2008.

Hamscher, W; van Ardenne, R.; Wallis, H.: 1 Handling Semantics in IT - Introduction into XML, XBRL and Ontologies, XBRL International, 2005, http://www.xbrl.org/2005/XBRL-CONF-CR2-2005-11-07.rtf, last call 07.08.2006.

Hamscher, W; Kannon, D. v.: Extensible Business Reporting Language (XBRL) Specification, XBRL International, 2000, http://www.xbrl.org/tr/2000-07-31/xbrl-2000-07-31.doc, last call 07.08.2008.

Hamscher, W.; Goodhand, M.; Hoffmann, C.; Homer, B.; Macdonald, J.; Shuetrim, G.; Wallis, H.: Financial Reporting Taxonomies Architecture 1.0, XBRL International, 2005, http://www.xbrl.org/technical/guidance/FRTA-RECOMMENDATION-2005-04-25+corrected-errata-2006-03-20.rtf, last call 18.07.2008.

Hoffmann, C.: Financial Reporting Using XBRL - IFRS and US GAAP Edition, Lulu, 2006.

Hoffman, C.; Strand, C.: XBRL Essentials – A nontechnical introduction to eXtensible Business Reporting Language (XBRL), the digital language of business reporting, American Institute of Certified Public Accountants, New York, 2001.

Hernández-Ros, I.; Wallis, H.: XBRL Dimensions 1.0, XBRL International, 2006, http://www.xbrl.org/Specification/XDT-CR4-2006-07-20.rtf, last call 09.08.2006.

Sommerville, I.: Software Engineering. 6th Edition. Pearson Studium. München, 2001.

Sutton, S. G.; Arnold, V.: Foundations and Frameworks for AIS Research, in Sutton, S. G.; Arnold, V.: Researching Accounting as an Information System Discipline, American Accounting Association, 2002.

Trites, G.: Interactive Data: The Impact on Assurance – New Challenges for the Auditing Profession, XBRL International, 2006.

Willis, M.; Hannon, N.; Combating Everyday Data Problems with XBRL, in: Strategic Finance, July 2005, pp. 57-59.